Praise for
PYTHON FOR KIDS

"Jason Briggs manages to successfully describe programming to kids without sounding like he's dumbing down the content. The lessons are well-constructed and leave the reader with a feeling of accomplishment in each chapter."
—Marziah Karch, Wired.com

"An excellent introduction to programming for anyone interested in learning to program, regardless of their age. The material is extremely well organized and presented, and makes for a great resource for either home or school."
—Roy Wood, *GeekDad*

"This book offers a good introduction to computer programming. . . . An excellent family bonding experience."
—Patrice Gans, *Education Week*

"By the end of the book, you have a fully-functional platform game running, and most likely a head full of ideas about your next game. *Python for Kids* is just as good an introduction for adults learning to code."
—Matthew Humphries, Geek.com

"Easy to read, provides sound programming advice and very clear explanations of how programming languages work. A great book for anyone who wants to break into programming without pangs of inadequacy."
—Sandra Henry-Stocker, *ITworld*

PYTHON
FOR KIDS

A PLAYFUL INTRODUCTION
TO PROGRAMMING

BY JASON R. BRIGGS

**no starch
press**

San Francisco

PYTHON FOR KIDS. Copyright © 2013 by Jason R. Briggs.

Printed in Korea

Fifth printing

17 16 15 14   5 6 7 8 9

ISBN-10: 1-59327-407-6
ISBN-13: 978-1-59327-407-8

Publisher: William Pollock
Production Editor: Serena Yang
Cover and Interior Design: Octopod Studios
Illustrator: Miran Lipovača
Developmental Editor: William Pollock
Technical Reviewers: Josh Pollock and Maria Fernandez
Copyeditor: Marilyn Smith
Compositor: Serena Yang
Proofreader: Greg Teague

For information on distribution, translations, or bulk sales, please contact No Starch Press, Inc. directly:
No Starch Press, Inc.
245 8th Street, San Francisco, CA 94103
phone: 415.863.9900; fax: 415.863.9950; info@nostarch.com; http://www.nostarch.com/

Library of Congress Cataloging-in-Publication Data

```
Briggs, Jason R.
  Python for kids : a playful introduction to programming / by Jason R. Briggs.
      pages cm
  Audience: 10+
  Includes index.
  ISBN 978-1-59327-407-8 -- ISBN 1-59327-407-6
 1.  Computer software--Juvenile literature. 2.  Computer programming--Juvenile literature. 3.  Python
(Computer program language)--Juvenile literature.  I. Title.
  QA76.52.B75 2013
  005.13'3--dc23
                                    2012044047
```

Production Date: February 7, 2014
Plant & Location: Printed by WeSP, South Korea
Job / Batch #: 012914

BRIEF CONTENTS

PART I: LEARNING TO PROGRAM

PART II: BOUNCE!

PART III: MR. STICK MAN RACES FOR THE EXIT

CONTENTS IN DETAIL

9
PYTHON'S BUILT-IN FUNCTIONS 109

10
USEFUL PYTHON MODULES 129

PART II: BOUNCE!

PART III: MR. STICK MAN RACES FOR THE EXIT

ABOUT THE AUTHOR

Jason R. Briggs has been a programmer since the age of eight, when he first learned BASIC on a Radio Shack TRS-80. He has written software professionally as a developer and systems architect and served as Contributing Editor for *Java Developer's Journal*. His articles have appeared in *JavaWorld*, *ONJava*, and *ONLamp*. *Python for Kids* is his first book.

Jason can be reached at *http://jasonrbriggs.com/* or by email at *mail@jasonrbriggs.com*.

ABOUT THE ILLUSTRATOR

Miran Lipovača is the author of *Learn You a Haskell for Great Good!*. He enjoys boxing, playing bass guitar, and, of course, drawing. He has a fascination with dancing skeletons and the number 71, and when he walks through automatic doors he pretends that he's actually opening them with his mind.

ABOUT THE TECHNICAL REVIEWERS

A recent graduate of The Nueva School, 15-year-old Josh Pollock is a freshman at Lick-Wilmerding High School in San Francisco. He first started programming in Scratch when he was 9 years old, began using TI-BASIC when he was in 6th grade, and moved on to Java and Python in 7th and UnityScript in 8th. In addition to programming, he loves playing the trumpet, developing computer games, and teaching people about interesting STEM topics.

Maria Fernandez has a master's degree in applied linguistics and has been interested in computers and technology for more than 20 years. She taught English to young refugee women with the Global Village Project in Georgia and currently resides in northern California working with ETS (Educational Testing Service).

ACKNOWLEDGMENTS

This must be what it's like when you get up on stage to accept an award, only to realize you've left the list of people you have to thank in your other trousers: You're guaranteed to forget someone, and that music will soon start rolling to quickly usher you off the stage.

So that being said, here's the (no doubt) incomplete list of people to whom I owe a huge debt of gratitude for helping make this book as good as I think it now is.

Thanks to the No Starch team, particularly Bill Pollock, for applying a liberal dose of "what-would-a-kid-think" while editing it. When you've been programming for a long time, it's all too easy to forget how difficult some of this stuff is for learners, and Bill was invaluable at pointing out those oft-overlooked, over-complicated parts. And thanks to Serena Yang, production manager extraordinaire; here's hoping you haven't torn out too much hair getting 300+ pages of code correctly colorized.

A big thank you must go to Miran Lipovača for utterly brilliant illustrations. Beyond brilliant. No really! If I had done the artwork, we'd be lucky to have the occasional smudged figure that doesn't resemble anything in particular. Is it a bear . . . ? Is it a dog . . . ? No, wait . . . is that supposed to be a tree?

Thanks to the reviewers. I apologize if some of your suggestions weren't implemented in the end. You were probably right, and I can only blame a personal character flaw for any probable goofs. Particular thanks to Josh for some great suggestions and some really good catches. And apologies to Maria for having to deal with occasionally dodgily formatted code.

Thanks to my wife and daughter, for putting up with a husband and father who had his nose buried in a computer screen even more than usual.

To Mum, for endless amounts of encouragement over the years.

Finally, thanks to my father, for buying a computer back in the 1970s and putting up with someone who wanted to use it as much as he did. None of this would have been possible without him.

INTRODUCTION

Why learn computer programming?

Programming fosters creativity, reasoning, and problem solving. The programmer gets the opportunity to create something from nothing, use logic to turn programming constructs into a form that a computer can run, and, when things don't work quite as well as expected, use problem solving to figure out what has gone wrong. Programming is a fun, sometimes challenging (and occasionally frustrating) activity, and the skills learned from it can be useful both in school and at work . . . even if your career has nothing to do with computers.

And, if nothing else, programming is a great way to spend an afternoon when the weather outside is dreary.

WHY PYTHON?

Python is an easy-to-learn programming language that has some really useful features for a beginning programmer. The code is quite easy to read when compared to other programming languages, and it has an interactive shell into which you can enter your programs and see them run. In addition to its simple language structure and an interactive shell with which to experiment, Python has some features that greatly augment the learning process and allow you to put together simple animations for creating your own games. One is the turtle module, inspired by Turtle graphics (used by the Logo programming language back in the 1960s) and designed for educational use. Another is the tkinter module, an interface for the Tk GUI toolkit, which provides a simple way to create programs with slightly more advanced graphics and animation.

HOW TO LEARN TO CODE

Like anything you try for the first time, it's always best to start with the basics, so begin with the first chapters and resist the urge to skip ahead to the later chapters. No one can play an orchestral symphony the first time they pick up an instrument. Student pilots don't start flying a plane before they understand the basic controls. Gymnasts aren't (usually) able to do back flips on their first try. If you jump ahead too quickly, not only will the basic ideas not stick in your head, but you'll also find the content of the later chapters more complicated than it actually is.

As you go through this book, try each of the examples, so you can see how they work. There are also programming puzzles at the end of most chapters for you to try, which will help improve your programming skills. Remember that the better you understand the basics, the easier it will be to understand more complicated ideas later on.

When you find something frustrating or too challenging, here are some things that I find helpful:

1. Break a problem down into smaller pieces. Try to understand what a small piece of code is doing, or think about only a small part of a difficult idea (focus on a small piece of code rather than trying to understand the whole thing at once).

2. If that still doesn't help, sometimes it's best to just leave it alone for a while. Sleep on it, and come back to it another day. This is a good way to solve many problems, and it can be particularly helpful for computer programmers.

WHO SHOULD READ THIS BOOK

This book is for anyone interested in computer programming, whether that's a child or an adult coming to programming for the first time. If you want to learn how to write your own software rather than just use the programs developed by others, *Python for Kids* is a great place to start.

In the following chapters, you'll find information to help you install Python, start the Python shell and perform basic calculations, print text on the screen and create lists, and perform simple control flow operations using if statements and for loops (and learn what if statements and for loops are!). You'll learn how to reuse code with functions, the basics of classes and objects, and descriptions of some of the many built-in Python functions and modules.

You'll find chapters on both simple and advanced turtle graphics, as well as on using the tkinter module to draw on the computer screen. There are programming puzzles of varying complexity at the ends of many chapters, which will help readers cement their newfound knowledge by giving them a chance to write small programs by themselves.

Once you've built up your fundamental programming knowledge, you'll learn how to write your own games. You'll develop two graphical games and learn about collision detection, events, and different animation techniques.

Most of the examples in this book use Python's IDLE (Integrated DeveLopment Environment) shell. IDLE provides syntax highlighting, copy-and-paste functionality (similar to what you would use in other applications), and an editor window where you can save your code for later use, which means IDLE works as both an interactive environment for experimentation and something a bit like a text editor. The examples will work just as well with the standard console and a regular text editor, but IDLE's syntax highlighting and slightly more user-friendly environment can aid understanding, so the very first chapter shows you how to set it up.

WHAT'S IN THIS BOOK

Here's a brief rundown of what you'll find in each chapter.

Chapter 1 is an introduction to programming with instructions for installing Python for the first time.

Chapter 2 introduces basic calculations and variables, and **Chapter 3** describes some of the basic Python types, such as strings, lists, and tuples.

Chapter 4 is the first taste of the turtle module. We'll jump from basic programming to moving a turtle (in the shape of an arrow) around the screen.

Chapter 5 covers the variations of conditions and if statements, and **Chapter 6** moves on to for loops and while loops.

Chapter 7 is where we start to use and create functions, and then in **Chapter 8** we cover classes and objects. We cover enough of the basic ideas to support some of the programming techniques we'll need in the games development chapters later on in the book. At this point, the material starts get a little more complicated.

Chapter 9 goes through most of the built-in functions in Python, and **Chapter 10** continues with a few modules (basically buckets of useful functionality) that are installed by default with Python.

Chapter 11 returns to the turtle module as the reader experiments with more complicated shapes. **Chapter 12** moves on to using the tkinter module for more advanced graphics creation.

In **Chapters 13** and **14**, we create our first game, "Bounce!," which builds on the knowledge gained from the preceding chapters, and in **Chapters 15–18**, we create another game, "Mr. Stick Man Races for the Exit." The game development chapters are where things could start to go seriously wrong. If all else fails, download the code from the companion website (*http://python-for-kids.com/*), and compare your code with these working examples.

In the **Afterword**, we wrap up with a look at PyGame and some other popular programming languages.

Finally, in the **Appendix**, you'll learn about Python's keywords in detail, and in the **Glossary**, you'll find definitions of the programming terms used throughout this book.

THE COMPANION WEBSITE

If you find that you need help as you read, try the companion site, *http://python-for-kids.com/,* where you'll find downloads for all the examples in this book and more programming puzzles. You'll also find solutions to all the programming puzzles in the book on the companion site, in case you get stumped or want to check your work.

HAVE FUN!

Remember as you work your way through this book that programming can be fun. Don't think of this as work. Think of programming as a way to create some fun games or applications that you can share with your friends or others.

Learning to program is a wonderful mental exercise and the results can be very rewarding. But most of all, whatever you do, have fun!

PART I

LEARNING TO PROGRAM

1

NOT ALL SNAKES SLITHER

A computer program is a set of instructions that causes a computer to perform some kind of action. It isn't the physical parts of a computer—like the wires, microchips, cards, hard drive, and such—but the hidden stuff running on that hardware. A computer program, which I'll usually refer to as just a *program*, is the set of commands that tell that dumb hardware what to do. *Software* is a collection of computer programs.

Without computer programs, almost every device you use daily would either stop working or be much less useful than it is now. Computer programs, in one form or another, control not only your personal computer but also video game systems, cell phones, and the GPS units in cars. Software also controls less obvious items like LCD TVs and their remote controllers, as well as some of the newest radios, DVD players, ovens, and some fridges. Even car engines, traffic lights, street lamps, train signals, electronic billboards, and elevators are controlled by programs.

Programs are a bit like thoughts. If you didn't have thoughts, you would probably just sit on the floor, staring vacantly and drooling down the front of your shirt. Your thought "get up off the floor" is an instruction, or command, that tells your body to stand up. In the same way, computer programs tell computers what to do.

If you know how to write computer programs, you can do all sorts of useful things. Sure, you may not be able to write programs to control cars, traffic lights, or your fridge (well, at least not at first), but you could create web pages, write your own games, or even make a program to help with your homework.

A FEW WORDS ABOUT LANGUAGE

Like humans, computers use multiple languages to communicate—in this case, programming languages. A *programming language* is simply a particular way to talk to a computer—a way to use instructions that both humans and the computer can understand.

There are programming languages named after people (like Ada and Pascal), those named using simple acronyms (like BASIC and FORTRAN), and even a few named after TV shows, like Python. Yes, the Python programming language was named after the *Monty Python's Flying Circus* TV show, not after python the snake.

NOTE   Monty Python's Flying Circus *was an alternative British comedy show first broadcast in the 1970s, and it remains hugely popular today among a certain audience. The show had sketches like "The Ministry of Silly Walks," "The Fish-Slapping Dance," and "The Cheese Shop" (which didn't sell any cheese).*

A number of things about the Python programming language make it extremely useful for beginners. Most importantly, you can use Python to write simple, efficient programs really quickly. Python doesn't use quite as many complicated symbols as other programming languages, which makes it easier to read and a lot friendlier for beginners. (That isn't to say Python doesn't use symbols—they're just not used quite as heavily as in many other languages.)

INSTALLING PYTHON

Installing Python is fairly straightforward. Here, we'll go over the steps for installing it on Windows 7, Mac OS X, and Ubuntu. When installing Python, you'll also set up a shortcut for the IDLE program, which is the *I*ntegrated *DeveL*opment *E*nvironment that lets you write programs for Python. If Python has already been installed on your computer, jump ahead to "Once You've Installed Python" on page 10.

INSTALLING PYTHON ON WINDOWS 7

To install Python for Microsoft Windows 7, point a web browser to *http://www.python.org/* and download the latest Windows installer for Python 3. Look for a section in the menu titled **Quick Links**, as shown here:

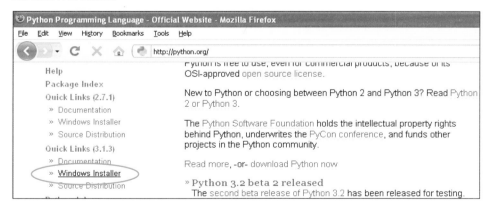

NOTE *The exact version of Python that you download is not important, as long as it starts with the number 3.*

After you download the Windows installer, double-click its icon, and then follow the instructions to install Python in the default location, as follows:

1. Select **Install for All Users**, and then click **Next**.
2. Leave the default directory unchanged, but note the name of the installation directory (probably *C:\Python31* or *C:\ Python32*). Click **Next**.
3. Ignore the Customize Python section of the installation, and click **Next**.

At the end of this process, you should have a Python 3 entry in your Start menu:

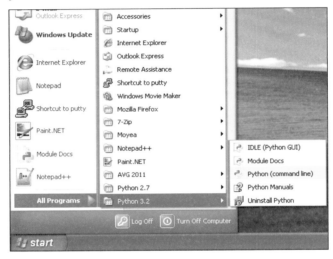

Next, follow these steps to add a Python 3 shortcut to your desktop:

1. Right-click your desktop, and select **New ▶ Shortcut** from the pop-up menu.
2. Enter the following in the box where it says **Type the location of the item** (make sure that the directory you enter is the same as the one you noted earlier):

```
c:\Python32\Lib\idlelib\idle.pyw -n
```

Your dialog should look like this:

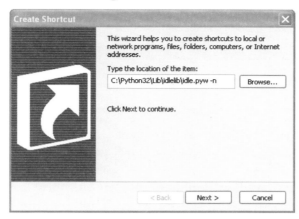

3. Click **Next** to move to the next dialog.

4. Enter the name as *IDLE*, and click **Finish** to create the shortcut.

Now you can skip to "Once You've Installed Python" on page 10 to get started with Python.

INSTALLING PYTHON ON MAC OS X

If you're using a Mac, you should find a version of Python pre-installed, but it's probably an older version of the language. To be sure that you're running the newest version, point your browser to *http://www.python.org/getit/* to download the latest installer for the Mac.

There are two different installers. The one you should download depends on which version of Mac OS X you have installed. (To find out, click the **Apple** icon in the top menu bar, and choose **About this Mac**.) Pick an installer as follows:

• If you're running a Mac OS X version between 10.3 and 10.6, download the 32-bit version of Python 3 for i386/PPC.

• If you're running Mac OS X version 10.6 or higher, download the 64-bit/32-bit version of Python 3 for x86-64.

Once the file has downloaded (it will have the filename extension .*dmg*), double-click it. You'll see a window showing the file's contents.

In this window, double-click *Python.mpkg*, and then follow the instructions to install the software. You'll be prompted for the administrator password for your Mac before Python installs. (Don't have the administrator password? Your parent may need to enter it.)

Next, you need to add a script to the desktop for launching Python's IDLE application, as follows:

1. Click the **Spotlight** icon, the small magnifying glass at the top-right corner of the screen.

2. In the box that appears, enter *Automator*.

3. Click the application that looks like a robot when it appears in the menu. It will either be in the section labeled Top Hit or in Applications.

4. Once Automator starts, select the **Application** template:

5. Click **Choose** to continue.

6. In the list of actions, find **Run Shell Script**, and drag it to the empty panel on the right. You'll see something like this:

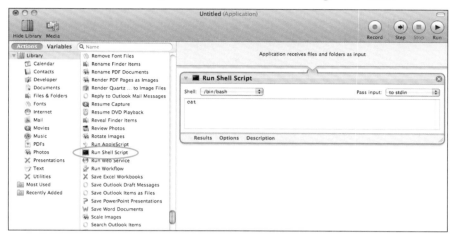

7. In the text box, you'll see the word *cat*. Select the word and replace it with the following text (everything from open to -n):

```
open -a "/Applications/Python 3.2/IDLE.app" --args -n
```

You may need to change the directory depending on the version of Python you installed.

8. Select **File ▸ Save**, and enter *IDLE* as the name.

9. Select **Desktop** from the Where dialog, and then click **Save**.

Now you can skip to "Once You've Installed Python" on page 10 to get started with Python.

INSTALLING PYTHON ON UBUNTU

Python comes preinstalled on the Ubuntu Linux distribution, but it may be an older version. Follow these steps to install Python 3 on Ubuntu 12.*x*:

1. Click the button for the Ubuntu Software Center in the Sidebar (it's the icon that looks like an orange bag—if you don't see it, you can always click the Dash Home icon and enter *Software* in the dialog).

2. Enter *Python* in the search box in the top-right corner of the Software Center.

3. In the list of software presented, select the latest version of IDLE, which is *IDLE (using Python 3.2)* in this example:

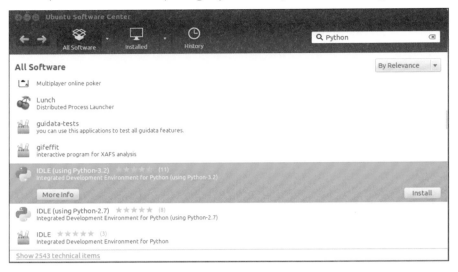

4. Click **Install**.

5. Enter your administrator password to install the software, and then click **Authenticate**. (Don't have the administrator password? Your parent may need to enter it.)

NOTE   *On some versions of Ubuntu you might only see* Python (v3.2) *in the main menu (rather than IDLE)—you can install this instead.*

Now that you've got the latest version of Python installed, let's give it a try.

ONCE YOU'VE INSTALLED PYTHON

You should now have an icon on your Windows or Mac OS X desktop labeled **IDLE**. If you're using Ubuntu, in the **Applications** menu, you should see a new group named **Programming** with the application **IDLE (using Python 3.2)** (or a later version).

Double-click the icon or choose the menu option, and you should see this window:

```
Python Shell
File  Edit  Debug  Options  Windows  Help
Python 3.2.2 (default, Sep  4 2011, 09:51:08) [MSC v.1500 32 bit (Intel)] on win
32
Type "copyright", "credits" or "license()" for more information.
==== No Subprocess ====
>>>
                                                                         Ln: 4 Col: 4
```

This is the *Python shell*, which is part of Python's integrated development environment. The three greater-than signs (>>>) are called the *prompt*.

Let's enter some commands at the prompt, beginning with the following:

```
>>> print("Hello World")
```

Make sure to include the double quotes (" "). Press ENTER on your keyboard when you're finished typing the line. If you've entered the command correctly, you should see something like this:

```
>>> print("Hello World")
Hello World
>>>
```

The prompt should reappear to let you know that the Python shell is ready to accept more commands.

Congratulations! You've just created your first Python program. The word print is a type of Python command called a *function*, and it prints out whatever is inside the parentheses to the screen. In essence, you have given the computer an instruction to display the words "Hello World"—an instruction that both you and the computer can understand.

SAVING YOUR PYTHON PROGRAMS

Python programs wouldn't be very useful if you needed to rewrite them every time you wanted to use them, never mind print them out so you could reference them. Sure, it might be fine to just rewrite short programs, but a large program, like a word processor, could contain millions of lines of code. Print that all out, and you could have well over 100,000 pages. Just imagine trying to carry that huge stack of paper home. Better hope that you won't meet up with a big gust of wind.

Luckily, we can save our programs for future use. To save a new program, open IDLE and choose **File ▶ New Window**. An empty window will appear, with ***Untitled*** in the menu bar. Enter the following code into the new shell window:

```
print("Hello World")
```

Now, choose **File ▶ Save**. When prompted for a filename, enter *hello.py*, and save the file to your desktop. Then choose **Run ▶ Run Module**. With any luck, your saved program should run, like this:

Now, if you close the shell window but leave the *hello.py* window open and then choose **Run ▶ Run Module**, the Python shell should reappear, and your program should run again. (To reopen the Python shell without running the program, choose **Run ▶ Python Shell**.)

After running the code, you'll find a new icon on your desktop labeled *hello.py*. If you double-click the icon, a black window will appear briefly and then vanish. What happened?

You're seeing the Python command-line console (similar to the shell) starting up, printing "Hello World," and then exiting. Here's what would appear if you had superhero-like speed vision and could see the window before it closed:

In addition to the menus, you can also use keyboard shortcuts to create a new shell window, save a file, and run a program:

- On Windows and Ubuntu, use CTRL-N to create a new shell window, use CTRL-S to save your file after you've finished editing, and press F5 to run your program.

- On Mac OS X, use ⌘-N to create a new shell window, use ⌘-S to save your file, and hold down the function (FN) key and press F5 to run your program.

WHAT YOU LEARNED

We began simply in this chapter with a Hello World application—the program nearly everyone starts with when they learn computer programming. In the next chapter, we'll do some more useful things with the Python shell.

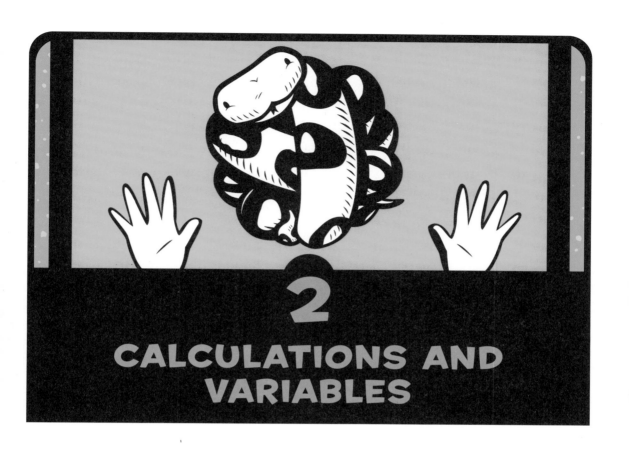

2
CALCULATIONS AND VARIABLES

Now that you have Python installed and know how to start the Python shell, you're ready to do something with it. We'll begin with some simple calculations and then move on to variables. *Variables* are a way of storing things in a computer program, and they can help you write useful programs.

CALCULATING WITH PYTHON

Normally, when asked to find the product of two numbers like 8 × 3.57, you would use a calculator or a pencil and paper. Well, how about using the Python shell to perform your calculation? Let's try it.

Start the Python shell by double-clicking the IDLE icon on your desktop or, if you're using Ubuntu, by clicking the IDLE icon in the Applications menu. At the prompt, enter this equation:

```
>>> 8 * 3.57
28.56
```

Notice that when entering a multiplication calculation in Python, you use the asterisk symbol (*) instead of a multiplication sign (×).

How about if we try an equation that's a bit more useful?

Suppose you are digging in your backyard and uncover a bag of 20 gold coins. The next day, you sneak down to the basement and stick the coins inside your grandfather's steam-powered replicating invention (luckily, you can just fit the 20 coins inside). You hear a whiz and a pop and, a few hours later, out shoot another 10 gleaming coins.

How many coins would you have in your treasure chest if you did this every day for a year? On paper, the equations might look like this:

$$10 \times 365 = 3650$$
$$20 + 3650 = 3670$$

Sure, it's easy enough to do these calculations on a calculator or on paper, but we can do all of these calculations with the Python shell as well. First, we multiply 10 coins by 365 days in a year to get 3650. Next, we add the original 20 coins to get 3670.

```
>>> 10 * 365
3650
>>> 20 + 3650
3670
```

Now, what if a raven spots the shiny gold sitting in your bedroom, and every week flies in and manages to steal three coins?

How many coins would you have left at the end of the year? Here's how this calculation looks in the shell:

```
>>> 3 * 52
156
>>> 3670 - 156
3514
```

First, we multiply 3 coins by 52 weeks in the year. The result is 156. We subtract that number from our total coins (3670), which tells us that we would have 3514 coins remaining at the end of the year.

This is a very simple program. In this book, you'll learn how to expand on these ideas to write programs that are even more useful.

PYTHON OPERATORS

You can do multiplication, addition, subtraction, and division in the Python shell, among other mathematical operations that we won't go into right now. The basic symbols used by Python to perform mathematical operations are called *operators*, as listed in Table 2-1.

Table 2-1: Basic Python Operators

Symbol	Operation
+	Addition
-	Subtraction
*	Multiplication
/	Division

The *forward slash* (/) is used for division because it's similar to the division line that you would use when writing a fraction. For example, if you had 100 pirates and 20 large barrels and you wanted to calculate how many pirates you could hide in each barrel, you could divide 100 pirates by 20 barrels (100 ÷ 20) by entering 100 / 20 in the Python shell. Just remember that the forward slash is the one whose top falls to the right.

THE ORDER OF OPERATIONS

We use parentheses in a programming language to control the order of operations. An *operation* is anything that uses an operator. Multiplication and division have a higher order than addition and subtraction, which means that they're performed first. In other words, if you enter an equation in Python, multiplication or division is performed before addition or subtraction.

For example, in the following equation, the numbers 30 and 20 are multiplied first, and the number 5 is added to their product.

```
>>> 5 + 30 * 20
605
```

This equation is another way of saying, "multiply 30 by 20, and then add 5 to the result." The result is 605. We can change the order of operations by adding parentheses around the first two numbers, like so:

```
>>> (5 + 30) * 20
700
```

The result of this equation is 700 (not 605) because the parentheses tell Python to do the operation in the parentheses first, and then do the operation outside the parentheses. This example is saying "add 5 to 30, and then multiply the result by 20."

Parentheses can be *nested*, which means that there can be parentheses inside parentheses, like this:

```
>>> ((5 + 30) * 20) / 10
70.0
```

In this case, Python evaluates the innermost parentheses first, then the outer ones, and then the final division operator.

In other words, this equation is saying, "add 5 to 30, then multiply the result by 20, and divide that result by 10." Here's what happens:

- Adding 5 to 30 gives 35.
- Multiplying 35 by 20 gives 700.
- Dividing 700 by 10 gives the final answer of 70.

If we had not used parentheses, the result would be slightly different:

```
>>> 5 + 30 * 20 / 10
65.0
```

In this case, 30 is first multiplied by 20 (giving 600), and then 600 is divided by 10 (giving 60). Finally, 5 is added to get the result of 65.

WARNING *Remember that multiplication and division always go before addition and subtraction, unless parentheses are used to control the order of operations.*

VARIABLES ARE LIKE LABELS

The word *variable* in programming describes a place to store information such as numbers, text, lists of numbers and text, and so on. Another way of looking at a variable is that it's like a label for something.

For example, to create a variable named fred, we use an equal sign (=) and then tell Python what information the variable should be the label for. Here, we create the variable fred and tell Python that it labels the number 100 (note that this doesn't mean that another variable can't have the same value):

```
>>> fred = 100
```

To find out what value a variable labels, enter print in the shell, followed by the variable name in parentheses, like this:

```
>>> print(fred)
100
```

We can also tell Python to change the variable fred so that it labels something else. For example, here's how to change fred to the number 200:

```
>>> fred = 200
>>> print(fred)
200
```

On the first line, we say that fred labels the number 200. In the second line, we ask what fred is labeling, just to confirm the change. Python prints the result on the last line.

We can also use more than one label (more than one variable) for the same item:

```
>>> fred = 200
>>> john = fred
>>> print(john)
200
```

In this example, we're telling Python that we want the name (or variable) john to label the same thing as fred by using the equal sign between john and fred.

Of course, fred probably isn't a very useful name for a variable because it most likely doesn't tell us anything about what the variable is used for. Let's call our variable number_of_coins instead of fred, like this:

```
>>> number_of_coins = 200
>>> print(number_of_coins)
200
```

This makes it clear that we're talking about 200 coins.

Variable names can be made up of letters, numbers, and the underscore character (_), but they can't start with a number. You can use anything from single letters (such as a) to long sentences for variable names. (A variable can't contain a space, so use an underscore to separate words.) Sometimes, if you're doing something quick, a short variable name is best. The name you choose should depend on how meaningful you need the variable name to be.

Now that you know how to create variables, let's look at how to use them.

USING VARIABLES

Remember our equation for figuring out how many coins you would have at the end of the year if you could magically create new coins with your grandfather's crazy invention in the basement? We have this equation:

```
>>> 20 + 10 * 365
3670
>>> 3 * 52
156
>>> 3670 - 156
3514
```

We can turn this into a single line of code:

```
>>> 20 + 10 * 365 – 3 * 52
3514
```

Now, what if we turn the numbers into variables? Try entering the following:

```
>>> found_coins = 20
>>> magic_coins = 10
>>> stolen_coins = 3
```

These entries create the variables found_coins, magic_coins, and stolen_coins.

Now, we can reenter the equation like this:

```
>>> found_coins + magic_coins * 365 - stolen_coins * 52
3514
```

You can see that this gives us the same answer. So who cares, right? Ah, but here's the magic of variables. What if you stick a scarecrow in your window, and the raven steals only two coins

instead of three? When we use a variable, we can simply change the variable to hold that new number, and it will change everywhere it is used in the equation. We can change the stolen_coins variable to 2 by entering this:

```
>>> stolen_coins = 2
```

We can then copy and paste the equation to calculate the answer again, like so:

1. Select the text to copy by clicking with the mouse and dragging from the beginning to the end of the line, as shown here:

```
*Python Shell*
File  Edit  Debug  Options  Windows  Help
Python 3.2.2 (default, Sep  4 2011, 09:51:08) [MSC v.1500 32 bit (Intel)] on win
32
Type "copyright", "credits" or "license()" for more information.
==== No Subprocess ====
>>> found_coins = 20
>>> magic_coins = 10
>>> stolen_coins = 3
>>> found_coins + magic_coins * 365 - stolen_coins * 52
3514
>>> stolen_coins = 2
                                                                    Ln: 7 Col: 55
```

2. Hold down the CTRL key (or, if you're using a Mac, the ⌘ key) and press C to copy the selected text. (You'll see this as CTRL-C from now on.)

3. Click the last prompt line (after stolen_coins = 2).

4. Hold down the CTRL key and press V to paste the selected text. (You'll see this as CTRL-V from now on.)

5. Press ENTER to see the new result:

```
Python Shell
File  Edit  Debug  Options  Windows  Help
Python 3.2.2 (default, Sep  4 2011, 09:51:08) [MSC v.1500 32 bit (Intel)] on win
32
Type "copyright", "credits" or "license()" for more information.
==== No Subprocess ====
>>> found_coins = 20
>>> magic_coins = 10
>>> stolen_coins = 3
>>> found_coins + magic_coins * 365 - stolen_coins * 52
3514
>>> stolen_coins = 2
>>> found_coins + magic_coins * 365 - stolen_coins * 52
3566
>>> |
                                                                    Ln: 12 Col: 4
```

Isn't that a lot easier than retyping the whole equation? It sure is.

You can try changing the other variables, and then copy (CTRL-C) and paste (CTRL-V) the calculation to see the effect of your changes. For example, if you bang the sides of your grandfather's invention at the right moment, and it spits out an extra 3 coins each time, you'll find that you end up with 4661 coins at the end of the year:

```
>>> magic_coins = 13
>>> found_coins + magic_coins * 365 - stolen_coins * 52
4661
```

Of course, using variables for a simple equation like this one is still only *slightly* useful. We haven't gotten to *really* useful yet. For now, just remember that variables are a way of labeling things so that you can use them later.

WHAT YOU LEARNED

In this chapter you learned how to do simple equations using Python operators and how to use parentheses to control the order of operations (the order in which Python evaluates the parts of the equations). We then created variables to label values and used those variables in our calculations.

3

STRINGS, LISTS, TUPLES, AND MAPS

In Chapter 2, we did some basic calculations with Python, and you learned about variables. In this chapter, we'll work with some other items in Python programs: strings, lists, tuples, and maps. You'll use strings to display messages in your programs (such as "Get Ready" and "Game Over" messages in a game). You'll also discover how lists, tuples, and maps are used to store collections of things.

STRINGS

When programming, we usually call text a *string*. Think of a string as a collection of letters, and the term makes sense. All the letters, numbers, and symbols in this book could be a string, and so could your name and address. In fact, the first Python program we created in Chapter 1 used a string: "Hello World."

CREATING STRINGS

In Python, we create a string by putting quotes around text because programming languages need to distinguish between different types of values. (We need to tell the computer whether a value is a number, a string, or something else.) For example, we could take our fred variable from Chapter 2 and use it to label a string:

```
fred = "Why do gorillas have big nostrils? Big fingers!!"
```

Then, to see what's inside fred, we could enter print(fred):

```
>>> print(fred)
Why do gorillas have big nostrils? Big fingers!!
```

You can also use single quotes to create a string, like this:

```
>>> fred = 'What is pink and fluffy? Pink fluff!!'
>>> print(fred)
What is pink and fluffy? Pink fluff!!
```

However, if you try to enter more than one line of text for your string using only a single (') or double quote (") or if you start with one type of quote and finish with another, you'll get an error message in the Python shell. For example, enter the following line:

```
>>> fred = "How do dinosaurs pay their bills?
```

You'll see this result:

```
SyntaxError: EOL while scanning string literal
```

This is an error message complaining about syntax because you did not follow the rules for ending a string with a single or double quote.

Syntax means the arrangement and order of words in a sentence or, in this case, the arrangement and order of words and symbols in a program. So SyntaxError means that you did something in an order Python was not expecting, or Python was expecting something that you missed. *EOL* means *end-of-line*, so the rest of the error message is telling you that Python hit the end of the line and did not find a double quote to close the string.

To use more than one line of text in your string (called a *multiline string*), use three single quotes ('''), and then hit ENTER between lines, like this:

```
>>> fred = '''How do dinosaurs pay their bills?
With tyrannosaurus checks!'''
```

Now let's print out the contents of fred to see if this worked:

```
>>> print(fred)
How do dinosaurs pay their bills?
With tyrannosaurus checks!
```

HANDLING PROBLEMS WITH STRINGS

Now consider this crazy example of a string, which causes Python to display an error message:

```
>>> silly_string = 'He said, "Aren't can't shouldn't wouldn't."'
SyntaxError: invalid syntax
```

In the first line, we try to create a string (defined as the variable silly_string) enclosed by single quotes, but also containing a mixture of single quotes in the words can't, shouldn't, and wouldn't, as well as double quotes. What a mess!

Remember that Python itself is not as smart as a human being, so all it sees is a string containing He said, "Aren, followed by a bunch of other characters that it doesn't expect. When Python sees a quotation mark (either a single or double quote), it expects a string to start following the first mark and the string to end after the next matching quotation mark (either single or double) on that line. In this case, the start of the string is the single quotation mark before He, and the end of the string, as far as Python is concerned, is the single quote after the n in Aren. IDLE highlights the point where things have gone wrong:

The last line of IDLE tells us what sort of error occurred—in this case, a syntax error.

Using double instead of single quotes still produces an error:

```
>>> silly_string = "He said, "Aren't can't shouldn't wouldn't.""
SyntaxError: invalid syntax
```

Here, Python sees a string bounded by double quotes, containing the letters He said, (and a space). Everything following that string (from Aren't on) causes the error:

This is because, from Python's perspective, all that extra stuff just isn't supposed to be there. Python looks for the next matching quote and doesn't know what you want it to do with anything that follows that quote on the same line.

The solution to this problem is a multiline string, which we learned about earlier, using *three* single quotes (' ' '), which allows us to combine double and single quotes in our string without causing errors. In fact, if we use three single quotes, we can put any combination of single and double quotes inside the string (as long as we don't try to put three single quotes there). This is what the error-free version of our string looks like:

```
silly_string = '''He said, "Aren't can't shouldn't wouldn't."'''
```

But wait, there's more. If you really want to use single or double quotes to surround a string in Python, instead of three single quotes, you can add a backslash (\) before each quotation mark within the string. This is called *escaping*. It's a way of saying to Python, "Yes, I know I have quotes inside my string, and I want you to ignore them until you see the end quote."

Escaping strings can make them harder to read, so it's probably better to use multiline strings. Still, you might come across snippets of code that use escaping, so it's good to know why the backslashes are there.

Here are a few examples of how escaping works:

```
❶ >>> single_quote_str = 'He said, "Aren\'t can\'t shouldn\'t wouldn\'t."'
❷ >>> double_quote_str = "He said, \"Aren't can't shouldn't wouldn't.\""
>>> print(single_quote_str)
He said, "Aren't can't shouldn't wouldn't."
>>> print(double_quote_str)
He said, "Aren't can't shouldn't wouldn't."
```

First, at ❶, we create a string with single quotes, using the backslash in front of the single quotes inside that string. At ❷, we create a string with double quotes, and use the backslash in front of those quotes in the string. In the lines that follow, we print the variables we've just created. Notice that the backslash character doesn't appear in the strings when we print them.

EMBEDDING VALUES IN STRINGS

If you want to display a message using the contents of a variable, you can embed values in a string using %s, which is like a marker for a value that you want to add later. (*Embedding values*, also referred to as *string substitution*, is programmer-speak for "inserting values.") For example, to have Python calculate or store the number of points you scored in a game, and then add it to a sentence like "I scored ___ points," use %s in the sentence in place of the value, and then tell Python that value, like this:

```
>>> myscore = 1000
>>> message = 'I scored %s points'
>>> print(message % myscore)
I scored 1000 points
```

Here, we create the variable myscore with the value 1000 and the variable message with a string that contains the words "I scored %s points," where %s is a placeholder for the number of points. On the next line, we call print(message) with the % symbol to tell Python to replace %s with the value stored in the variable myscore. The result of printing this message is I scored 1000 points. We don't need to use a variable for the value. We could do the same example and just use print(message % 1000).

We can also pass in different values for the %s placeholder, using different variables, as in this example:

```
>>> joke_text = '%s: a device for finding furniture in the dark'
>>> bodypart1 = 'Knee'
>>> bodypart2 = 'Shin'
>>> print(joke_text % bodypart1)
Knee: a device for finding furniture in the dark
>>> print(joke_text % bodypart2)
Shin: a device for finding furniture in the dark
```

Here, we create three variables. The first, joke_text, includes the string with the %s marker. The other variables are bodypart1 and bodypart2. We can print the variable joke_text, and once again use the % operator to replace it with the contents of the variables bodypart1 and bodypart2 to produce different messages.

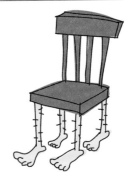

You can also use more than one placeholder in a string, like this:

```
>>> nums = 'What did the number %s say to the number %s? Nice belt!!'
>>> print(nums % (0, 8))
What did the number 0 say to the number 8? Nice belt!!
```

When using more than one placeholder, be sure to wrap the replacement values in parentheses, as shown in the example. The order of the values is the order in which they'll be used in the string.

MULTIPLYING STRINGS

What is 10 multiplied by 5? The answer is 50, of course. But what's 10 multiplied by a? Here's Python's answer:

```
>>> print(10 * 'a')
aaaaaaaaaa
```

Python programmers might use this approach to line up strings with a specific number of spaces when displaying messages in the shell, for example. How about printing a letter in the shell (select **File ▸ New Window**, and enter the following code):

```
spaces = ' ' * 25
print('%s 12 Butts Wynd' % spaces)
print('%s Twinklebottom Heath' % spaces)
print('%s West Snoring' % spaces)
print()
print()
print('Dear Sir')
print()
print('I wish to report that tiles are missing from the')
print('outside toilet roof.')
print('I think it was bad wind the other night that blew them away.')
print()
print('Regards')
print('Malcolm Dithering')
```

Once you've typed the code into the shell window, select **File ▸ Save As**. Name your file *myletter.py*. You can then run the code (as we've done previously) by selecting **Run ▸ Run Module**.

From now on, when you see Save As: somefilename.py *above a chunk of code, you'll know you need to select* **File ▸ New Window**, *enter the code into the window that appears, and then save it as we did in this example.*

In the first line of this example, we create the variable spaces by multiplying a space character by 25. We then use that variable in the next three lines to align the text to the right of the shell. You can see the result of these print statements below:

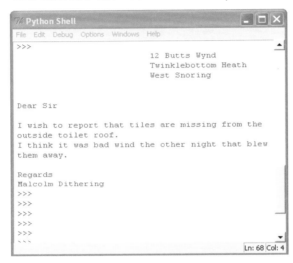

In addition to using multiplication for alignment, we can also use it to fill the screen with annoying messages. Try this example for yourself:

```
>>> print(1000 * 'snirt')
```

LISTS ARE MORE POWERFUL THAN STRINGS

"Spider legs, toe of frog, eye of newt, bat wing, slug butter, and snake dandruff" is not quite a normal shopping list (unless you happen to be a wizard), but we'll use it as our first example of the differences between strings and lists.

We could store this list of items in the `wizard_list` variable using a string like this:

```
>>> wizard_list = 'spider legs, toe of frog, eye of newt, bat wing,
slug butter, snake dandruff'
>>> print(wizard_list)
spider legs, toe of frog, eye of newt, bat wing, slug butter, snake
dandruff
```

But we could also create a *list*, a somewhat magical kind of Python object that we can manipulate. Here's what these items would look like written as a list:

```
>>> wizard_list = ['spider legs', 'toe of frog', 'eye of newt',
              'bat wing', 'slug butter', 'snake dandruff']
>>> print(wizard_list)
['spider legs', 'toe of frog', 'eye of newt', 'bat wing', 'slug
butter', 'snake dandruff']
```

Creating a list takes a bit more typing than creating a string, but a list is more useful than a string because it can be manipulated. For example, we could print the third item in the `wizard_list` (eye of newt) by entering its position in the list (called the *index position*) inside square brackets ([ ]), like this:

```
>>> print(wizard_list[2])
eye of newt
```

Huh? Isn't it the third item on the list? Yes, but lists start at index position 0, so the first item in a list is 0, the second is 1, and the third is 2. That may not make a lot of sense to humans, but it does to computers.

We can also change an item in a list much more easily than we could in a string. Perhaps instead of eye of newt we needed a snail tongue. Here's how we would do that with our list:

```
>>> wizard_list[2] = 'snail tongue'
>>> print(wizard_list)
['spider legs', 'toe of frog', 'snail tongue', 'bat wing', 'slug
butter', 'snake dandruff']
```

This sets the item in index position 2, previously eye of newt, to snail tongue.

Another option is to show a subset of the items in the list. We do this by using a colon (:) inside square brackets. For example, enter the following to see the third to fifth items in a list (a brilliant set of ingredients for a lovely sandwich):

```
>>> print(wizard_list[2:5])
['snail tongue', 'bat wing', 'slug butter']
```

Writing [2:5] is the same as saying, "show the items from index position 2 up to (but not including) index position 5"—or in other words, items 2, 3, and 4.

Lists can be used to store all sorts of items, like numbers:

```
>>> some_numbers = [1, 2, 5, 10, 20]
```

They can also hold strings:

```
>>> some_strings = ['Which', 'Witch', 'Is', 'Which']
```

They might have mixtures of numbers and strings:

```
>>> numbers_and_strings = ['Why', 'was', 6, 'afraid', 'of', 7,
                          'because', 7, 8, 9]
>>> print(numbers_and_strings)
['Why', 'was', 6, 'afraid', 'of', 7, 'because', 7, 8, 9]
```

And lists might even store other lists:

```
>>> numbers = [1, 2, 3, 4]
>>> strings = ['I', 'kicked', 'my', 'toe', 'and', 'it', 'is', 'sore']
>>> mylist = [numbers, strings]
>>> print(mylist)
[[1, 2, 3, 4], ['I', 'kicked', 'my', 'toe', 'and', 'it', 'is', 'sore']]
```

This list-within-list example creates three variables: numbers with four numbers, strings with eight strings, and mylist using numbers and strings. The third list (mylist) has only two elements because it's a list of variable names, not the contents of the variables.

ADDING ITEMS TO A LIST

To add items to a list, we use the append function. A *function* is a chunk of code that tells Python to do something. In this case, append adds an item to the end of a list.

For example, to add a bear burp (I'm sure there is such a thing) to the wizard's shopping list, do this:

```
>>> wizard_list.append('bear burp')
>>> print(wizard_list)
['spider legs', 'toe of frog', 'snail tongue', 'bat wing', 'slug butter', 'snake dandruff', 'bear burp']
```

You can keep adding more magical items to the wizard's list in the same way, like so:

```
>>> wizard_list.append('mandrake')
>>> wizard_list.append('hemlock')
>>> wizard_list.append('swamp gas')
```

Now the wizard's list looks like this:

```
>>> print(wizard_list)
['spider legs', 'toe of frog', 'snail tongue', 'bat wing', 'slug butter', 'snake dandruff', 'bear burp', 'mandrake', 'hemlock', 'swamp gas']
```

The wizard is clearly ready to work some serious magic!

REMOVING ITEMS FROM A LIST

To remove items from a list, use the del command (short for *delete*). For example, to remove the sixth item in the wizard's list, snake dandruff, do this:

```
>>> del wizard_list[5]
>>> print(wizard_list)
['spider legs', 'toe of frog', 'snail tongue', 'bat wing', 'slug butter', 'bear burp', 'mandrake', 'hemlock', 'swamp gas']
```

NOTE   *Remember that positions start at zero, so* wizard_list[5] *actually refers to the sixth item in the list.*

And here's how to remove the items we just added (mandrake, hemlock, and swamp gas):

```
>>> del wizard_list[8]
>>> del wizard_list[7]
>>> del wizard_list[6]
>>> print(wizard_list)
['spider legs', 'toe of frog', 'snail tongue', 'bat wing', 'slug
butter', 'bear burp']
```

LIST ARITHMETIC

We can join lists by adding them, just like adding numbers, using a plus (+) sign. For example, suppose we have two lists: list1, containing the numbers 1 through 4, and list2, containing some words. We can add them using print and the + sign, like so:

```
>>> list1 = [1, 2, 3, 4]
>>> list2 = ['I', 'tripped', 'over', 'and', 'hit', 'the', 'floor']
>>> print(list1 + list2)
[1, 2, 3, 4, 'I', 'tripped', 'over', 'and', 'hit', 'the', 'floor']
```

We can also add the two lists and set the result equal to another variable.

```
>>> list1 = [1, 2, 3, 4]
>>> list2 = ['I', 'ate', 'chocolate', 'and', 'I', 'want', 'more']
>>> list3 = list1 + list2
>>> print(list3)
[1, 2, 3, 4, 'I', 'ate', 'chocolate', 'and', 'I', 'want', 'more']
```

And we can multiply a list by a number. For example, to multiply list1 by 5, we write list1 * 5:

```
>>> list1 = [1, 2]
>>> print(list1 * 5)
[1, 2, 1, 2, 1, 2, 1, 2, 1, 2]
```

This is actually telling Python to repeat list1 five times, resulting in 1, 2, 1, 2, 1, 2, 1, 2, 1, 2.

On the other hand, division (/) and subtraction (-) give only errors, as in these examples:

```
>>> list1 / 20
Traceback (most recent call last):
  File "<pyshell>", line 1, in <module>
    list1 / 20
TypeError: unsupported operand type(s) for /: 'list' and 'int'

>>> list1 - 20
Traceback (most recent call last):
  File "<pyshell>", line 1, in <module>
    list1 - 20
TypeError: unsupported operand type(s) for -: 'list' and 'int'
```

But why? Well, joining lists with + and repeating lists with * are straightforward enough operations. These concepts also make sense in the real world. For example, if I were to hand you two paper shopping lists and say, "Add these two lists," you might write out all the items on another sheet of paper in order, end to end. The same might be true if I said, "Multiply this list by 3." You could imagine writing a list of all of the list's items three times on another sheet of paper.

But how would you divide a list? For example, consider how you would divide a list of six numbers (1 through 6) in two. Here are just three different ways:

```
[1, 2, 3]        [4, 5, 6]
[1]              [2, 3, 4, 5, 6]
[1, 2, 3, 4]     [5, 6]
```

Would we divide the list in the middle, split it after the first item, or just pick some random place and divide it there? There's no simple answer, and when you ask Python to divide a list, it doesn't know what to do, either. That's why it responds with an error.

The same goes for adding anything other than a list to a list. You can't do that either. For example, here's what happens when we try to add the number 50 to list1:

```
>>> list1 + 50
Traceback (most recent call last):
  File "<pyshell>", line 1, in <module>
    list1 + 50
TypeError: can only concatenate list (not "int") to list
```

Why do we get an error here? Well, what does it mean to add 50 to a list? Does it mean add 50 to each item? But what if the items aren't numbers? Does it mean add the number 50 to the end or beginning of the list?

In computer programming, commands should work in exactly the same way every time you enter them. That dumb computer sees things only in black and white. Ask it to make a complicated decision, and it throws up its hands with errors.

TUPLES

A *tuple* is like a list that uses parentheses, as in this example:

```
>>> fibs = (0, 1, 1, 2, 3)
>>> print(fibs[3])
2
```

Here we define the variable fibs as the numbers 0, 1, 1, 2, and 3. Then, as with a list, we print the item in index position 3 in the tuple using print(fibs[3]).

The main difference between a tuple and a list is that a tuple cannot change once you've created it. For example, if we try to replace the first value in the tuple fibs with the number 4 (just as we replaced values in our wizard_list), we get an error message:

```
>>> fibs[0] = 4
Traceback (most recent call last):
  File "<pyshell>", line 1, in <module>
    fibs[0] = 4
TypeError: 'tuple' object does not support item assignment
```

Why would you use a tuple instead of a list? Basically because sometimes it is useful to use something that you know can never change. If you create a tuple with two elements inside, it will always have those two elements inside.

PYTHON MAPS WON'T HELP YOU FIND YOUR WAY

In Python, a *map* (also referred to as a *dict*, short for *dictionary*) is a collection of things, like lists and tuples. The difference between maps and lists or tuples is that each item in a map has a *key* and a corresponding *value*.

For example, say we have a list of people and their favorite sports. We could put this information into a Python list, with the person's name followed by their sport, like so:

```
>>> favorite_sports = ['Ralph Williams, Football',
                       'Michael Tippett, Basketball',
                       'Edward Elgar, Baseball',
                       'Rebecca Clarke, Netball',
                       'Ethel Smyth, Badminton',
                       'Frank Bridge, Rugby']
```

If I asked you what Rebecca Clarke's favorite sport is, you could skim through that list and find the answer is netball. But what if the list included 100 (or many more) people?

Now, if we store this same information in a map, with the person's name as the key and their favorite sport as the value, the Python code would look like this:

```
>>> favorite_sports = {'Ralph Williams' : 'Football',
                       'Michael Tippett' : 'Basketball',
                       'Edward Elgar' : 'Baseball',
                       'Rebecca Clarke' : 'Netball',
                       'Ethel Smyth' : 'Badminton',
                       'Frank Bridge' : 'Rugby'}
```

We use colons to separate each key from its value, and each key and value is surrounded by single quotes. Notice, too, that the items in a map are enclosed in braces ({}), not parentheses or square brackets.

The result is a map (each key maps to a particular value), as shown in Table 3-1.

Table 3-1: Keys Pointing to Values in a Map of Favorite Sports

Key	Value
Ralph Williams	Football
Michael Tippett	Basketball
Edward Elgar	Baseball
Rebecca Clarke	Netball
Ethel Smyth	Badminton
Frank Bridge	Rugby

Now, to get Rebecca Clarke's favorite sport, we access our map favorite_sports using her name as the key, like so:

```
>>> print(favorite_sports['Rebecca Clarke'])
Netball
```

And the answer is netball.

To delete a value in a map, use its key. For example, here's how to remove Ethel Smyth:

```
>>> del favorite_sports['Ethel Smyth']
>>> print(favorite_sports)
{'Rebecca Clarke': 'Netball', 'Michael Tippett': 'Basketball', 'Ralph
Williams': 'Football', 'Edward Elgar': 'Baseball', 'Frank Bridge':
'Rugby'}
```

To replace a value in a map, we also use its key:

```
>>> favorite_sports['Ralph Williams'] = 'Ice Hockey'
>>> print(favorite_sports)
{'Rebecca Clarke': 'Netball', 'Michael Tippett': 'Basketball', 'Ralph
Williams': 'Ice Hockey', 'Edward Elgar': 'Baseball', 'Frank Bridge':
'Rugby'}
```

We replace the favorite sport of Football with Ice Hockey by using the key Ralph Williams.

As you can see, working with maps is kind of like working with lists and tuples, except that you can't join maps with the plus operator (+). If you try to do that, you'll get an error message:

```
>>> favorite_sports = {'Rebecca Clarke': 'Netball',
                       'Michael Tippett': 'Basketball',
                       'Ralph Williams': 'Ice Hockey',
                       'Edward Elgar': 'Baseball',
                       'Frank Bridge': 'Rugby'}
>>> favorite_colors = {'Malcolm Warner' : 'Pink polka dots',
                       'James Baxter' : 'Orange stripes',
                       'Sue Lee' : 'Purple paisley'}
>>> favorite_sports + favorite_colors
Traceback (most recent call last):
  File "<stdin>", line 1, in <module>
TypeError: unsupported operand type(s) for +: 'dict' and 'dict'
```

Joining maps doesn't make sense to Python, so it just throws up its hands.

WHAT YOU LEARNED

In this chapter, you learned how Python uses strings to store text, and how it uses lists and tuples to handle multiple items. You saw that the items in lists can be changed, and that you can join one list to another list, but that the values in a tuple cannot change. You also learned how to use maps to store values with keys that identify them.

PROGRAMMING PUZZLES

The following are a few experiments you can try yourself. The answers can be found at *http://python-for-kids.com/*.

#1: FAVORITES

Make a list of your favorite hobbies and give the list the variable name games. Now make a list of your favorite foods and name the variable foods. Join the two lists and name the result favorites. Finally, print the variable favorites.

#2: COUNTING COMBATANTS

If there are 3 buildings with 25 ninjas hiding on each roof and 2 tunnels with 40 samurai hiding inside each tunnel, how many ninjas and samurai are about to do battle? (You can do this with one equation in the Python shell.)

#3: GREETINGS!

Create two variables: one that points to your first name and one that points to your last name. Now create a string and use placeholders to print your name with a message using those two variables, such as "Hi there, Brando Ickett!"

4
DRAWING WITH TURTLES

A *turtle* in Python is sort of like a turtle in the real world. We know a turtle as a reptile that moves around very slowly and carries its house on its back. In the world of Python, a turtle is a small, black arrow that moves slowly around the screen. Actually, considering that a Python turtle leaves a trail as it moves around the screen, it's actually less like a turtle and more like a snail or a slug.

The turtle is a nice way to learn some of the basics of computer graphics, so in this chapter, we'll use a Python turtle to draw some simple shapes and lines.

USING PYTHON'S TURTLE MODULE

A *module* in Python is a way of providing useful code to be used by another program (among other things, the module can contain functions we can use). We'll learn more about modules in Chapter 7. Python has a special module called turtle that we can use to learn how computers draw pictures on a screen. The turtle module is a way of programming vector graphics, which is basically just drawing with simple lines, dots, and curves.

Let's see how the turtle works. First, start the Python shell by clicking the desktop icon (or if you're using Ubuntu, select **Applications ▸ Programming ▸ IDLE**). Next, tell Python to use the turtle by importing the turtle module, as follows:

```
>>> import turtle
```

Importing a module tells Python that you want to use it.

If you're using Ubuntu and you get an error at this point, you might need to install tkinter. To do so, open the Ubuntu Software Center and enter python-tk *in the search box. "Tkinter – Writing Tk Applications with Python" should appear in the window. Click* **Install** *to install this package.*

CREATING A CANVAS

Now that we have imported the turtle module, we need to create a canvas—a blank space to draw on, like an artist's canvas. To do so, we call the function Pen from the turtle module, which automatically creates a canvas (we'll learn more about what a function is later). Enter this into the Python shell:

```
>>> t = turtle.Pen()
```

You should see a blank box (the canvas), with an arrow in the center, something like this:

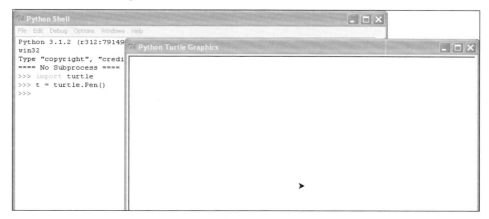

The arrow in the middle of the screen is the turtle, and you're right—it isn't very turtle-like.

If the Turtle window appears behind the Python Shell window, you may find that it doesn't seem to be working properly. When you move your mouse over the Turtle window, the cursor turns into an hourglass, like this:

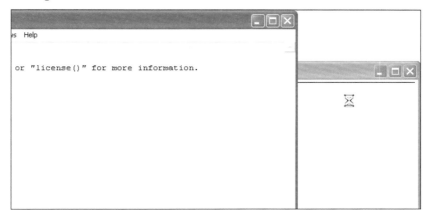

This could happen for several reasons: you haven't started the shell from the icon on your desktop (if you're using Windows or a Mac), you clicked IDLE (Python GUI) in the Windows Start menu, or IDLE isn't installed correctly. Try exiting and restarting the shell from the desktop icon. If that fails, try using the Python console instead of the shell, as follows:

- In Windows, select **Start ▸ All Programs**, and then in the **Python 3.2** group, click **Python (command line)**.
- In Mac OS X, click the Spotlight icon at the top-right corner of the screen and enter *Terminal* in the input box. Then enter *python* when the terminal opens.
- In Ubuntu, open the terminal from your **Applications** menu and enter *python*.

MOVING THE TURTLE

You send instructions to the turtle by using functions available on the variable t we just created, similar to using the Pen function in the turtle module. For example, the forward instruction tells the turtle to move forward. To tell the turtle to advance 50 pixels, enter the following command:

```
>>> t.forward(50)
```

You should see something like this:

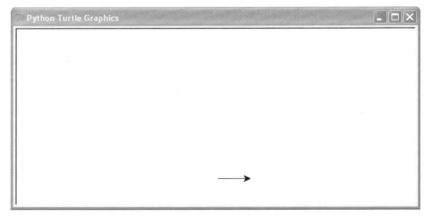

The turtle has moved forward 50 pixels. A *pixel* is a single point on the screen—the smallest element that can be represented. Everything you see on your computer monitor is made up of pixels, which are tiny, square dots. If you could zoom in on the canvas and the line drawn by the turtle, you would be able to see that the arrow representing the turtle's path is just a bunch of pixels. That's simple computer graphics.

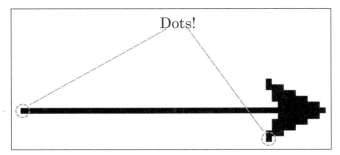

Now we'll tell the turtle to turn left 90 degrees with the following command:

```
>>> t.left(90)
```

If you haven't learned about degrees yet, here's how to think about them. Imagine that you're standing in the center of a circle.

- The direction you're facing is 0 degrees.
- If you hold out your left arm, that's 90 degrees left.
- If you hold out your right arm, that's 90 degrees right.

You can see this 90-degree turn to the left or right here:

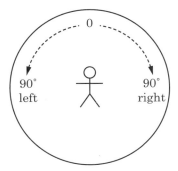

If you continue around the circle to the right from where your right arm is pointing, 180 degrees is directly behind you, 270 degrees is the direction your left arm is pointing, and 360 degrees is back where you started; degrees go from 0 to 360. The degrees in a full circle, when turning to the right, can be seen here in 45-degree increments:

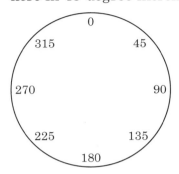

When Python's turtle turns left, it swivels around to face the new direction (just as if you turned your body to face where your arm is pointing 90 degrees left).

The t.left(90) command points the arrow up (since it started by pointing to the right):

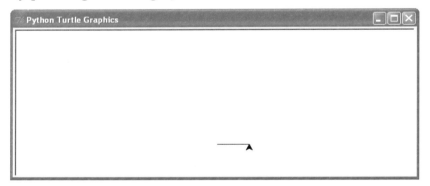

NOTE   *When you call t.left(90), it's the same as calling t.right(270). This is also true of calling t.right(90), which is the same as t.left(270). Just imagine that circle and follow along with the degrees.*

Now we'll draw a square. Add the following code to the lines you've already entered:

```
>>> t.forward(50)
>>> t.left(90)
```

```
>>> t.forward(50)
>>> t.left(90)
>>> t.forward(50)
>>> t.left(90)
```

Your turtle should have drawn a square and should now be facing in the same direction it started:

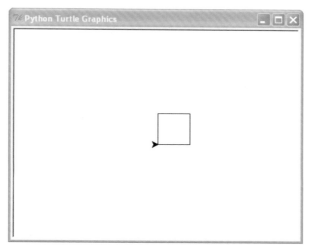

To erase the canvas, enter reset. This clears the canvas and puts the turtle back at its starting position.

```
>>> t.reset()
```

You can also use clear, which just clears the screen and leaves the turtle where it is.

```
>>> t.clear()
```

We can also turn our turtle right or move it backward. We can use up to lift the pen off the page (in other words, tell the turtle to stop drawing), and down to start drawing. These functions are written in the same way as the others we've used.

Let's try another drawing using some of these commands. This time, we'll have the turtle draw two lines. Enter the following code:

```
>>> t.reset()
>>> t.backward(100)
>>> t.up()
>>> t.right(90)
```

```
>>> t.forward(20)
>>> t.left(90)
>>> t.down()
>>> t.forward(100)
```

First, we reset the canvas and move the turtle back to its starting position with t.reset(). Next, we move the turtle backward 100 pixels with t.backward(100), and then use t.up() to pick up the pen and stop drawing.

Then, with the command t.right(90), we turn the turtle right 90 degrees to point down, toward the bottom of the screen, and with t.forward(20), we move forward 20 pixels. Nothing is drawn because of the use of up command on the third line. We turn the turtle left 90 degrees to face right with t.left(90), and then with the down command, we tell the turtle to put the pen back down and start drawing again. Finally, we draw a line forward, parallel to the first line we drew, with t.forward(100). The two parallel lines we've drawn end up looking like this:

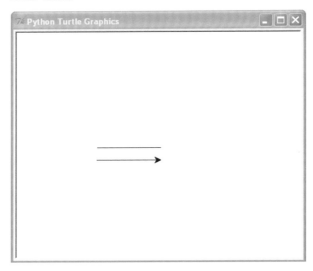

WHAT YOU LEARNED

In this chapter, you learned how to use Python's turtle module. We drew some simple lines, using left and right turns and forward and backward commands. You found out how to stop the turtle from drawing using up, and start drawing again with down. You also discovered that the turtle turns by degrees.

PROGRAMMING PUZZLES

Try drawing some of the following shapes with the turtle. The answers can be found at *http://python-for-kids.com/*.

#1: A RECTANGLE

Create a new canvas using the turtle module's Pen function and then draw a rectangle.

#2: A TRIANGLE

Create another canvas, and this time, draw a triangle. Look back at the diagram of the circle with the degrees ("Moving the Turtle" on page 46) to remind yourself which direction to turn the turtle using degrees.

#3: A BOX WITHOUT CORNERS

Write a program to draw the four lines shown here (the size isn't important, just the shape):

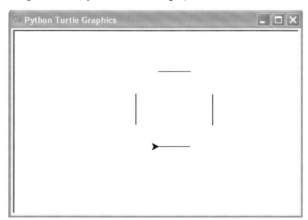

5
ASKING QUESTIONS WITH IF AND ELSE

In programming, we often ask yes or no questions, and decide to do something based on the answer. For example, we might ask, "Are you older than 20?" and if the answer is yes, respond with "You are too old!"

These sorts of questions are called *conditions*, and we combine these conditions and the responses into *if statements*. Conditions can be more complicated than a single question, and if statements can also be combined with multiple questions and different responses based on the answer to each question.

In this chapter, you'll learn how to use if statements to build programs.

IF STATEMENTS

An if statement might be written in Python like this:

```
>>> age = 13
>>> if age > 20:
        print('You are too old!')
```

An if statement is made up of the if keyword, followed by a condition and a colon (:), as in if age > 20:. The lines following the colon must be in a block, and if the answer to the question is yes (or *true*, as we say in Python programming), the commands in the block will be run. Now, let's explore how to write blocks and conditions.

A BLOCK IS A GROUP OF PROGRAMMING STATEMENTS

A *block* of code is a grouped set of programming statements. For example, when if age > 20: is true, you might want to do more than just print "You are too old!" Perhaps you want to print out a few other choice sentences, like this:

```
>>> age = 25
>>> if age > 20:
        print('You are too old!')
        print('Why are you here?')
        print('Why aren\'t you mowing a lawn or sorting papers?')
```

This block of code is made up of three `print` statements that are run only if the condition age > 20 is found to be true. Each line in the block has four spaces at the beginning, when you compare it with the `if` statement above it. Let's look at that code again, with visible spaces:

```
>>> age = 25
>>> if age > 20:
    ⬚⬚⬚⬚print('You are too old!')
    ⬚⬚⬚⬚print('Why are you here?')
    ⬚⬚⬚⬚print('Why aren\'t you mowing a lawn or sorting papers?')
```

In Python, *whitespace*, such as a tab (inserted when you press the TAB key) or a space (inserted when you press the spacebar), is meaningful. Code that is at the same position (indented the same number of spaces from the left margin) is grouped into a block, and whenever you start a new line with more spaces than the previous one, you are starting a new block that is part of the previous one, like this:

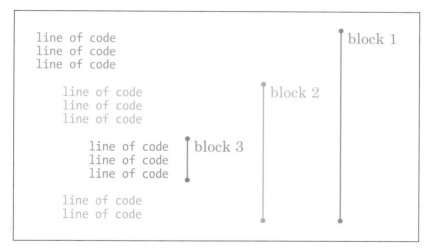

We group statements together into blocks because they are related. The statements need to be run together.

When you change the indentation, you're generally creating new blocks. The following example shows three separate blocks that are created just by changing the indentation.

```
line of code                        │ block 1
line of code
line of code

    line of code    │ block 2
    line of code
    line of code

line of code
line of code
line of code

    line of code    │ block 3
    line of code
    line of code
```

Here, even though blocks 2 and 3 have the same indentation, they are considered different blocks because there is a block with less indentation (fewer spaces) between them.

For that matter, a block with four spaces on one line and six spaces on the next will produce an *indentation error* when you run it, because Python expects you to use the same number of spaces for all the lines in a block. So if you start a block with four spaces, you should consistently use four spaces for that block. Here's an example:

```
>>> if age > 20:
    ▯▯▯▯print('You are too old!')
    ▯▯▯▯▯▯print('Why are you here?')
```

I've made the spaces visible so that you can see the differences. Notice that the third line has six spaces instead of four.

When we try to run this code, IDLE highlights the line where it sees a problem with a red block and displays an explanatory SyntaxError message:

```
>>> age = 25
>>> if age > 20:
        print('You are too old!')
        ▮print('Why are you here?')
SyntaxError: unexpected indent
```

Python didn't expect to see two extra spaces at the beginning of the second print line.

Use consistent spacing to make your code easier to read. If you start writing a program and put four spaces at the beginning of a block, keep using four spaces at the beginning of the other blocks in your program. Also, be sure to indent each line in the same block with the same number of spaces.

CONDITIONS HELP US COMPARE THINGS

A *condition* is a programming statement that compares things and tells us whether the criteria set by the comparison are either True (yes) or False (no). For example, age > 10 is a condition, and is another way of saying, "Is the value of the age variable greater than 10?" This is also a condition: hair_color == 'mauve', which is another way of saying, "Is the value of the hair_color variable mauve?"

We use symbols in Python (called *operators*) to create our conditions, such as equal to, greater than, and less than. Table 5-1 lists some symbols for conditions.

Table 5-1: Symbols for Conditions

Symbol	Definition
==	Equal to
!=	Not equal to
>	Greater than
<	Less than
>=	Greater than or equal to
<=	Less than or equal to

For example, if you are 10 years old, the condition your_age == 10 would return True; otherwise, it would return False. If you are 12 years old, the condition your_age > 10 would return True.

Be sure to use a double equal sign (==) when defining an equal-to condition.

Let's try a few more examples. Here, we set our age as equal to 10 and then write a conditional statement that will print "You are too old for my jokes!" if age is greater than 10:

```
>>> age = 10
>>> if age > 10:
        print('You are too old for my jokes!')
```

What happens when we type this into IDLE and press ENTER?

Nothing.

Because the value returned by age is not greater than 10, Python does not execute (run) the print block. However, if we had set the variable age to 20, the message would be printed.

Now let's change the previous example to use a greater-than-or-equal-to (>=) condition:

```
>>> age = 10
>>> if age >= 10:
        print('You are too old for my jokes!')
```

You should see "You are too old for my jokes!" printed to the screen because the value of age is equal to 10.

Next, let's try using an equal-to (==) condition:

```
>>> age = 10
>>> if age == 10:
        print('What\'s brown and sticky? A stick!!')
```

You should see the message "What's brown and sticky? A stick!!" printed to the screen.

IF-THEN-ELSE STATEMENTS

In addition to using if statements to do something when a condition is met (True), we can also use if statements to do something when a condition is not true. For example, we might print one message to the screen if your age is 12 and another if it's not 12 (False).

The trick here is to use an if-then-else statement, which essentially says "*If* something is true, then do this; or *else*, do that."

Let's create an if-then-else statement. Enter the following into the shell:

```
>>> print("Want to hear a dirty joke?")
Want to hear a dirty joke?
```

```
>>> age = 12
>>> if age == 12:
        print("A pig fell in the mud!")
else:
        print("Shh. It's a secret.")

A pig fell in the mud!
```

Because we've set the age variable to 12, and the condition is asking whether age is equal to 12, you should see the first print message on the screen. Now try changing the value of age to a number other than 12, like this:

```
>>> print("Want to hear a dirty joke?")
Want to hear a dirty joke?
>>> age = 8
>>> if age == 12:
        print("A pig fell in the mud!")
else:
        print("Shh. It's a secret.")

Shh. It's a secret.
```

This time, you should see the second print message.

IF AND ELIF STATEMENTS

We can extend an if statement even further with elif (which is short for else-if). For example, we can check if a person's age is 10, 11, or 12 (and so on) and have our program do something different based on the answer. These statements are different from if-then-else statements in that there can be more than one elif in the same statement:

```
      >>> age = 12
❶  >>> if age == 10:
❷          print("What do you call an unhappy cranberry?")
          print("A blueberry!")
```

```
❸ elif age == 11:
        print("What did the green grape say to the blue grape?")
        print("Breathe! Breathe!")
❹ elif age == 12:
❺       print("What did 0 say to 8?")
        print("Hi guys!")
  elif age == 13:
        print("Why wasn't 10 afraid of 7?")
        print("Because rather than eating 9, 7 8 pi.")
  else:
        print("Huh?")

What did 0 say to 8? Hi guys!
```

In this example, the if statement on the second line checks to see if the value of the age variable is equal to 10 at ❶. The print statement that follows at ❷ is run if age is equal to 10. However, since we've set age equal to 12, the computer jumps to the next if statement at ❸ and checks if the value of age is equal to 11. It isn't, so the computer jumps to the next if statement at ❹ to see if age is equal to 12. It is, so this time, the computer executes the print command at ❺.

When you enter this code in the IDLE, it will automatically indent, so be sure to press the BACKSPACE or DELETE key once you've typed each print statement, so that your if, elif, and else statements will start at the far-left margin. This is the same position the if statement would be in if the prompt (>>>) were absent.

COMBINING CONDITIONS

You can combine conditions by using the keywords and and or, which produces shorter and simpler code. Here's an example of using or:

```
>>> if age == 10 or age == 11 or age == 12 or age == 13:
        print('What is 13 + 49 + 84 + 155 + 97? A headache!')
else:
        print('Huh?')
```

In this code, if any of the conditions on the first line are true (in other words, if age is 10, 11, 12, *or* 13), the block of code on the next line beginning with print will run.

If the conditions in the first line are not true (else), Python moves to the block in the last line, displaying Huh? on the screen.

To shrink this example even further, we could use the and keyword, along with the greater than or equal-to operator (>=) and less-than-or-equal-to operator (<=), as follows:

```
>>> if age >= 10 and age <= 13:
        print('What is 13 + 49 + 84 + 155 + 97? A headache!')
else:
        print('Huh?')
```

Here, if age is greater than or equal to 10 *and* less than or equal to 13, as defined on the first line with if age >= 10 and age <= 13:, the block of code beginning with print on the following line will run. For example, if the value of age is 12, then What is 13 + 49 + 84 + 155 + 97? A headache! will be printed to the screen, because 12 is more than 10 and less than 13.

VARIABLES WITH NO VALUE—NONE

Just as we can assign numbers, strings, and lists to a variable, we can also assign nothing, or an empty value, to a variable. In Python, an empty value is referred to as None, and it is the absence of value. And it's important to note that the value None is different from the value 0 because it is the absence of a value, rather than a number with a value of 0. The only value that a variable has when we give it the empty value None is nothing. Here's an example:

```
>>> myval = None
>>> print(myval)
None
```

Assigning a value of None to a variable is a way of saying that the variable no longer has any value (or rather, that it no longer labels a value). Setting a variable to None is also a way to define a variable without setting its value. You might do this when you know you're going to need a variable later in your program, but you want to define all your variables at the beginning. Programmers often define their variables at the beginning of a program because placing them there makes it easy to see the names of all the variables used by a chunk of code.

You can check for None in an if statement as well, as in the following example:

```
>>> myval = None
>>> if myval == None:
        print("The variable myval doesn't have a value")

The variable myval doesn't have a value
```

This is useful when you only want to calculate a value for a variable if it hasn't already been calculated.

THE DIFFERENCE BETWEEN STRINGS AND NUMBERS

User input is what a person enters on the keyboard—whether that's a character, a pressed arrow or ENTER key, or anything else. User input comes into Python as a string, which means that when you type the number 10 on your keyboard, Python saves the number 10 into a variable as a string, not a number.

What's the difference between the number 10 and the string '10'? Both look the same to us, with the only difference being that one is surrounded by quotes. But to a computer, the two are very different.

For example, suppose that we compare the value of the variable age to a number in an `if` statement, like this:

```
>>> if age == 10:
        print("What's the best way to speak to a monster?")
        print("From as far away as possible!")
```

Then we set the variable age to the number 10:

```
>>> age = 10
>>> if age == 10:
        print("What's the best way to speak to a monster?")
        print("From as far away as possible!")
What's the best way to speak to a monster?
From as far away as possible!
```

As you can see, the `print` statement executes.

Next, we set age to the string `'10'` (with quotes), like this:

```
>>> age = '10'
>>> if age == 10:
        print("What's the best way to speak to a monster?")
        print("From as far away as possible!")
```

Here, the code in the `print` statement doesn't run because Python doesn't see the number in quotes (a string) as a number.

Fortunately, Python has magic functions that can turn strings into numbers and numbers into strings. For example, you can convert the string `'10'` into a number with `int`:

```
>>> age = '10'
>>> converted_age = int(age)
```

The variable `converted_age` would now hold the number 10.

To convert a number into a string, use `str`:

```
>>> age = 10
>>> converted_age = str(age)
```

In this case, `converted_age` would hold the string 10 instead of the number 10.

Remember that `if age == 10` statement that didn't print anything when the variable was set to a string (`age = '10'`)? If we convert the variable first, we get an entirely different result:

```
>>> age = '10'
>>> converted_age = int(age)
>>> if converted_age == 10:
        print("What's the best way to speak to a monster?")
        print("From as far away as possible!")
What's the best way to speak to a monster?
From as far away as possible!
```

But hear this: If you try to convert a number with a decimal point, you'll get an error because the `int` function expects an integer.

```
>>> age = '10.5'
>>> converted_age = int(age)
Traceback (most recent call last):
    File "<pyshell#35>", line 1, in <module>
    converted_age = int(age)
ValueError: invalid literal for int() with base 10: '10.5'
```

A `ValueError` is what Python uses to tell you that the value you have tried to use isn't appropriate. To fix this, use the function `float` instead of `int`. The `float` function can handle numbers that aren't integers.

```
>>> age = '10.5'
>>> converted_age = float(age)
>>> print(converted_age)
10.5
```

You will also get a `ValueError` if you try to convert a string that doesn't contain a number in digits:

```
>>> age = 'ten'
>>> converted_age = int(age)
Traceback (most recent call last):
    File "<pyshell#1>", line 1, in <module>
```

```
converted_age = int(age)
ValueError: invalid literal for int() with base 10: 'ten'
```

WHAT YOU LEARNED

In this chapter, you learned how to work with `if` statements to create blocks of code that are executed only when particular conditions are true. You saw how to extend `if` statements using `elif` so that different sections of code will execute as a result of different conditions, and how to use the `else` keyword to execute code if none of the conditions turn out to be true. You also learned how to combine conditions using the `and` and `or` keywords so that you can see if numbers fall in a range, and how to change strings into numbers with `int`, `str`, and `float`. And you discovered that nothing (`None`) has meaning in Python and can be used to reset variables to their initial, empty state.

PROGRAMMING PUZZLES

Try the following puzzles using `if` statement and conditions. The answers can be found at *http://python-for-kids.com/*.

#1: ARE YOU RICH?

What do you think the following code will do? Try to figure out the answer without typing it into the shell, and then check your answer.

```
>>> money = 2000
>>> if money > 1000:
        print("I'm rich!!")
else:
        print("I'm not rich!!")
            print("But I might be later...")
```

#2: TWINKIES!

Create an `if` statement that checks whether a number of Twinkies (in the variable `twinkies`) is less than 100 or greater than 500. Your program should print the message "Too few or too many" if the condition is true.

#3: JUST THE RIGHT NUMBER

Create an if statement that checks whether the amount of money contained in the variable money is between 100 and 500 *or* between 1,000 and 5,000.

#4: I CAN FIGHT THOSE NINJAS

Create an if statement that prints the string "That's too many" if the variable ninjas contains a number that's less than 50, prints "It'll be a struggle, but I can take 'em" if it's less than 30, and prints "I can fight those ninjas!" if it's less than 10. You might try out your code with:

```
>>> ninjas = 5
```

6

GOING LOOPY

Nothing is worse than having to do the same thing over and over again. There's a reason why some people count sheep when they're having trouble falling asleep, and it has nothing to do with the amazing sleep-inducing powers of woolly mammals. It's because endlessly repeating something is boring, and your mind can drop off to sleep more easily if you're not focusing on something interesting.

Programmers don't particularly like repeating themselves either, unless they're also trying to fall asleep. Thankfully, most programming languages have what is called a for loop, which repeats things like other programming statements and blocks of code automatically.

In this chapter, we'll look at for loops, as well as another type of loop that Python offers: the while loop.

USING FOR LOOPS

To print hello five times in Python, you *could* do the following:

```
>>> print("hello")
hello
>>> print("hello")
hello
>>> print("hello")
hello
>>> print("hello")
hello
>>> print("hello")
hello
```

But this is rather tedious. Instead, you can use a for loop to reduce the amount of typing and repetition, like this:

```
❶ >>> for x in range(0, 5):
❷         print('hello')

hello
hello
hello
hello
hello
```

The range function at ❶ can be used to create a list of numbers ranging from a starting number up to the number just before the ending number. That may sound a little confusing. Let's combine the range function with the list function to see exactly how this works. The range function doesn't actually create a list of numbers; it returns an *iterator*, which is a type of Python object specially designed to work with loops. However, if we combine range with list, we get a list of numbers.

```
>>> print(list(range(10, 20)))
[10, 11, 12, 13, 14, 15, 16, 17, 18, 19]
```

In the case of the for loop, the code at ❶ is actually telling Python to do the following:

- Start counting from 0 and stop before reaching 5.
- For each number we count, store the value in the variable x.

Then Python executes the block of code at ❷. Note that there are four additional spaces at the beginning of line ❷ (when you compare with line ❶). IDLE will have automatically indented this for you.

When we hit ENTER after the second line, Python prints "hello" five times.

We could also use the x in our print statement to count the hellos:

```
>>> for x in range(0, 5):
        print('hello %s' % x)
hello 0
hello 1
hello 2
hello 3
hello 4
```

If we get rid of the for loop again, our code might look something like this:

```
>>> x = 0
>>> print('hello %s' % x)
hello 0
>>> x = 1
>>> print('hello %s' % x)
hello 1
>>> x = 2
>>> print('hello %s' % x)
hello 2
```

```
>>> x = 3
>>> print('hello %s' % x)
hello 3
>>> x = 4
>>> print('hello %s' % x)
hello 4
```

So using the loop has actually saved us from writing eight extra lines of code. Good programmers hate doing things more than once, so the for loop is one of the more popular statements in a programming language.

You don't need to stick to using the range and list functions when making for loops. You could also use a list you've already created, such as the shopping list from Chapter 3, as follows:

```
>>> wizard_list = ['spider legs', 'toe of frog', 'snail tongue',
                   'bat wing', 'slug butter', 'bear burp']
>>> for i in wizard_list:
        print(i)
spider legs
toe of frog
snail tongue
bat wing
slug butter
bear burp
```

This code is a way of saying, "For each item in wizard_list, store the value in the variable i, and then print the contents of that variable." Again, if we got rid of the for loop, we would need to do something like this:

```
>>> wizard_list = ['spider legs', 'toe of frog', 'snail tongue',
                   'bat wing', 'slug butter', 'bear burp']
>>> print(wizard_list[0])
spider legs
>>> print(wizard_list[1])
toe of frog
>>> print(wizard_list[2])
snail tongue
```

```
>>> print(wizard_list[3])
bat wing
>>> print(wizard_list[4])
slug butter
>>> print(wizard_list[5])
bear burp
```

So once again, the loop has saved us a lot of typing.

Let's create another loop. Type the following code into the shell. It should automatically indent the code for you.

```
❶ >>> hugehairypants = ['huge', 'hairy', 'pants']
❷ >>> for i in hugehairypants:
❸        print(i)
❹        print(i)
❺
❻ huge
   huge
   hairy
   hairy
   pants
   pants
```

In the first line ❶, we create a list containing 'huge', 'hairy', and 'pants'. In the next line ❷, we loop through the items in that list, and each item is then assigned to the variable i. We print the contents of the variable twice in the next two lines (❸ and ❹). Pressing ENTER on the next blank line ❺ tells Python to end the block, and it then runs the code and prints each element of the list twice ❻.

Remember that if you enter the wrong number of spaces, you'll end up with an error message. If you entered the preceding code with an extra space on the fourth line ❹, Python would display an indentation error:

```
>>> hugehairypants = ['huge', 'hairy', 'pants']
>>> for i in hugehairypants:
        print(i)
        █print(i)

SyntaxError: unexpected indent
```

As you learned in Chapter 5, Python expects the number of spaces in a block to be consistent. It doesn't matter how many spaces you insert, as long as you use the same number for every new line (plus it makes the code easier for humans to read).

Here's a more complicated example of a for loop with two blocks of code:

```
>>> hugehairypants = ['huge', 'hairy', 'pants']
>>> for i in hugehairypants:
        print(i)
        for j in hugehairypants:
                print(j)
```

Where are the blocks in this code? The first block is the first for loop:

```
hugehairypants = ['huge', 'hairy', 'pants']
for i in hugehairypants:
    print(i)                    #
    for j in hugehairypants:  # These lines are the FIRST block.
        print(j)                #
```

The second block is the single print line in the second for loop:

```
❶ hugehairypants = ['huge', 'hairy', 'pants']
  for i in hugehairypants:
      print(i)
❷     for j in hugehairypants:
❸         print(j)                    # This line is also the SECOND block.
```

Can you figure out what this little bit of code is going to do?

After a list called hugehairypants is created at ❶, we can tell from the next two lines that it's going to loop through the items in the list and print out each one. However, at ❷, it will loop over the list again, this time assigning the value to the variable j, and then print each item again at ❸. The code at ❷ and ❸ is still part of the for loop, which means they will be executed for each item as the for loop goes through the list.

So when this code runs, we should see huge followed by huge, hairy, pants, and then hairy followed by huge, hairy, pants, and so on.

Enter the code into the Python shell and see for yourself:

```
>>> hugehairypants = ['huge', 'hairy', 'pants']
>>> for i in hugehairypants:
❶       print(i)
        for j in hugehairypants:
❷           print(j)


◈ huge
  huge
  hairy
  pants
◈ hairy
  huge
  hairy
  pants
◈ pants
  huge
  hairy
  pants
```

Python enters the first loop and prints an item from the list at ❶. Next, it enters the second loop and prints all the items in the list at ❷. Then it continues with the print(i) command, printing the next item in the list, and then prints the complete list again with print(j). In the output, the lines marked ◈ are printed by the print(i) statement. The unmarked lines are printed by print(j).

How about something more practical than printing silly words? Remember that calculation we came up with in Chapter 2 to work out how many gold coins you would have at the end of the year if you used your grandfather's crazy invention to duplicate coins? It looked like this:

```
>>> 20 + 10 * 365 – 3 * 52
```

This represents 20 found coins plus 10 magic coins multiplied by 365 days in the year, minus the 3 coins a week stolen by the raven.

It might be useful to see how your pile of gold coins will increase each week. We can do this with another for loop, but first, we need to change the value of our magic_coins variable so it represents the total number of magic coins per week. That's 10 magic coins per day times 7 days in a week, so magic_coins should be 70:

```
>>> found_coins = 20
>>> magic_coins = 70
>>> stolen_coins = 3
```

We can see our treasure increase each week by creating another variable, called coins, and using a loop:

```
   >>> found_coins = 20
   >>> magic_coins = 70
   >>> stolen_coins = 3
❶ >>> coins = found_coins
❷ >>> for week in range(1, 53):
❸        coins = coins + magic_coins - stolen_coins
❹        print('Week %s = %s' % (week, coins))
```

At ❶, the variable coins is loaded with the value of the variable found_coins; this is our starting number. The next line at ❷ sets up the for loop, which will run the commands in the block (the block is made up of the lines at ❸ and ❹). Each time it loops, the variable week is loaded with the next number in the range of 1 through 52.

The line at ❸ is a bit more complicated. Basically, each week we want to add the number of coins we've magically created and subtract the number of coins that were stolen by the raven. Think of the variable coins as something like a treasure chest. Every week, the new coins are piled into the chest. So this line really means, "Replace the contents of the variable coins with the number of my current coins, plus what I've created this week." Basically, the equal sign (=) is a bossy piece of code that says, "Work out some stuff on the right first, and then save it for later, using the name on the left."

The line at ❹ is a print statement using placeholders, which prints the week number and the total number of coins (so far) to the screen. (If that doesn't make sense to you, reread "Embedding

Values in Strings" on page 30.) So, if you run this program, you'll see something like this:

```
Python Shell                                                    _ □ X
File  Edit  Debug  Options  Windows  Help
Python 3.2.2 (default, Sep  4 2011, 09:51:08) [MSC v.1500 32 bit (Intel)] on win
32
Type "copyright", "credits" or "license()" for more information.
==== No Subprocess ====
>>> found_coins = 20
>>> magic_coins = 70
>>> stolen_coins = 3
>>> coins = found_coins
>>> for week in range(1, 53):
        coins = coins + magic_coins - stolen_coins
        print('Week %s = %s' % (week, coins))


Week 1 = 87
Week 2 = 154
Week 3 = 221
Week 4 = 288
Week 5 = 355
Week 6 = 422
Week 7 = 489
Week 8 = 556
Week 9 = 623
Week 10 = 690
Week 11 = 757
Week 12 = 824
Week 13 = 891
Week 14 = 958
Week 15 = 1025
Week 16 = 1092
Week 17 = 1159
Week 18 = 1226
                                                              Ln: 43 Col: 0
```

WHILE WE'RE TALKING ABOUT LOOPING . . .

A for loop isn't the only kind of loop you can make in Python. There's also the while loop. A for loop is a loop of a specific length, whereas a while loop is a loop that is used when you don't know ahead of time when it needs to stop looping.

Imagine a staircase with 20 steps. The staircase is indoors, and you know you can easily climb 20 steps. A for loop is like that.

```
>>> for step in range(0, 20):
        print(step)
```

Now imagine a staircase going up a mountainside. The mountain is really tall, and you might run out of energy before you reach the top, or the weather might turn bad, forcing you to stop. This is what a while loop is like.

```
step = 0
while step < 10000:
    print(step)
    if tired == True:
        break
    elif badweather == True:
        break
    else:
        step = step + 1
```

If you try to enter and run this code, you'll get an error. Why? The error happens because we haven't created the variables tired and badweather. Although there isn't enough code here to actually make a working program, it does demonstrate a basic example of a while loop.

We start by creating a variable called step with step = 0. Next, we create a while loop that checks whether the value of the variable step is less than 10,000 (step < 10000), which is the total number of steps from the bottom of the mountain to the top. As long as step is less than 10,000, Python will execute the rest of the code.

With print(step), we print the value of the variable and then check whether the value of the variable tired is True with if tired == True:. (True is called a Boolean value, which we'll learn about in Chapter 8.) If it is, we use the break keyword to exit the loop. The break keyword is a way of jumping out of a loop (in other words, stopping it) immediately, and it works with both while and for loops. Here it has the effect of jumping out of the block and would move to any commands that appeared after the line step = step + 1.

The line elif badweather == True: checks to see if the variable badweather is set to True. If so, the break keyword exits the loop. If neither tired nor badweather is True (else), we add 1 to the step variable with step = step + 1, and the loop continues.

So the steps of a while loop are as follows:

1. Check the condition.
2. Execute the code in the block.
3. Repeat.

More commonly, a while loop might be created with a couple of conditions, rather than just one, like this:

```
❶ >>> x = 45
❷ >>> y = 80
❸ >>> while x < 50 and y < 100:
        x = x + 1
        y = y + 1
        print(x, y)
```

Here, we create a variable x with the value 45 at ❶, and a variable y with the value 80 at ❷. The loop checks for two conditions at ❸: whether x is less than 50 and whether y is less than 100. While both conditions are true, the lines that follow are executed, adding 1 to both variables and then printing them. Here's the output of this code:

```
46 81
47 82
48 83
49 84
50 85
```

Can you figure out how this works?

We start counting at 45 for the variable x and at 80 for the variable y, and then increment (add 1 to each variable) every time the code in the loop is run. The loop will run as long as x is less than 50 and y is less than 100. After looping five times (1 is added to each variable each time), the value in x reaches 50. Now the first condition (x < 50) is no longer true, so Python knows to stop looping.

Another common use of a while loop is to create semi-eternal loops. This is a type of loop that could go on forever, but actually continues until something happens in the code to break out of it. Here's an example:

```
while True:
    lots of code here
    lots of code here
    lots of code here
    if some_value == True:
        break
```

The condition for the `while` loop is just `True`, which is always true, so the code in the block will always run (thus, the loop is eternal). Only if the variable `some_value` is true will Python break out of the loop. You can see a better example of this in "Using randint to Pick a Random Number" on page 134, but you might want to wait until you've read Chapter 7 before taking a look at it.

WHAT YOU LEARNED

In this chapter, we used loops to perform repetitive tasks without all the repetition. We told Python what we wanted repeated by writing the tasks inside blocks of code, which we put inside loops. We used two types of loops: `for` loops and `while` loops, which are similar but can be used in different ways. We also used the `break` keyword to stop looping—that is, to break out of a loop.

PROGRAMMING PUZZLES

Here are some examples of loops that you can try out for yourself. The answers can be found at *http://python-for-kids.com/*.

#1: THE HELLO LOOP

What do you think the following code will do? First, guess what will happen, and then run the code in Python to see if you were right.

```
>>> for x in range(0, 20):
        print('hello %s' % x)
        if x < 9:
            break
```

#2: EVEN NUMBERS

Create a loop that prints even numbers until it reaches your year of age or, if your age is an odd number, prints out odd numbers until it reaches your age. For example, it might print out something like this:

```
2
4
6
8
10
12
14
```

#3: MY FIVE FAVORITE INGREDIENTS

Create a list containing five different sandwich ingredients, such as the following:

```
>>> ingredients = ['snails', 'leeches', 'gorilla belly-button lint',
                   'caterpillar eyebrows', 'centipede toes']
```

Now create a loop that prints out the list (including the numbers):

```
1 snails
2 leeches
3 gorilla belly-button lint
4 caterpillar eyebrows
5 centipede toes
```

#4: YOUR WEIGHT ON THE MOON

If you were standing on the moon right now, your weight would be 16.5 percent of what it is on Earth. You can calculate that by multiplying your Earth weight by 0.165.

If you gained a kilo in weight every year for the next 15 years, what would your weight be when you visited the moon each year and at the end of the 15 years? Write a program using a for loop that prints your moon weight for each year.

7

RECYCLING YOUR CODE WITH FUNCTIONS AND MODULES

Think about how much stuff you throw away each day: water bottles, soda cans, potato chip bags, plastic sandwich wrappers, bags that held carrot sticks or apple slices, shopping bags, newspapers, magazines, and so on. Now imagine what would happen if all of that trash just got dumped in a pile at the end of your driveway, without separating out the paper, the plastic, and the tin cans.

Of course, you probably recycle as much as possible, which is good, because no one likes to climb over a pile of trash on the way to school. Rather than sitting in an enormous, gross pile, those glass bottles that you recycle are melted down and turned into new jars and bottles; paper is pulped into recycled paper; and plastic is turned into heavier plastic goods. So we reuse things we would otherwise throw away.

In the programming world, reuse is just as important. Obviously, your program won't disappear under a pile of garbage, but if you don't reuse some of what you're doing, you'll eventually wear your fingers down to painful stubs through overtyping. Reuse also makes your code shorter and easier to read.

As you'll learn in this chapter, Python offers a number of different ways to reuse code.

USING FUNCTIONS

You've already seen one of the ways to recycle Python code. In the previous chapter, we used the functions range and list to make Python count.

```
>>> list(range(0, 5))
[0,1,2,3,4]
```

If you know how to count, it's not too hard to create a list of consecutive numbers by typing them yourself, but the larger the list, the more typing you need to do. However, if you use functions, you can just as easily create a list with a thousand numbers.

Here's an example that uses the list and range functions to produce a list of numbers:

```
>>> list(range(0, 1000))
[0,1,2,3,4,5,6,7,8,9,10,11,12,13,14,15,16...,997,998,999]
```

Functions are chunks of code that tell Python to do something. They are one way to reuse code—you can use functions in your programs again and again.

When you're writing simple programs, functions are handy. Once you start writing long, more complicated programs, like games, functions are *essential* (assuming you want to finish writing your program this century).

PARTS OF A FUNCTION

A function has three parts: a *name*, *parameters*, and a *body*. Here's an example of a simple function:

```
>>> def testfunc(myname):
        print('hello %s' % myname)
```

The name of this function is testfunc. It has a single parameter, myname, and its body is the block of code immediately following the line beginning with def (short for define). A *parameter* is a variable that exists only while a function is being used.

You can run the function by calling its name, using parentheses around the parameter value:

```
>>> testfunc('Mary')
hello Mary
```

The function could take two, three, or any number of parameters, instead of just one:

```
>>> def testfunc(fname, lname):
        print('Hello %s %s' % (fname, lname))
```

The two values for these parameters are separated by a comma:

```
>>> testfunc('Mary', 'Smith')
Hello Mary Smith
```

We could also create some variables first and then call the function with them:

```
>>> firstname = 'Joe'
>>> lastname = 'Robertson'
>>> testfunc(firstname, lastname)
Hello Joe Robertson
```

A function is often used to return a value, using a return statement. For example, you could write a function to calculate how much money you were saving:

```
>>> def savings(pocket_money, paper_route, spending):
        return pocket_money + paper_route - spending
```

This function takes three parameters. It adds the first two (pocket_money and paper_route) and subtracts the last (spending). The result is returned and can be assigned to a variable (the same way we set other values to variables) or printed:

```
>>> print(savings(10, 10, 5))
15
```

VARIABLES AND SCOPE

A variable that's inside the body of a function can't be used again when the function has finished running because it exists only inside the function. In the world of programming, this is called *scope*.

Let's look at a simple function that uses a couple of variables but doesn't have any parameters:

```
❶ >>> def variable_test():
        first_variable = 10
        second_variable = 20
❷        return first_variable * second_variable
```

In this example, we create the function called variable_test at ❶, which multiplies two variables (first_variable and second_variable) and returns the result at ❷.

```
>>> print(variable_test())
200
```

If we call this function using print, we get the result: 200. However, if we try to print the contents of first_variable (or second_variable, for that matter) outside of the block of code in the function, we get an error message:

```
>>> print(first_variable)
Traceback (most recent call last):
  File "<pyshell#50>", line 1, in <module>
    print(first_variable)
NameError: name 'first_variable' is not defined
```

If a variable is defined outside the function, it has a different scope. For example, let's define a variable before we create our function, and then try using it inside the function:

```
❶ >>> another_variable = 100
  >>> def variable_test2():
          first_variable = 10
          second_variable = 20
❷         return first_variable * second_variable * another_variable
```

In this code, even though the variables first_variable and second_variable can't be used outside the function, the variable another_variable (which was created outside the function at ❶) can be used inside it at ❷.

Here's the result of calling this function:

```
>>> print(variable_test2())
20000
```

Now, suppose you were building a spaceship out of something economical like used tin cans. You think you can flatten 2 cans a week to create the curved walls of your spaceship, but you'll need something like 500 cans to finish the fuselage. We can easily write a function to help work out how long it will take to flatten 500 cans if we do 2 cans a week.

Let's create a function to show how many cans we've flattened each week up to a year. Our function will take the number of cans as a parameter:

```
>>> def spaceship_building(cans):
        total_cans = 0
        for week in range(1, 53):
            total_cans = total_cans + cans
            print('Week %s = %s cans' % (week, total_cans))
```

On the first line of the function, we create a variable called total_cans and set its value to 0. We then create a loop for the weeks in the year and add the number of cans flattened each week. This block of code makes up the content of our function. But there's also another block of code in this function: its last two lines, which make up the block of the for loop.

Let's try entering that function in the shell and calling it with different values for the number of cans:

```
>>> spaceship_building(2)

Week 1 = 2 cans
Week 2 = 4 cans
Week 3 = 6 cans
Week 4 = 8 cans
Week 5 = 10 cans
Week 6 = 12 cans
Week 7 = 14 cans
Week 8 = 16 cans
Week 9 = 18 cans
Week 10 = 20 cans
(continues on...)

>>> spaceship_building(13)
Week 1 = 13 cans
Week 2 = 26 cans
Week 3 = 39 cans
Week 4 = 52 cans
Week 5 = 65 cans
(continues on...)
```

This function can be reused with different values for the number of cans per week, which is a bit more efficient than retyping the for loop every time you want to try it with different numbers.

Functions can also be grouped together into modules, which is where Python becomes really useful, as opposed to just mildly useful.

USING MODULES

Modules are used to group functions, variables, and other things together into larger, more powerful programs. Some modules are built in to Python, and you can download other modules separately. You'll find modules to help you write games (such as tkinter, which is built in, and PyGame, which is not), modules for manipulating images (such as PIL, the Python Imaging Library), and modules for drawing three-dimensional graphics (such as Panda3D).

Modules can be used to do all sorts of useful things. For example, if you were designing a simulation game, and you wanted the world of the game to change realistically, you could calculate the current date and time using a built-in module called time:

```
>>> import time
```

Here, the import command is used to tell Python that we want to use the module time.

We can then call functions that are available in this module, using the dot symbol. (Remember that we used functions like this to work with the turtle module in Chapter 4, such as t.forward(50).) For example, here's how we might call the asctime function with the time module:

```
>>> print(time.asctime())
'Mon Nov 5 12:40:27 2012'
```

The function asctime is a part of the time module that returns the current date and time, as a string.

Now suppose that you want to ask someone using your program to enter a value, perhaps their date of birth or their age. You can do this using a print statement, to display a message, and the sys (short for *system*) module, which contains utilities for interacting with the Python system itself. First, we import the sys module:

```
>>> import sys
```

Inside the sys module is a special *object* called stdin (for *standard input*), which provides a rather useful function called readline. The readline function is used to read a line of text typed on the keyboard until you press ENTER. (We'll look at how objects work in Chapter 8.) To test readline, enter the following code in the shell:

```
>>> import sys
>>> print(sys.stdin.readline())
```

If you then type some words and press ENTER, those words will be printed out in the shell.

Think back to the code we wrote in Chapter 5, using an if statement:

```
>>> if age >= 10 and age <= 13:
        print('What is 13 + 49 + 84 + 155 + 97? A headache!')
else:
        print('Huh?')
```

Rather than creating the variable age and giving it a specific value before the if statement, we can now ask someone to enter the value instead. But first, let's turn the code into a function:

```
>>> def silly_age_joke(age):
        if age >= 10 and age <= 13:
                print('What is 13 + 49 + 84 + 155 + 97? A headache!')
        else:
                print('Huh?')
```

Now you can call the function by entering its name, and then tell it what number to use by entering the number in parentheses. Does it work?

```
>>> silly_age_joke(9)
Huh?
>>> silly_age_joke(10)
What is 13 + 49 + 84 + 155 + 97? A headache!
```

It works! Now let's make the function ask for a person's age. (You can add to or change a function as many times as you want.)

```
>>> def silly_age_joke():
        print('How old are you?')
❶       age = int(sys.stdin.readline())
❷       if age >= 10 and age <= 13:
            print('What is 13 + 49 + 84 + 155 + 97? A headache!')
        else:
            print('Huh?')
```

Did you recognize the function int at ❶, which converts a string to a number? We included that function because readline() returns whatever someone enters as a string, but we want a number so that we can compare it with the numbers 10 and 13 at ❷. To try this yourself, call the function without any parameters, and then type a number when How old are you? appears:

```
>>> silly_age_joke()
How old are you?
10
What is 13 + 49 + 84 + 155 + 97? A headache!
>>> silly_age_joke()
How old are you?
15
Huh?
```

WHAT YOU LEARNED

In this chapter, you've seen how to make reusable chunks of code in Python with functions and how to use functions provided by modules. You learned how the scope of variables controls whether they can be seen inside or outside of functions, and how to create functions using the def keyword. You also found out how to import modules so you can use their contents.

PROGRAMMING PUZZLES

Give the following examples a try, to experiment with creating your own functions. The answers can be found at *http://python-for-kids.com/*.

#1: BASIC MOON WEIGHT FUNCTION

In Chapter 6, one programming puzzle was to create a for loop to determine your weight on the moon over a period of 15 years. That for loop could easily be turned into a function. Try creating a function that takes a starting weight and increases the weight amount each year. You might call the new function using code like this:

```
>>> moon_weight(30, 0.25)
```

#2: MOON WEIGHT FUNCTION AND YEARS

Take the function you've just created, and change it to work out the weight over different periods, such as 5 years or 20 years. Be sure to change the function so that it takes three arguments: initial weight, weight gained each year, and number of years:

```
>>> moon_weight(90, 0.25, 5)
```

#3: MOON WEIGHT PROGRAM

Instead of a simple function, where you pass in the values as parameters, you can make a mini-program that prompts for the values using sys.stdin.readline(). In this case, you call the function without any parameters at all:

```
>>> moon_weight()
```

The function will display a message asking for the starting weight, then a second message asking for the amount the weight will increase each year, and finally a message asking for the number of years. You would see something like the following:

```
Please enter your current Earth weight
45
Please enter the amount your weight might increase each year
0.4
Please enter the number of years
12
```

Remember to import the sys module first before creating your function:

```
>>> import sys
```

8

HOW TO USE CLASSES AND OBJECTS

Why is a giraffe like a sidewalk? Because both a giraffe and a sidewalk are *things*, known in the English language as *nouns* and in Python as *objects*.

The idea of *objects* is an important one in the world of computers. Objects are a way of organizing code in a program and breaking things down to make it easier to think about complex ideas. (We used an object in Chapter 4 when we worked with the turtle—Pen.)

To really understand how objects work in Python, we need to think about types of objects. Let's start with giraffes and sidewalks.

A giraffe is a type of mammal, which is a type of animal. A giraffe is also an animate object—it's alive.

Now consider a sidewalk. There's not much to say about a sidewalk other than it's not a living thing. Let's call it an inanimate object (in other words, it's not alive). The terms *mammal*, *animal*, *animate*, and *inanimate* are all ways of classifying things.

BREAKING THINGS INTO CLASSES

In Python, objects are defined by *classes*, which we can think of as a way to classify objects into groups. Here is a tree diagram of the classes that giraffes and sidewalks would fit into based on our preceding definitions:

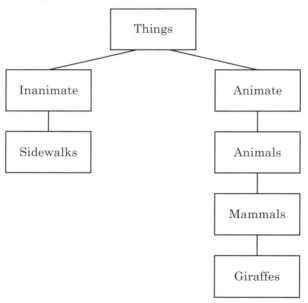

The main class is `Things`. Below the `Things` class, we have `Inanimate` and `Animate`. These are further broken down into just `Sidewalks` for `Inanimate`, and `Animals`, `Mammals`, and `Giraffes` for `Animate`.

We can use classes to organize bits of Python code. For example, consider the `turtle` module. All the things that Python's `turtle` module can do—such as moving forward, moving backward, turning left, and turning right—are functions in the `Pen` class. An object can be thought of as a member of a class, and we can create any number of objects for a class—which we will get to shortly.

Now let's create the same set of classes as shown in our tree diagram, starting from the top. We define classes using the `class` keyword followed by a name. Since `Things` is the broadest class, we'll create it first:

```
>>> class Things:
        pass
```

We name the class `Things` and use the `pass` statement to let Python know that we're not going to give any more information. `pass` is used when we want to provide a class or function but don't want to fill in the details at the moment.

Next, we'll add the other classes and build some relationships between them.

CHILDREN AND PARENTS

If a class is a part of another class, then it's a *child* of that class, and the other class is its *parent*. Classes can be both children of and parents to other classes. In our tree diagram, the class above another class is its parent, and the class below it is its child. For example, `Inanimate` and `Animate` are both children of the class `Things`, meaning that `Things` is their parent.

To tell Python that a class is a child of another class, we add the name of the parent class in parentheses after the name of our new class, like this:

```
>>> class Inanimate(Things):
        pass

>>> class Animate(Things):
        pass
```

Here, we create a class called `Inanimate` and tell Python that its parent class is `Things` with the code `class Inanimate(Things)`. Next, we create a class called `Animate` and tell Python that its parent class is also `Things`, using `class Animate(Things)`.

Let's try the same thing with the `Sidewalks` class. We create the `Sidewalks` class with the parent class `Inanimate` like so:

```
>>> class Sidewalks(Inanimate):
        pass
```

And we can organize the `Animals`, `Mammals`, and `Giraffes` classes using their parent classes as well:

```
>>> class Animals(Animate):
        pass

>>> class Mammals(Animals):
        pass

>>> class Giraffes(Mammals):
        pass
```

ADDING OBJECTS TO CLASSES

We now have a bunch of classes, but what about putting some things into those classes? Say we have a giraffe named Reginald. We know that he belongs in the class `Giraffes`, but what do we use, in programming terms, to describe single giraffe called Reginald? We call Reginald an *object* of the class `Giraffes` (you may also see the term *instance* of the class). To "introduce" Reginald to Python, we use this little snippet of code:

```
>>> reginald = Giraffes()
```

This code tells Python to create an object in the `Giraffes` class and assign it to the variable `reginald`. Like a function, the class name is followed by parentheses. Later in this chapter we'll see how to create objects and use parameters in the parentheses.

But what does the `reginald` object do? Well, nothing at the moment. To make our objects useful, when we create our classes, we also need to define functions that can be used with the objects in that class. Rather than just using the `pass` keyword immediately after the class definition, we can add function definitions.

DEFINING FUNCTIONS OF CLASSES

Chapter 7 introduced functions as a way to reuse code. When we define a function that is associated with a class, we do so in the same way that we define any other function, except that we indent it beneath the class definition. For example, here's a normal function that isn't associated with a class:

```
>>> def this_is_a_normal_function():
        print('I am a normal function')
```

And here are a couple of functions that belong to a class:

```
>>> class ThisIsMySillyClass:
        def this_is_a_class_function():
            print('I am a class function')
        def this_is_also_a_class_function():
            print('I am also a class function. See?')
```

ADDING CLASS CHARACTERISTICS AS FUNCTIONS

Consider the child classes of the Animate class we defined on page 95. We can add *characteristics* to each class to describe what it is and what it can do. A characteristic is a trait that all of the members of the class (and its children) share.

For example, what do all animals have in common? Well, to start with, they all breathe. They also move and eat. What about mammals? Mammals all feed their young with milk. And they breathe, move, and eat. We know that giraffes eat leaves from high up in trees, and like all mammals, they feed their young with milk, breathe, move, and eat food. When we add these characteristics to our tree diagram, we get something like this:

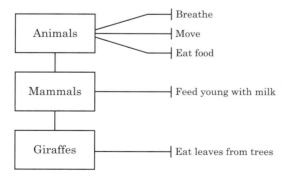

These characteristics can be thought of as actions, or *functions*— things that an object of that class can do.

To add a function to a class, we use the def keyword. So the Animals class will look like this:

```
>>> class Animals(Animate):
        def breathe(self):
            pass
        def move(self):
            pass
        def eat_food(self):
            pass
```

In the first line of this listing, we define the class as we did before, but instead of using the pass keyword on the next line, we define a function called breathe, and give it one parameter: self. The self parameter is a way for one function in the class to call another function in the class (and in the parent class). We will see this parameter in use later.

On the next line, the pass keyword tells Python we're not going to provide any more information about the breathe function because it's going to do nothing for now. Then we add the functions move and eat_food, which also do nothing for now. We'll re-create our classes shortly and put some proper code in the functions. This is a common way to develop programs. Often, programmers will create classes with functions that do nothing as a way to figure out what the class should do, before getting into the details of the individual functions.

We can also add functions to the other two classes, Mammals and Giraffes. Each class will be able to use the characteristics (the functions) of its parent. This means that you don't need to make one really complicated class; you can put your functions in the highest parent where the characteristic applies. (This is a good way to make your classes simpler and easier to understand.)

```
>>> class Mammals(Animals):
        def feed_young_with_milk(self):
            pass

>>> class Giraffes(Mammals):
        def eat_leaves_from_trees(self):
            pass
```

WHY USE CLASSES AND OBJECTS?

We've now added functions to our classes, but why use classes and objects at all, when you could just write normal functions called breathe, move, eat_food, and so on?

To answer that question, we'll use our giraffe called Reginald, which we created earlier as an object of the Giraffes class, like this:

```
>>> reginald = Giraffes()
```

Because reginald is an object, we can call (or run) functions provided by his class (the Giraffes class) and its parent classes. We call functions on an object by using the dot operator and the name of the function. To tell Reginald the giraffe to move or eat, we can call the functions like this:

```
>>> reginald = Giraffes()
>>> reginald.move()
>>> reginald.eat_leaves_from_trees()
```

Suppose Reginald has a giraffe friend named Harold. Let's create another Giraffes object called harold:

```
>>> harold = Giraffes()
```

Because we're using objects and classes, we can tell Python exactly which giraffe we're talking about when we want to run the move function. For example, if we wanted to make Harold move but leave Reginald in place, we could call the move function using our harold object, like this:

```
>>> harold.move()
```

In this case, only Harold would be moving.

Let's change our classes a little to make this a bit more obvious. We'll add a print statement to each function, instead of using pass:

```
>>> class Animals(Animate):
        def breathe(self):
            print('breathing')
        def move(self):
            print('moving')
        def eat_food(self):
            print('eating food')
```

```
>>> class Mammals(Animals):
        def feed_young_with_milk(self):
            print('feeding young')

>>> class Giraffes(Mammals):
        def eat_leaves_from_trees(self):
            print('eating leaves')
```

Now when we create our reginald and harold objects and call functions on them, we can see something actually happen:

```
>>> reginald = Giraffes()
>>> harold = Giraffes()
>>> reginald.move()
moving
>>> harold.eat_leaves_from_trees()
eating leaves
```

On the first two lines, we create the variables reginald and harold, which are objects of the Giraffes class. Next, we call the move function on reginald, and Python prints moving on the following line. In the same way, we call the eat_leaves_from_trees function on harold, and Python prints eating leaves. If these were real giraffes, rather than objects in a computer, one giraffe would be walking, and the other would be eating.

OBJECTS AND CLASSES IN PICTURES

How about taking a more graphical approach to objects and classes?

Let's return to the turtle module we toyed with in Chapter 4. When we use turtle.Pen(), Python creates an object of the Pen class that is provided by the turtle module (similar to our reginald and harold objects in the previous section). We can create two turtle objects (named Avery and Kate), just as we created two giraffes:

```
>>> import turtle
>>> avery = turtle.Pen()
>>> kate = turtle.Pen()
```

Each turtle object (avery and kate) is a member of the Pen class.

Now here's where objects start to become powerful. Having created our turtle objects, we can call functions on each, and they will draw independently. Try this:

```
>>> avery.forward(50)
>>> avery.right(90)
>>> avery.forward(20)
```

With this series of instructions, we tell Avery to move forward 50 pixels, turn right 90 degrees, and move forward 20 pixels so that she finishes facing downward. Remember that turtles always start off facing to the right.

Now it's time to move Kate.

```
>>> kate.left(90)
>>> kate.forward(100)
```

We tell Kate to turn left 90 degrees, and then move forward 100 pixels so that she ends facing up.

So far, we have a line with arrowheads moving in two different directions, with the head of each arrow representing a different turtle object: Avery pointing down, and Kate facing up.

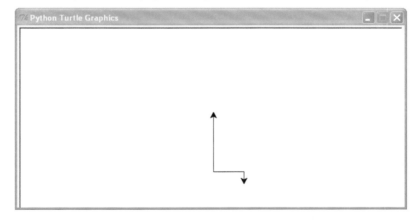

Now let's add another turtle, Jacob, and move him, too, without bugging Kate or Avery.

```
>>> jacob = turtle.Pen()
>>> jacob.left(180)
>>> jacob.forward(80)
```

First, we create a new Pen object called jacob, then we turn him left 180 degrees, and then move him forward 80 pixels. Our drawing now looks like this, with three turtles:

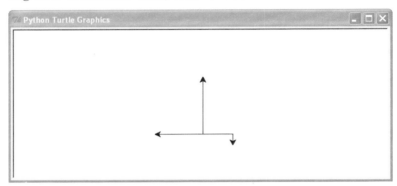

Remember that every time we call turtle.Pen() to create a turtle, we add a new, independent object. Each object is still an instance of the class Pen, and we can use the same functions on each object, but because we're using objects, we can move each turtle independently. Like our independent giraffe objects (Reginald and Harold), Avery, Kate, and Jacob are independent turtle objects. If we create a new object with the same variable name as an object we've already created, the old object won't necessarily vanish. Try it for yourself: Create another Kate turtle and try moving it around.

OTHER USEFUL FEATURES OF OBJECTS AND CLASSES

Classes and objects make it easy to group functions. They're also really useful when we want to think about a program in smaller chunks.

For example, consider a really large software application, like a word processor or a 3D computer game. It's nearly impossible for most people to understand large programs like these as a whole because there's just so much code. But break these monster programs into smaller pieces, and each piece starts to make sense—as long as you know the language, of course!

When writing a large program, breaking it up also allows you to divide the work among other programmers. The most complicated programs that you use (like your web browser) were written by many people, or teams of people, working on different parts at the same time around the world.

Now imagine that we want to expand some of the classes we've created in this chapter (Animals, Mammals, and Giraffes), but we have too much work to do, and we want our friends to help. We could divide the work of writing the code so that one person worked on the Animals class, another on the Mammals class, and still another on the Giraffes class.

INHERITED FUNCTIONS

Those of you who have been paying attention may realize that whoever ends up working on the Giraffes class is lucky, because any functions created by the people working on the Animals and Mammals classes can also be used by the Giraffes class. The Giraffes class *inherits* functions from the Mammals class, which, in turn, inherits from the Animals class. In other words, when we create a giraffe object, we can use functions defined in the Giraffes class, as well as functions defined in the Mammals and Animals classes. And, by the same token, if we create a mammal object, we can use functions defined in the Mammals class as well as its parent class Animals.

Take a look at the relationship between the Animals, Mammals, and Giraffes classes again. The Animals class is the parent of the Mammals class, and Mammals is the parent of Giraffes.

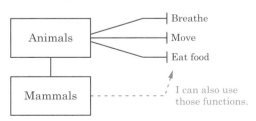

Even though Reginald is an object of the Giraffes class, we can still call the move function that we defined in the Animals class because functions defined in any parent class are available to its child classes:

```
>>> reginald = Giraffes()
>>> reginald.move()
moving
```

In fact, all of the functions we defined in both the Animals and Mammals classes can be called from our reginald object because the functions are inherited:

```
>>> reginald = Giraffes()
>>> reginald.breathe()
breathing
>>> reginald.eat_food()
eating food
>>> reginald.feed_young_with_milk()
feeding young
```

FUNCTIONS CALLING OTHER FUNCTIONS

When we call functions on an object, we use the object's variable name. For example, here's how to call the move function on Reginald the giraffe:

```
>>> reginald.move()
```

To have a function in the Giraffes class call the move function, we would use the self parameter instead. The self parameter is a way for one function in the class to call another function. For example, suppose we add a function called find_food to the Giraffes class:

```
>>> class Giraffes(Mammals):
        def find_food(self):
            self.move()
            print("I've found food!")
            self.eat_food()
```

We have now created a function that combines two other functions, which is quite common in programming. Often, you will write a function that does something useful, which you can then use inside another function. (We'll do this in Chapter 13, where we'll write more complicated functions to create a game.)

Let's use `self` to add some functions to the `Giraffes` class:

```
>>> class Giraffes(Mammals):
        def find_food(self):
            self.move()
            print("I've found food!")
            self.eat_food()
        def eat_leaves_from_trees(self):
            self.eat_food()
        def dance_a_jig(self):
            self.move()
            self.move()
            self.move()
            self.move()
```

We use the `eat_food` and `move` functions from the parent `Animals` class to define `eat_leaves_from_trees` and `dance_a_jig` for the `Giraffes` class because these are inherited functions. By adding functions that call other functions in this way, when we create objects of these classes, we can call a single function that does more than just one thing. You can see what happens when we call the `dance_a_jig` function below—our giraffe moves 4 times (that is, the text "moving" is printed 4 times):

```
>>> reginald = Giraffes()
>>> reginald.dance_a_jig()
moving
moving
moving
moving
```

INITIALIZING AN OBJECT

Sometimes when creating an object, we want to set some values (also called *properties*) for later use. When we *initialize* an object, we are getting it ready to be used.

For example, suppose we want to set the number of spots on our giraffe objects when they are created—that is, when they're initialized. To do this, we create an __init__ function (notice that there are two underscore characters on each side, for a total of four).

This is a special type of function in Python classes and must have this name. The init function is a way to set the properties for an object when the object is first created, and Python will automatically call this function when we create a new object. Here's how to use it:

```
>>> class Giraffes:
        def __init__(self, spots):
            self.giraffe_spots = spots
```

First, we define the init function with two parameters, self and spots, with the code def __init__(self, spots):. Just like the other functions we have defined in the class, the init function also needs to have self as the first parameter. Next, we set the parameter spots to an object variable (its property) called giraffe_spots using the self parameter, with the code self.giraffe_spots = spots. You might think of this line of code as saying, "Take the value of the parameter spots and save it for later (using the object variable giraffe_spots)." Just as one function in a class can call another function using the self parameter, variables in the class are also accessed using self.

Next, if we create a couple of new giraffe objects (Ozwald and Gertrude) and display their number of spots, you can see the initialization function in action:

```
>>> ozwald = Giraffes(100)
>>> gertrude = Giraffes(150)
>>> print(ozwald.giraffe_spots)
100
>>> print(gertrude.giraffe_spots)
150
```

First, we create an instance of the Giraffes class, using the parameter value 100. This has the effect of calling the __init__ function and using 100 for the value of the spots parameter. Next, we create another instance of the Giraffes class, this time with 150. Finally, we print the object variable giraffe_spots for each of our giraffe objects, and we see that the results are 100 and 150. It worked!

Remember, when we create an object of a class, such as ozwald above, we can refer to its variables or functions using the dot operator and the name of the variable or function we want to use (for example, `ozwald.giraffe_spots`). But when we're creating functions inside a class, we refer to those same variables (and other functions) using the `self` parameter (`self.giraffe_spots`).

WHAT YOU LEARNED

In this chapter, we used classes to create categories of things and made objects (instances) of those classes. You learned how the child of a class inherits the functions of its parent, and that even though two objects are of the same class, they're not necessarily clones. For example, a giraffe object can have its own number of spots. You learned how to call (or run) functions on an object and how object variables are a way of saving values in those objects. Finally, we used the `self` parameter in functions to refer to other functions and variables. These concepts are fundamental to Python, and you'll see them again and again as you read the rest of this book.

PROGRAMMING PUZZLES

Some of the ideas in this chapter will start to make sense the more you use them. Try them out with the following examples, and then find the answers at *http://python-for-kids.com/*.

#1: THE GIRAFFE SHUFFLE

Add functions to the `Giraffes` class to move the giraffe's left and right feet forward and backward. A function for moving the left foot forward might look like this:

```
>>> def left_foot_forward(self):
        print('left foot forward')
```

Then create a function called `dance` to teach Reginald to dance (the function will call the four foot functions you've just created). The result of calling this new function will be a simple dance:

```
>>> reginald = Giraffes()
>>> reginald.dance()
left foot forward
left foot back
right foot forward
right foot back
left foot back
```

```
right foot back
right foot forward
left foot forward
```

#2: TURTLE PITCHFORK

Create the following picture of a sideways pitchfork using four
turtle Pen objects (the exact length of the lines isn't important).
Remember to import the turtle module first!

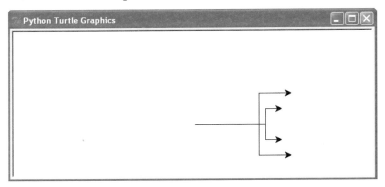

9

PYTHON'S BUILT-IN FUNCTIONS

Python has a well-stocked box of programming tools, including a large number of functions and modules that are ready-made for you to use. Like a trusty hammer or a bicycle wrench, these built-in tools—chunks of code, really—can make writing programs a lot easier.

As you learned in Chapter 7, modules need to be imported before they can be used. Python's *built-in functions* don't need to be imported first; they're available as soon as the Python shell starts. In this chapter, we'll look at some of the more useful built-in functions, and then focus on one: the open function, which lets you open files in order to read and write from them.

USING BUILT-IN FUNCTIONS

We'll look at 12 built-in functions that are commonly used by Python programmers. I'll describe what they do and how to use them, and then show examples of how they can help in your programs.

THE ABS FUNCTION

The abs function returns the *absolute value* of a number, which is the value of a number without its sign. For example, the absolute value of 10 is 10, and the absolute value of −10 is 10.

To use the abs function, simply call it with a number or variable as its parameter, like this:

```
>>> print(abs(10))
10
>>> print(abs(-10))
10
```

You might use the abs function to do something like calculate an absolute amount of movement of a character in a game, no matter in which the direction that character is traveling. For example, say the character takes three steps to his right (positive 3) and then ten steps to his left (negative 10, or −10). If we didn't care about the direction (positive or negative), the absolute value of these numbers would be 3 and 10. You might use this in a board game where you roll two dice and then move your character a maximum number of steps in any direction, based on the total of the dice. Now, if we store the number of steps in a variable, we can determine if the character is moving with the code

below. We might want to display some information when the player has decided to move (in this case, we'll just display "Character is moving"):

```
>>> steps = -3
>>> if abs(steps) > 0:
        print('Character is moving')
```

If we hadn't used abs, the if statement might look like this:

```
>>> steps = -3
>>> if steps < 0 or steps > 0:
        print('Character is moving')
```

As you can see, using abs makes the if statement just a little shorter and easier to understand.

THE BOOL FUNCTION

The name bool is short for *Boolean*, the word programmers use to describe a type of data that can have one of two possible values, usually either true or false.

The bool function takes a single parameter and returns either True or False based on its value. When using bool for numbers, 0 returns False, while any other number returns True. Here's how you might use bool with various numbers:

```
>>> print(bool(0))
False
>>> print(bool(1))
True
>>> print(bool(1123.23))
True
>>> print(bool(-500))
True
```

When you use bool for other values, like strings, it returns False if there's no value for the string (in other words, the keyword None or an empty string). Otherwise, it will return True, as shown here:

```
>>> print(bool(None))
False
>>> print(bool('a'))
True
```

```
>>> print(bool(' '))
True
>>> print(bool('What do you call a pig doing karate? Pork Chop!'))
True
```

The `bool` function will also return `False` for lists, tuples, and maps that do not contain any values, or `True` when they do:

```
>>> my_silly_list = []
>>> print(bool(my_silly_list))
False
>>> my_silly_list = ['s', 'i', 'l', 'l', 'y']
>>> print(bool(my_silly_list))
True
```

You might use `bool` when you need to decide whether a value has been set or not. For example, if we ask people using our program to enter the year they were born, our `if` statement could use `bool` to test the value they enter:

```
>>> year = input('Year of birth: ')
Year of birth:
>>> if not bool(year.rstrip()):
        print('You need to enter a value for your year of birth')
You need to enter a value for your year of birth
```

The first line of this example uses `input` to store what someone enters on the keyboard as the variable year. Pressing ENTER on the next line (without typing anything else) stores the value of the ENTER key in the variable. (We used `sys.stdin.readline()` back in Chapter 7, which is another way to do the same thing.)

On the following line, the `if` statement checks the Boolean value of the variable after using the `rstrip` function (which removes any spaces and ENTER characters from the end of the string). Because the user didn't enter anything in this example, the `bool` function returns false. Because this `if` statement uses the `not` keyword, it is a way of saying, "do this if the function does not return true," and so the code prints `You need to enter a value for your year of birth` on the next line.

THE DIR FUNCTION

The dir function (short for *directory*) returns information about any value. Basically, it tells you the functions that can be used with that value in alphabetical order.

For example, to display the functions that are available for a list value, enter this:

```
>>> dir(['a', 'short', 'list'])
['__add__', '__class__', '__contains__', '__delattr__',
'__delitem__', '__doc__', '__eq__', '__format__', '__ge__',
'__getattribute__', '__getitem__', '__gt__', '__hash__', '__iadd__',
'__imul__', '__init__', '__iter__', '__le__', '__len__', '__lt__',
'__mul__', '__ne__', '__new__', '__reduce__', '__reduce_ex__',
'__repr__', '__reversed__', '__rmul__', '__setattr__', '__setitem__',
'__sizeof__', '__str__', '__subclasshook__', 'append', 'count',
'extend', 'index', 'insert', 'pop', 'remove', 'reverse', 'sort']
```

The dir function works on pretty much anything, including strings, numbers, functions, modules, objects, and classes. But sometimes the information it returns may not be very useful. For example, if you call dir on the number 1, it displays a number of special functions (those that start and end with underscores) used by Python itself, which isn't really useful (you can usually ignore most of them):

```
>>> dir(1)
['__abs__', '__add__', '__and__', '__bool__', '__ceil__',
'__class__', '__delattr__', '__divmod__', '__doc__', '__eq__',
'__float__', '__floor__', '__floordiv__', '__format__', '__ge__',
'__getattribute__', '__getnewargs__', '__gt__', '__hash__',
'__index__', '__init__', '__int__', '__invert__', '__le__',
'__lshift__', '__lt__', '__mod__', '__mul__', '__ne__', '__neg__',
'__new__', '__or__', '__pos__', '__pow__', '__radd__', '__rand__',
'__rdivmod__', '__reduce__', '__reduce_ex__', '__repr__',
'__rfloordiv__', '__rlshift__', '__rmod__', '__rmul__', '__ror__',
'__round__', '__rpow__', '__rrshift__', '__rshift__', '__rsub__',
'__rtruediv__', '__rxor__', '__setattr__', '__sizeof__', '__str__',
'__sub__', '__subclasshook__', '__truediv__', '__trunc__',
'__xor__', 'bit_length', 'conjugate', 'denominator', 'imag',
'numerator', 'real']
```

The dir function can be useful when you have a variable and quickly want to find out what you can do with it. For example, run dir using the variable popcorn containing a string value, and you get the list of functions provided by the string class (all strings are members of the string class):

```
>>> popcorn = 'I love popcorn!'
>>> dir(popcorn)
['__add__', '__class__', '__contains__', '__delattr__', '__doc__',
'__eq__', '__format__', '__ge__', '__getattribute__', '__getitem__',
'__getnewargs__', '__gt__', '__hash__', '__init__', '__iter__',
'__le__', '__len__', '__lt__', '__mod__', '__mul__', '__ne__',
'__new__', '__reduce__', '__reduce_ex__', '__repr__', '__rmod__',
'__rmul__', '__setattr__', '__sizeof__', '__str__',
'__subclasshook__', 'capitalize', 'center', 'count', 'encode',
'endswith', 'expandtabs', 'find', 'format', 'format_map', 'index',
'isalnum', 'isalpha', 'isdecimal', 'isdigit', 'isidentifier',
'islower', 'isnumeric', 'isprintable', 'isspace', 'istitle',
'isupper', 'join', 'ljust', 'lower', 'lstrip', 'maketrans', 'parti-
tion', 'replace', 'rfind', 'rindex', 'rjust', 'rpartition',
'rsplit', 'rstrip', 'split', 'splitlines', 'startswith', 'strip',
'swapcase', 'title', 'translate', 'upper', 'zfill']
```

At this point, you could use help to get a short description of any function in the list. Here's an example of running help against the upper function:

```
>>> help(popcorn.upper)
Help on built-in function upper:

upper(...)
    S.upper() -> str
    Return a copy of S converted to uppercase.
```

The information returned can be a little confusing, so let's take a closer look. The ellipsis (...) means that upper is a built-in function of the string class and, in this case, takes no parameters. The arrow (->) on the next line means that this function returns a string (str). The last line offers a brief description of what the function does.

THE EVAL FUNCTION

The eval function (short for *evaluate*) takes a string as a parameter and runs it as though it were a Python expression. For example, eval('print("wow")') will actually run the statement print("wow").

The eval function works only with simple expressions, such as the following:

```
>>> eval('10*5')
50
```

Expressions that are split over more than one line (such as if statements) generally won't evaluate, as in this example:

```
>>> eval('''if True:
        print("this won't work at all")''')
Traceback (most recent call last):
  File "<stdin>", line 1, in <module>
  File "<string>", line 1
    if True: print("this won't work at all')
    ^
SyntaxError: invalid syntax
```

The eval function is often used to turn user input into Python expressions. For example, you could write a simple calculator program that reads equations entered into Python and then calculates (evaluates) the answers.

Since user input is read in as a string, Python needs to convert it into numbers and operators before doing any calculations. The eval function makes that conversion easy:

```
>>> your_calculation = input('Enter a calculation: ')
Enter a calculation: 12*52
>>> eval(your_calculation)
624
```

In this example, we use `input` to read what the user enters into the variable `your_calculation`. On the next line, we enter the expression `12*52` (perhaps your age multiplied by the number of weeks in a year). We use `eval` to run this calculation, and the result is printed on the final line.

THE EXEC FUNCTION

The exec function is like `eval`, except that you can use it to run more complicated programs. The difference between the two is that eval returns a value (something that you can save in a variable), whereas exec does not. Here's an example:

```
>>> my_small_program = '''print('ham')
print('sandwich')'''
>>> exec(my_small_program)
ham
sandwich
```

In the first two lines, we create a variable with a multiline string containing two `print` statements, and then use `exec` to run the string.

You could use exec to run mini programs that your Python program reads in from files—really, programs inside programs! This can be quite useful when writing long, complicated applications. For example, you could create a Dueling Robots game, where two robots move around a screen and try to attack each other. Players of the game would provide the instructions for their robot as mini Python programs. The Dueling Robots game would read in these scripts and use exec to run.

THE FLOAT FUNCTION

The `float` function converts a string or a number into a *floating-point* number, which is a number with a decimal place (also called a *real number*). For example, the number 10 is an *integer* (also called a *whole number*), but 10.0, 10.1, and 10.253 are all floating-point numbers (also called *floats*).

You might use floating point numbers (rather than integers) if you were writing a problem that calculated monetary amounts. Floats are also used in graphics programs (3D games, for example), to calculate how, and where, to draw things on the screen.

You can convert a string to a float simply by calling float:

```
>>> float('12')
12.0
```

You can use a decimal place in a string as well:

```
>>> float('123.456789')
123.456789
```

You might use float to convert values entered into your program into proper numbers, which is particularly useful when you need to compare the value a person enters with other values. For example, to check whether a person's age is above a certain number, we could do this:

```
>>> your_age = input('Enter your age: ')
Enter your age: 20
>>> age = float(your_age)
>>> if age > 13:
        print('You are %s years too old' % (age - 13))
You are 7.0 years too old
```

THE INT FUNCTION

The int function converts a string or a number into a whole number (or integer), which basically means that everything after the decimal point is dropped. For example, here's how to convert a floating-point number into a plain integer:

```
>>> int(123.456)
123
```

This example converts a string to an integer:

```
>>> int('123')
123
```

But try to convert a string containing a floating-point number into an integer, and you get an error message. For example, here we try to convert a string containing a floating-point number using the int function:

```
>>> int('123.456')
Traceback (most recent call last):
  File "<pyshell>", line 1, in <module>
    int('123.456')
ValueError: invalid literal for int() with base 10: '123.456'
```

As you can see, the result is a ValueError message.

THE LEN FUNCTION

The len function returns the length of an object or, in the case of a string, the number of characters in the string. For example, to get the length of this is a test string, you would do this:

```
>>> len('this is a test string')
21
```

When used with a list or a tuple, len returns the number of items in that list or tuple:

```
>>> creature_list = ['unicorn', 'cyclops', 'fairy', 'elf', 'dragon',
                'troll']
>>> print(len(creature_list))
6
```

Used with a map, len also returns the number of items in the map:

```
>>> enemies_map = {'Batman' : 'Joker',
               'Superman' : 'Lex Luthor',
               'Spiderman' : 'Green Goblin'}
>>> print(len(enemies_map))
3
```

The len function is particularly useful when you're working with loops. For example, we could use it to display the index positions of the elements in a list like this:

```
>>> fruit = ['apple', 'banana', 'clementine', 'dragon fruit']
❶ >>> length = len(fruit)
❷ >>> for x in range(0, length):
❸         print('the fruit at index %s is %s' % (x, fruit[x]))

the fruit at index 0 is apple
the fruit at index 1 is banana
the fruit at index 2 is clementine
the fruit at index 3 is dragon fruit
```

Here, we store the length of the list in the variable length at ❶, and then use that variable in the range function to create our loop at ❷. At ❸, as we loop through each item in the list, we print a message showing the item's index position and value. You could also use the len function, if you had a list of strings and wanted to print every second or third item in the list.

THE MAX AND MIN FUNCTIONS

The max function returns the largest item in a list, tuple, or string. For example, here's how to use it with a list of numbers:

```
>>> numbers = [5, 4, 10, 30, 22]
>>> print(max(numbers))
30
```

A string with the characters separated by commas or spaces will also work:

```
>>> strings = 's,t,r,i,n,g,S,T,R,I,N,G'
>>> print(max(strings))
t
```

As this example shows, letters are ranked alphabetically, and lowercase letters come after uppercase letters, so *t* is more than *T*.

But you don't have to use lists, tuples, or strings. You can also call the max function directly, and enter the items that you want to compare into the parentheses as parameters:

```
>>> print(max(10, 300, 450, 50, 90))
450
```

The min function works like max, except that it returns the smallest item in the list, tuple, or string. Here's our list of numbers example using min instead of max:

```
>>> numbers = [5, 4, 10, 30, 22]
>>> print(min(numbers))
4
```

Suppose you were playing a guessing game with a team of four players, and each had to guess a number that was less than your number. If any player guesses above your number, all players lose, but if they all guess lower, they win. We could use max to quickly find whether all of the guesses are lower, like so:

```
>>> guess_this_number = 61
>>> player_guesses = [12, 15, 70, 45]
>>> if max(player_guesses) > guess_this_number:
        print('Boom! You all lose')
else:
        print('You win')

Boom! You all lose
```

In this example, we store the number to guess using the variable guess_this_number. The team members' guesses are stored in the list player_guesses. The if statement checks the maximum guess against the number in guess_this_number, and if any player guesses over the number, we print the message "Boom! You all lose."

THE RANGE FUNCTION

The range function, as we've seen before, is mainly used in for loops, to loop through a section of code a specific number of times. The first two parameters given to range are called the *start* and the *stop*. You saw range with these two parameters in the earlier example of using the len function to work with a loop.

The numbers that range generates begin with the number given as the first parameter and end with the number that's one less than the second parameter. For example, the following shows what happens when we print the numbers that range creates between 0 and 5:

```
>>> for x in range(0, 5):
        print(x)

0
1
2
3
4
```

The range function actually returns a special object called an *iterator* that repeats an action a number of times. In this case, it returns the next highest number each time it is called.

You can convert the iterator into a list (using the function list). If you then print the returned value when calling range, you'll see the numbers it contains as well:

```
>>> print(list(range(0, 5)))
[0, 1, 2, 3, 4]
```

You can also add a third parameter to range, called *step*. If the step value is not included, the number 1 is used as the step by default. But what happens when we pass in the number 2 as the step? Here's the result:

```
>>> count_by_twos = list(range(0, 30, 2))
>>> print(count_by_twos)
[0, 2, 4, 6, 8, 10, 12, 14, 16, 18, 20, 22, 24, 26, 28]
```

Each number in the list increases by two from the previous number, and the list ends with the number 28, which is 2 less than 30. You can also use negative steps:

```
>>> count_down_by_twos = list(range(40, 10, -2))
>>> print(count_down_by_twos)
[40, 38, 36, 34, 32, 30, 28, 26, 24, 22, 20, 18, 16, 14, 12]
```

THE SUM FUNCTION

The sum function adds items in a list and returns the total. Here's an example:

```
>>> my_list_of_numbers = list(range(0, 500, 50))
>>> print(my_list_of_numbers)
[0, 50, 100, 150, 200, 250, 300, 350, 400, 450]
>>> print(sum(my_list_of_numbers))
2250
```

On the first line, we create a list of numbers between 0 and 500, using range with a step of 50. Next, we print the list to see the result. Finally, passing the variable my_list_of_numbers to the sum function with print(sum(my_list_of_numbers)) adds all the items in the list, giving the total of 2250.

WORKING WITH FILES

Python files are the same as other files on your computer: documents, pictures, music, games . . . indeed, everything on your computer is stored as files.

Let's look at how to open and work with files in Python by using the built-in function open. But first we need to create a new file to play with.

CREATING A TEST FILE

We'll experiment with a text file we'll call *test.txt*. Follow the steps for the operating system you're using.

CREATING A NEW FILE IN WINDOWS

If you're using Windows, follow these steps to create *test.txt*:

1. Select **Start ▸ All Programs ▸ Accessories ▸ Notepad**.
2. Enter a few lines into the empty file.
3. Select **File ▸ Save**.
4. When the dialog appears, select the *C:* drive by double-clicking **My Computer** and then double-clicking **Local Disk (C:)**.
5. Double-click the *Users* folder and then double-click your username.
6. Enter *test.txt* in the **File name** box at the bottom of the dialog.
7. Finally, click the **Save** button.

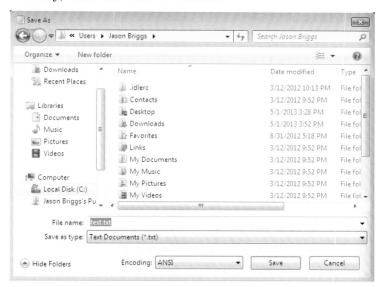

CREATING A NEW FILE IN MAC OS X

If you're using a Mac, follow these steps to create *test.txt*:

1. Click the **Spotlight** icon in the menu bar at the top of the screen.
2. Enter *TextEdit* in the search box that appears.

3. TextEdit should appear in the Applications section. Click it to open the editor (you can also find TextEdit in the Applications folder in Finder).

4. Type a few lines of text into the empty file.

5. Select **Format ▸ Make Plain Text**.

6. Select **File ▸ Save**.

7. In the **Save As** box, enter *test.txt*.

8. In the Places list, click your username—the name you logged in with or the name of the person who owns the computer you're using.

9. Finally, click the **Save** button.

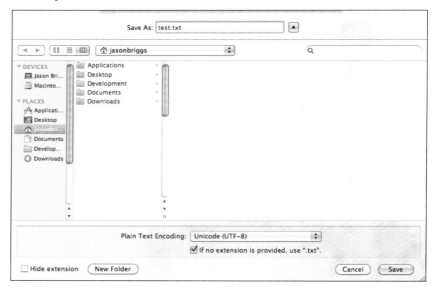

CREATING A NEW FILE IN UBUNTU

If you're using Ubuntu, follow these steps to create *test.txt*:

1. Open your editor, which is usually called Text Editor. If you haven't used it before, search for it in the **Applications** menu.

2. Enter a few lines of text in the editor.

3. Select **File ▸ Save**.

4. In the **Name** box, enter *test.txt* for the filename. Your home directory may already be selected in the box labeled **Save in Folder**, but if not, click it in the Places list. (Your home directory is the username that you are logged in with.)

5. Click the **Save** button.

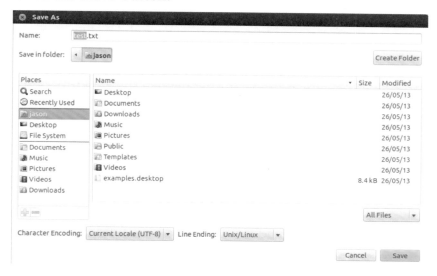

OPENING A FILE IN PYTHON

Python's built-in open function opens a file in the Python shell and displays its contents. How you tell the function which file to open depends on your operating system. Look over the example for a Windows file, and then read the Mac- or Ubuntu-specific section if you're using one of those systems.

OPENING A WINDOWS FILE

If you're using Windows, enter the following code to open *test.txt*:

```
>>> test_file = open('c:\\Users\\<your username>\\test.txt')
>>> text = test_file.read()
>>> print(text)
There once was a boy named Marcelo
Who dreamed he ate a marshmallow
He awoke with a start
As his bed fell apart
And he found he was a much rounder fellow
```

On the first line, we use open, which returns a file object with functions for working with files. The parameter we use with the open function is a string telling Python where to find the file. If you're using Windows, you saved *test.txt* to your user directory on the *C:* drive, so you specify the location of your file as c:\\Users\\<your username>\\test.txt.

The two backslashes in the Windows filename tell Python that the backslash is just that, and not some sort of command. (As you learned in Chapter 3, backslashes on their own have a special meaning in Python, particularly in strings.) We save the file object to the variable test_file.

On the second line, we use the read function, provided by the file object, to read the contents of the file and store it in the variable text. We print the variable on the final line to display the contents of the file.

OPENING A MAC OS X FILE

If you are using Mac OS X, you'll need to enter a different location on the first line of the Windows example to open *test.txt*. Use the username you clicked when saving the text file in the string. For example, if the username is *sarahwinters*, the open parameter should look like this:

```
>>> test_file = open('/Users/sarahwinters/test.txt')
```

OPENING AN UBUNTU FILE

If you are using Ubuntu, you'll need to enter a different location on the first line of the Windows example to open *test.txt*. Use the username you clicked when saving the text file. For example, if the username is *jacob*, the open parameter should look like this:

```
>>> test_file = open('/home/jacob/test.txt')
```

WRITING TO FILES

The file object returned by open has other functions besides read. We can create a new, empty file by using a second parameter, the string 'w', when we call the function:

```
>>> test_file = open('c:\\myfile.txt', 'w')
```

The parameter 'w' tells Python that we want to write to the file object, rather than read from it.

We can now add information to this new file using the write function:

```
>>> test_file = open('c:\\myfile.txt', 'w')
>>> test_file.write('this is my test file')
20
```

Finally, we need to tell Python when we're finished writing to the file, using the close function:

```
>>> test_file = open('c:\\myfile.txt', 'w')
>>> test_file.write('What is green and loud? A froghorn!')
>>> test_file.close()
```

Now, if you open the file with your text editor, you should see that it contains the text "What is green and loud? A froghorn!" Or, you can use Python to read it again:

```
>>> test_file = open('myfile.txt')
>>> print(test_file.read())
What is green and loud? A froghorn!
```

WHAT YOU LEARNED

In this chapter, you learned about Python's built-in functions, such as float and int, which can turn numbers with decimal points into integers and vice versa. You also saw how the len function can make looping easier, and how Python can be used to open files in order to read from them and write to them.

PROGRAMMING PUZZLES

Try the following examples to experiment with some of Python's built-in functions. Find the answers at *http://python-for-kids.com/*.

#1: MYSTERY CODE

What will be the result of running the following code? Guess, and then run the code to see if you're right.

```
>>> a = abs(10) + abs(-10)
>>> print(a)
>>> b = abs(-10) + -10
>>> print(b)
```

#2: A HIDDEN MESSAGE

Try using dir and help to find out how to break a string into words, and then create a small program to print every other word in the following string, starting with the first word (this):

```
"this if is you not are a reading very this good then way you to have
hide done a it message wrong"
```

#3: COPYING A FILE

Create a Python program to copy a file. (Hint: You'll need to open the file that you want to copy, read it in, and then create a new file—the copy.) Check that your program works by printing the contents of the new file on the screen.

10
USEFUL PYTHON MODULES

As you learned in Chapter 7, a Python module is any combination of functions, classes, and variables. Python uses modules to group functions and classes in order to make them easier to use. For example, the turtle module, which we used in previous chapters, groups functions and classes that are used to create a canvas for a turtle to draw on the screen.

When you import a module into a program, you can use all of its contents. For example, when we imported the turtle module in Chapter 4, we had access to the Pen class, which we used to create an object representing the turtle's canvas:

```
>>> import turtle
>>> t = turtle.Pen()
```

Python has a lot of modules for doing all sorts of different tasks. In this chapter, we'll look at some of the most useful ones and try some of their functions.

MAKING COPIES WITH THE COPY MODULE

The copy module contains functions for creating copies of objects. Usually, when writing a program, you'll create new objects, but sometimes it's useful to create a copy of an object, and then use that copy to create a new object, particularly when the process of creating an object takes several steps.

For example, suppose we have an Animal class, with an __init__ function that takes the parameters species, number_of_legs, and color.

```
>>> class Animal:
        def __init__(self, species, number_of_legs, color):
            self.species = species
            self.number_of_legs = number_of_legs
            self.color = color
```

We could create a new object in the class Animal using the following code. Let's create a pink hippogriff with six legs, called harry.

```
>>> harry = Animal('hippogriff', 6, 'pink')
```

Suppose we want a herd of pink hippogriffs with six legs? We could repeat the previous code over and over again, or use `copy`, which can be found in the `copy` module:

```
>>> import copy
>>> harry = Animal('hippogriff', 6, 'pink')
>>> harriet = copy.copy(harry)
>>> print(harry.species)
hippogriff
>>> print(harriet.species)
hippogriff
```

In this example, we create an object and label it with the variable `harry`, and then we create a copy of that object and label it `harriet`. These are two completely different objects, even though they have the same species. This saves only a bit of typing, but when the objects are a lot more complicated, being able to copy them can be useful.

We can also create and `copy` a list of `Animal` objects.

```
>>> harry = Animal('hippogriff', 6, 'pink')
>>> carrie = Animal('chimera', 4, 'green polka dots')
>>> billy = Animal('bogill', 0, 'paisley')
>>> my_animals = [harry, carrie, billy]
>>> more_animals = copy.copy(my_animals)
>>> print(more_animals[0].species)
hippogriff
>>> print(more_animals[1].species)
chimera
```

In the first three lines, we create three `Animal` objects and store them in `harry`, `carrie`, and `billy`. On the fourth line, we add these objects to the list `my_animals`. Next, we use `copy` to create a new list, `more_animals`. Finally, we print the species of the first two objects (`[0]` and `[1]`) in the `more_animals` list and see that they're the same as in the original list: `hippogriff` and `chimera`. We've made a copy of the list without needing to create the objects all over again.

But look what happens if we change the species of one of our Animal objects in the original my_animals list (hippogriff to ghoul). Python changes the species in more_animals, too.

```
>>> my_animals[0].species = 'ghoul'
>>> print(my_animals[0].species)
ghoul
>>> print(more_animals[0].species)
ghoul
```

That's odd. Didn't we change the species in my_animals only? Why did the species change in both lists?

The species changed because copy actually makes a *shallow copy*, which means it doesn't copy objects inside the objects we copied. Here, it has copied the main list object but not the individual objects inside the list. So we end up with a new list that does not have its own new objects—the list more_animals has the same three objects inside it.

By the same token, if we add a new animal to the first list (my_animals), it doesn't appear in the copy (more_animals). As proof, print the length of each list after adding another animal, like this:

```
>>> sally = Animal('sphinx', 4, 'sand')
>>> my_animals.append(sally)
>>> print(len(my_animals))
4
>>> print(len(more_animals))
3
```

As you can see, when we append a new animal to the first list, my_animals, it isn't added to the copy of that list, more_animals. When we use len and print the results, the first list has four elements and the second has three.

Another function in the copy module, deepcopy, actually creates copies of all objects inside the object being copied. When we use deepcopy to copy my_animals, we get a new list complete with copies of all of its objects. As a result, changes to one of our original Animal objects won't affect the objects in the new list. Here's an example:

```
>>> more_animals = copy.deepcopy(my_animals)
>>> my_animals[0].species = 'wyrm'
>>> print(my_animals[0].species)
wyrm
```

```
>>> print(more_animals[0].species)
ghoul
```

When we change the species of the first object in the original
list from ghoul to wyrm, the copied list doesn't change, as we can see
when we print the species of the first object in each list.

KEEPING TRACK OF KEYWORDS WITH THE KEYWORD MODULE

A Python *keyword* is any word in Python that is part of the language itself, such as if, else, and for. The keyword module contains
a function named iskeyword and a variable called kwlist. The function iskeyword returns true if any string is a Python keyword. The
variable kwlist returns a list of all Python keywords.

Notice in the following code that the function iskeyword returns
true for the string if and false for the string ozwald. You can see
the full list of keywords when we print the contents of the variable,
which is useful because keywords don't always stay the same. New
versions (or older versions) of Python may have different keywords.

```
>>> import keyword
>>> print(keyword.iskeyword('if'))
True
>>> print(keyword.iskeyword('ozwald'))
False
>>> print(keyword.kwlist)
['False', 'None', 'True', 'and', 'as', 'assert', 'break', 'class',
'continue', 'def', 'del', 'elif', 'else', 'except', 'finally',
'for', 'from', 'global', 'if', 'import', 'in', 'is', 'lambda',
'nonlocal', 'not', 'or', 'pass', 'raise', 'return', 'try', 'while',
'with', 'yield']
```

You can find a description of each keyword in the Appendix.

GETTING RANDOM NUMBERS WITH THE RANDOM MODULE

The random module contains a number of functions that are useful
for generating random numbers—kind of like asking the computer
to "pick a number." The most useful functions in the random module
are randint, choice, and shuffle.

USING RANDINT TO PICK A RANDOM NUMBER

The randint function picks a random number between a range of numbers, say between 1 and 100, between 100 and 1000, or between 1000 and 5000. Here's an example:

```
>>> import random
>>> print(random.randint(1, 100))
58
>>> print(random.randint(100, 1000))
861
>>> print(random.randint(1000, 5000))
3795
```

You might use randint to do something like create a simple (and annoying) guessing game, using a while loop, like this:

```
>>> import random
>>> num = random.randint(1, 100)
❶ >>> while True:
❷         print('Guess a number between 1 and 100')
❸         guess = input()
❹         i = int(guess)
❺         if i == num:
              print('You guessed right')
❻             break
❼         elif i < num:
              print('Try higher')
❽         elif i > num:
              print('Try lower')
```

First, we import the random module, and then we set the variable num to a random number using randint with a range of 1 to 100. We then create a while loop at ❶ that will loop forever (or at least until the player guesses the number).

Next, we print a message at ❷, and then use input to get input from the user, which we store in the variable guess at ❸. We convert the input to a number using int, and save it in the variable i at ❹. Then we compare it with the randomly selected number at ❺.

If the input and the randomly generated number are equal, we print "You guessed right," and then exit the loop at ❻. If the numbers aren't equal, we check to see if the number the player guessed is higher than the random number at ❼, or lower at ❽, and print a hint message accordingly.

This code is a bit long, so you may want to type it into a new shell window or create a text document, save it, and then run it in IDLE. Here's a reminder of how to open and run a saved program:

1. Start IDLE and choose **File ▸ Open**.

2. Browse to the directory where you saved the file, and click the filename to select it.

3. Click **Open**.

4. After the new window opens, choose **Run ▸ Run Module**.

Here's what happens when we run the program:

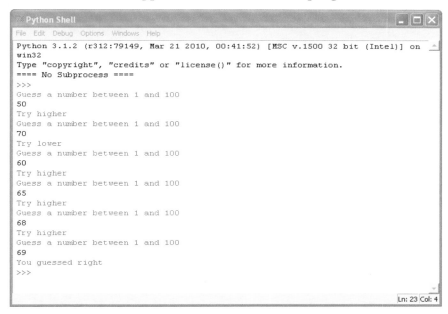

USING CHOICE TO PICK A RANDOM ITEM FROM A LIST

If you want to pick a random item from a list instead of a random number from a given range, you can use choice. For example, you might want Python to choose your dessert for you.

```
>>> import random
>>> desserts = ['ice cream', 'pancakes', 'brownies', 'cookies',
        'candy']
```

```
>>> print(random.choice(desserts))
brownies
```

Looks like you'll be having brownies—not a bad choice at all.

USING SHUFFLE TO SHUFFLE A LIST

The shuffle function shuffles a list, mixing up the items. If you're working along in IDLE and you just imported random and created the desserts list in the previous example, you could skip right to the random.shuffle command in the following code.

```
>>> import random
>>> desserts = ['ice cream', 'pancakes', 'brownies', 'cookies',
            'candy']
>>> random.shuffle(desserts)
>>> print(desserts)
['pancakes', 'ice cream', 'candy', 'brownies', 'cookies']
```

You can see the results of the shuffle when we print the list—the order is completely different. If you were writing a card game, you might use this to shuffle a list representing a deck of cards.

CONTROLLING THE SHELL WITH THE SYS MODULE

The sys module contains system functions that you can use to control the Python shell itself. Here, we'll look at how to use exit function, stdin and stdout objects, and version variable.

EXITING THE SHELL WITH THE EXIT FUNCTION

The exit function is a way of stopping the Python shell or console. Enter the following code, and you'll be prompted with a dialog asking if you want to exit. Click **Yes**, and the shell will shut down.

```
>>> import sys
>>> sys.exit()
```

This won't work if you're not using the modified version of IDLE that we set up in Chapter 1. Instead, you'll get an error, like this:

```
>>> import sys
>>> sys.exit()
Traceback (most recent call last):
  File "<pyshell#1>", line 1, in <module>
    sys.exit()
SystemExit
```

READING WITH THE STDIN OBJECT

The stdin object (short for *standard input*) in the sys module prompts a user to enter information to be read into the shell and used by the program. As you learned in Chapter 7, this object has a readline function, which is used to read a line of text typed on the keyboard until the user presses ENTER. It works like the input function that we used in the random number guessing game earlier in this chapter. For example, enter the following:

```
>>> import sys
>>> v = sys.stdin.readline()
He who laughs last thinks slowest
```

Python will store the string He who laughs last thinks slowest in the variable v. To confirm this, print the contents of v:

```
>>> print(v)
He who laughs last thinks slowest
```

One of the differences between input and the readline function is that with readline, you can specify the number of characters to read as a parameter (however, at the moment this works only in the console, not when you're running in the shell). For example:

```
>>> v = sys.stdin.readline(13)
He who laughs last thinks slowest
>>> print(v)
He who laughs
```

WRITING WITH THE STDOUT OBJECT

Unlike stdin, the stdout object (short for *standard output*) can be used to write messages to the shell (or console), rather than reading them in. In some ways, it's the same as print, but stdout is a file object, so it has the same functions we used in Chapter 9, such as write. Here's an example:

```
>>> import sys
>>> sys.stdout.write("What does a fish say when it swims into a wall?
Dam.")
What does a fish say when it swims into a wall? Dam.52
```

Notice that when write finishes, it returns a count of the number of characters it has written. You can see 52 printed into the shell at the end of the message. We could save this value to a variable in order to record, over time, how many characters we have written to the screen.

WHICH VERSION OF PYTHON AM I USING?

The variable version displays your version of Python, which can be useful if you want to make sure you're up-to-date. Some programmers like to print information when their programs start up. For example, you might put the version of Python into an About window of your program, like this:

```
>>> import sys
>>> print(sys.version)
3.1.2 (r312:79149, Mar 21 2013, 00:41:52) [MSC v.1500 32 bit (Intel)]
```

DOING TIME WITH THE TIME MODULE

Python's time module contains functions for displaying the time, though not necessarily as you might expect. Try this:

```
>>> import time
>>> print(time.time())
1300139149.34
```

The number returned by the call to
time() is actually the number of seconds
since January 1, 1970, at 00:00:00 AM
to be exact. On its own, this unusual reference point may not seem immediately

useful, but it can serve a purpose. For example, to find out how
long parts of your program take to run, you can record the time at
the beginning and end, and compare the values. Let's try this to
find out how long it will take to print all numbers from 0 to 999.

First, create a function like this:

```
>>> def lots_of_numbers(max):
        for x in range(0, max):
            print(x)
```

Next, call the function with max set to 1000:

```
>>> lots_of_numbers(1000)
```

Then work out how long the function takes by modifying our
program with the time module.

```
>>> def lots_of_numbers(max):
❶       t1 = time.time()
❷       for x in range(0, max):
            print(x)
❸       t2 = time.time()
❹       print('it took %s seconds' % (t2-t1))
```

Calling the program again, we get the following result (which
will vary depending on the speed of your system):

```
>>> lots_of_numbers(1000)
0
1
2
3
.
.
.
997
998
999
it took 50.159196853637695 seconds
```

Here's how this works: The first time we call the `time()` function, we assign the value returned to the variable t1 at ❶. We then loop and print all the numbers in the third and fourth lines at ❷. After the loop, we again call `time()`, and assign the value returned to the variable t2 at ❸. Since it took several seconds for the loop to complete, the value in t2 will be higher than t1 because more seconds will have passed since January 1, 1970. Subtracting t1 from t2 as we do at ❹, we get the number of seconds it took to print all those numbers.

CONVERTING A DATE WITH ASCTIME

The function `asctime` takes a date as a tuple and converts it into something more readable. (Remember that a tuple is like a list with items that you can't change.) As you saw in Chapter 7, calling `asctime` without any parameters will display the current date and time in a readable form.

```
>>> import time
>>> print(time.asctime())
Mon Mar 11 22:03:41 2013
```

To call `asctime` with a parameter, we first create a tuple with values for the date and time. For example, here we assign the tuple to the variable t:

```
>>> t = (2007, 5, 27, 10, 30, 48, 6, 0, 0)
```

The values in the sequence are year, month, day, hours, minutes, seconds, day of the week (0 is Monday, 1 is Tuesday, and so on), day of the year (we put 0 as a placeholder), and whether or not it is daylight saving time (0 if it isn't; 1 if it is). Calling `asctime` with a similar tuple, we get this:

```
>>> import time
>>> t = (2020, 2, 23, 10, 30, 48, 6, 0, 0)
>>> print(time.asctime(t))
Sun Feb 23 10:30:48 2020
```

GETTING THE DATE AND TIME WITH LOCALTIME

Unlike `asctime`, the function `localtime` returns the current date and time as an object, with the values in roughly the same order as asctime input. If you print the object, you'll see the name of the class, and each of the values labeled as tm_year, tm_mon (for month), tm_mday (for day of the month), tm_hour, and so on.

```
>>> import time
>>> print(time.localtime())
time.struct_time(tm_year=2020, tm_mon=2, tm_mday=23, tm_hour=22,
tm_min=18, tm_sec=39, tm_wday=0, tm_yday=73, tm_isdst=0)
```

To print the current year and month, you can use their index positions (as with the tuple we used with asctime). Based on our example, we know that year is in the first position (position 0) and month is in the second position (1). Therefore, we use year = t[0] and month = t[1], like this:

```
>>> t = time.localtime()
>>> year = t[0]
>>> month = t[1]
>>> print(year)
2020
>>> print(month)
2
```

And we see that we're in the second month of 2020.

TAKING SOME TIME OFF WITH SLEEP

The function sleep is quite useful when you want to delay or slow down your program. For example, to print every second from 1 to 61, we could use the following loop:

```
>>> for x in range(1, 61):
        print(x)
```

This code will rapidly print all numbers from 1 to 60. However, we can tell Python to sleep for a second between each print statement, like this:

```
>>> for x in range(1, 61):
        print(x)
        time.sleep(1)
```

This adds a delay between the display of each number. In Chapter 12, we'll use the sleep function to make an animation a bit more realistic.

USING THE PICKLE MODULE TO SAVE INFORMATION

The pickle module is used to convert Python objects into something that can be written into a file and then easily read back out. You might find pickle useful if you're writing a game and want to save information about a player's progress. For example, here's how we might add a save feature to a game:

```
>>> game_data = {
    'player-position' : 'N23 E45',
    'pockets' : ['keys', 'pocket knife', 'polished stone'],
    'backpack' : ['rope', 'hammer', 'apple'],
    'money' : 158.50
}
```

Here, we create a Python map containing the player's current position in our imaginary game, a list of the items in the player's pockets and backpack, and the amount of money the player is carrying. We can save this map to a file by opening the file for writing and then calling pickle's dump function, like this:

```
❶ >>> import pickle
❷ >>> game_data = {
    'player-position' : 'N23 E45',
    'pockets' : ['keys', 'pocket knife', 'polished stone'],
    'backpack' : ['rope', 'hammer', 'apple'],
    'money' : 158.50
    }
❸ >>> save_file = open('save.dat', 'wb')
❹ >>> pickle.dump(game_data, save_file)
❺ >>> save_file.close()
```

We import the pickle module first at ❶, and create a map of our game data at ❷. At ❸, we open the file *save.dat* with the parameter wb, which tells Python to write the file in binary mode (you might need to save this in a directory like */Users/malcolmozwald, /home/susanb/* or *C:\\Users\JimmyIpswich*, as we did in Chapter 9. At ❹, we use dump to pass in the map and the file variable as two parameters. Finally, at ❺, we close the file, because we're finished with it.

NOTE *Plain text files contain only characters that humans can read. Images, music files, movies, and pickled Python objects have information that isn't always readable by humans, so they're known as binary files. If you were to open the* save.dat *file, you would see that it doesn't look like a text file; it looks like a jumbled mixture of normal text and special characters.*

We can unpickle objects we've written to the file using pickle's load function. When we unpickle something, we reverse the pickle process: We take the information written into the file and convert it back into values that our program can use. The process is similar to using the dump function.

```
>>> load_file = open('save.dat', 'rb')
>>> loaded_game_data = pickle.load(load_file)
>>> load_file.close()
```

First, we open the file using rb as the parameter, which means read binary. We then pass the file to load and set the return value to the variable loaded_game_data. Finally, we close the file.

To prove that our saved data has been loaded correctly, print the variable:

```
>>> print(loaded_game_data)
{'money': 158.5, 'backpack': ['rope', 'hammer', 'apple'],
'player-position': 'N23 E45', 'pockets': ['keys', 'pocket knife',
'polished stone']}
```

WHAT YOU LEARNED

In this chapter, you learned how Python modules group functions, classes, and variables, and how to use these functions by importing modules. You've seen how to copy objects, generate random numbers, and randomly shuffle lists of objects, as well as how to work with time in Python. Finally, you learned how to save and load information from a file using `pickle`.

PROGRAMMING PUZZLES

Try the following to practice using Python's modules. Check your answers at *http://python-for-kids.com/*.

#1: COPIED CARS

What will the following code print?

```
>>> import copy
>>> class Car:
        pass

>>> car1 = Car()
>>> car1.wheels = 4
>>> car2 = car1
>>> car2.wheels = 3
>>> print(car1.wheels)
```
What is printed here?
```
>>> car3 = copy.copy(car1)
>>> car3.wheels = 6
>>> print(car1.wheels)
```
What is printed here?

#2: PICKLED FAVORITES

Create a list of your favorite things, and then use `pickle` to save them to a file called *favorites.dat*. Close the Python shell, and then reopen it and display your list of favorites by loading the file.

11
MORE TURTLE GRAPHICS

Let's take another look at the turtle module we began using in Chapter 4. As you'll see in this chapter, in Python, turtles can do a lot more than just draw plain black lines. For example, you can use them to draw more advanced geometric shapes, create different colors, and even fill your shapes with color.

STARTING WITH THE BASIC SQUARE

We've already learned how to make the turtle draw simple shapes. Before using the turtle, we need to import the turtle module and create the Pen object:

```
>>> import turtle
>>> t = turtle.Pen()
```

Here's the code we used to create a square in Chapter 4:

```
>>> t.forward(50)
>>> t.left(90)
>>> t.forward(50)
>>> t.left(90)
>>> t.forward(50)
>>> t.left(90)
>>> t.forward(50)
```

In Chapter 6, you learned about for loops. With our newfound knowledge, we can make this somewhat tedious code for a square simpler using a for loop:

```
>>> t.reset()
>>> for x in range(1, 5):
        t.forward(50)
        t.left(90)
```

On the first line, we tell the Pen object to reset itself. Next, we start a for loop that will count from 1 to 4 with the code range(1, 5). Then, with the following lines, in each run of the loop, we move forward 50 pixels and turn left 90 degrees. Because we've used a for loop, this code is a little shorter than the previous version—ignoring the reset line, we've gone from six lines down to three.

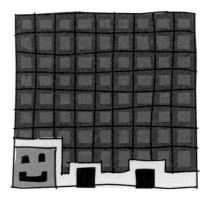

DRAWING STARS

Now, with a few simple changes to our for loop, we can create something even more interesting. Type in the following:

```
>>> t.reset()
>>> for x in range(1, 9):
        t.forward(100)
        t.left(225)
```

This code produces an eight-point star:

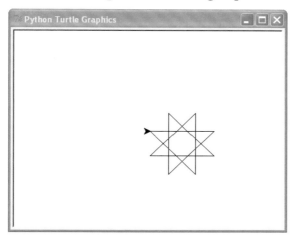

The code itself is very similar to the code we used to draw a square, with a few exceptions:

- Rather than looping four times with range(1, 5), we loop eight times with range(1, 9).
- Rather than moving forward 50 pixels, we move forward 100 pixels.
- Rather than turning 90 degrees, we turn 225 degrees to the left.

Now let's develop our star just a bit more. By using a 175-degree angle and looping 37 times, we can make a star with even more points, using this code:

```
>>> t.reset()
>>> for x in range(1, 38):
        t.forward(100)
        t.left(175)
```

Here's the result of running this code:

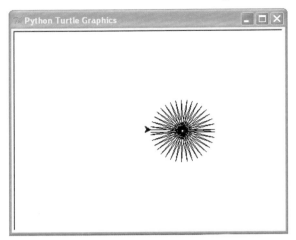

While we're playing with stars, here's the code to produce a spiraling star:

```
>>> t.reset()
>>> for x in range(1, 20):
        t.forward(100)
        t.left(95)
```

By changing the degree of the turn and reducing the number of loops, the turtle ends up drawing quite a different style of star:

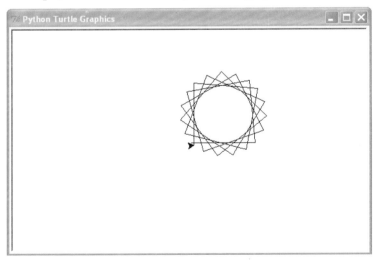

Using similar code, we can create a variety of shapes, from a basic square to a spiral star. As you can see, by using for loops, we've made it much simpler to draw these shapes. Without for loops, our code would have required a lot of tedious typing.

Now let's use an if statement to control how the turtle will turn and draw another star variation. In this example, we want the turtle to turn one angle the first time, and then another angle the next time.

```
>>> t.reset()
>>> for x in range(1, 19):
        t.forward(100)
        if x % 2 == 0:
            t.left(175)
        else:
            t.left(225)
```

Here, we create a loop that will run 18 times (range(1, 19)) and tell the turtle to move forward 100 pixels (t.forward(100)). New here is the if statement (if x % 2 == 0:). This statement checks to see if the variable x contains an even number by using a *modulo* operator, the % in the expression x % 2 == 0, which is a way of saying, "x mod 2" is equal to 0.

The expression x % 2 essentially says, "What is the amount left over when you divide the number in variable x into two equal parts?" For example, if we were to divide 5 balls into two parts, we would get two groups of 2 balls (making a total of 4 balls), and the remainder (the amount left over) would be 1 ball, as shown here.

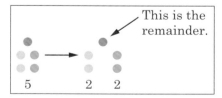

This is the remainder.

5   2   2

If we divided 13 balls into two parts, we would get two groups of 6 balls with 1 ball remaining:

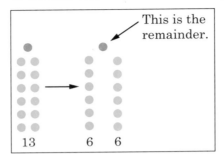

When we check to see if the remainder equals zero after dividing x by 2, we are actually asking whether it can be broken into two parts with no remainder. This method is a nice way to see if a number in a variable is even, because even numbers can always be divided into two equal parts.

On the fifth line of our code, we tell the turtle to turn left 175 degrees (t.left(175)) if the number in x is even (if x % 2 == 0:); otherwise (else), on the final line, we tell it to turn 225 degrees (t.left(225)).

Here's the result of running this code:

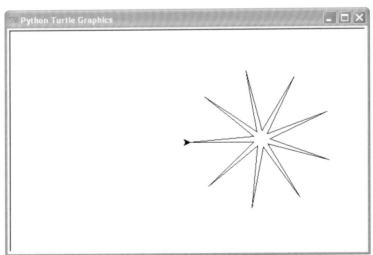

DRAWING A CAR

The turtle can do more than just draw stars and simple geometric shapes. For our next example, we'll draw a rather primitive-looking car. First, we draw the body of the car. In IDLE, select **File ▸ New Window**, and then enter the following code in the window.

```
t.reset()
t.color(1,0,0)
t.begin_fill()
t.forward(100)
t.left(90)
t.forward(20)
t.left(90)
t.forward(20)
t.right(90)
t.forward(20)
t.left(90)
t.forward(60)
t.left(90)
t.forward(20)
t.right(90)
t.forward(20)
t.left(90)
t.forward(20)
t.end_fill()
```

Next, we draw the first wheel.

```
t.color(0,0,0)
t.up()
t.forward(10)
t.down()
t.begin_fill()
t.circle(10)
t.end_fill()
```

Finally, we draw the second wheel.

```
t.setheading(0)
t.up()
t.forward(90)
t.right(90)
t.forward(10)
t.setheading(0)
```

```
t.begin_fill()
t.down()
t.circle(10)
t.end_fill()
```

Select **File** ▸ **Save As**. Give the file a name, such as *car.py*. Select **Run** ▸ **Run Module** to try out the code. And here's our car:

You may have noticed that a few new turtle functions have snuck into this code:

- color is used to change the color of the pen.
- begin_fill and end_fill are used to fill in an area of the canvas with a color.
- circle draws a circle of a particular size.
- setheading turns the turtle to face a particular direction.

Let's take a look at how we can use these functions to add color to our drawings.

COLORING THINGS IN

The color function takes three parameters. The first specifies the amount of red, the second the amount of green, and the third the amount of blue. For example, to get the bright red of the car, we used color(1,0,0), which tells the turtle to use a 100 percent red pen.

This red, green, and blue color recipe is called *RGB*. It's the way that colors are represented on your computer monitor, and the relative mix of these primary colors produces other colors, just like when you mix blue and red paint to make purple or yellow and red to make orange. The colors red, green, and blue are called *primary* colors because you cannot mix other shades to produce them.

Although we're not using paint when we create colors on a computer monitor (we're using light), it may help to understand this RGB recipe by thinking about three pots of paint: one red, one green, and one blue. Each pot is full, and we give each full pot a value of 1 (or 100 percent). We then mix all of the red paint and all of the green paint in a vat to produce yellow (that's 1 and 1 of each, or 100 percent of each color).

Now let's return to the world of code. To draw a yellow circle with the turtle, we would use 100 percent of both the red and green paint, but no blue, like this:

```
>>> t.color(1,1,0)
>>> t.begin_fill()
>>> t.circle(50)
>>> t.end_fill()
```

The 1,1,0 in the first line represents 100 percent red, 100 percent green, and 0 percent blue. On the next line, we tell the turtle to fill the shapes it draws with this RGB color (t.begin_fill), and then we tell it to draw a circle with (t.circle). On the final line, end_fill tells the turtle to fill the circle with the RGB color.

A FUNCTION TO DRAW A FILLED CIRCLE

To make it easier to experiment with different colors, let's create a function from the code we used to draw a filled circle.

```
>>> def mycircle(red, green, blue):
        t.color(red, green, blue)
        t.begin_fill()
        t.circle(50)
        t.end_fill()
```

We can draw a bright green circle by using only the green paint, with this code:

```
>>> mycircle(0, 1, 0)
```

Or we can draw a darker green circle by using only half the green paint (0.5):

```
>>> mycircle(0, 0.5, 0)
```

To play with the RGB colors on your screen, try drawing a circle first with full red then half red (1 and 0.5), and then with full blue and finally half blue, like this:

```
>>> mycircle(1, 0, 0)
>>> mycircle(0.5, 0, 0)
>>> mycircle(0, 0, 1)
>>> mycircle(0, 0, 0.5)
```

NOTE   *If your canvas starts to get cluttered, use t.reset() to delete your old drawings. Also remember that you can move the turtle without drawing lines by using t.up() to lift the pen (use t.down() to set it back down again).*

Various combinations of red, green, and blue will produce a huge variety of colors, like gold:

```
>>> mycircle(0.9, 0.75, 0)
```

Here's light pink:

```
>>> mycircle(1, 0.7, 0.75)
```

And here are two versions for different shades of orange:

```
>>> mycircle(1, 0.5, 0)
>>> mycircle(0.9, 0.5, 0.15)
```

Try mixing some colors yourself!

CREATING PURE BLACK AND WHITE

What happens when you turn off all the lights at night? Everything goes black. The same thing happens with colors on a computer. No light means no color, so a circle with 0 for all of the primary colors creates black:

```
>>> mycircle(0, 0, 0)
```

Here's the result:

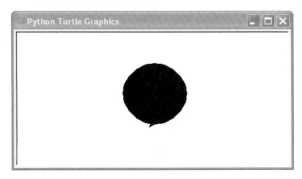

The opposite is true if you use 100 percent of all three colors. In this case, you get white. Enter the following to wipe out your black circle:

```
>>> mycircle(1, 1, 1)
```

A SQUARE-DRAWING FUNCTION

You've seen that we fill shapes with color by telling the turtle to start filling using begin_fill, and the shapes are filled only once we use the end_fill function. Now we'll try a few more experiments with shapes and filling. Let's use the square-drawing function from the beginning of the chapter and pass it the size of the square as a parameter.

```
>>> def mysquare(size):
        for x in range(1, 5):
            t.forward(size)
            t.left(90)
```

Test your function by calling it with size 50, like so:

```
>>> mysquare(50)
```

This produces a small square:

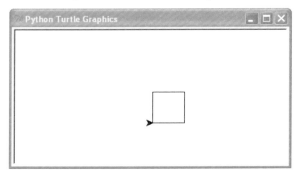

Now let's try our function with different sizes. The following code creates five consecutive squares of size 25, 50, 75, 100, and 125.

```
>>> t.reset()
>>> mysquare(25)
>>> mysquare(50)
>>> mysquare(75)
>>> mysquare(100)
>>> mysquare(125)
```

Here's what those squares should look like:

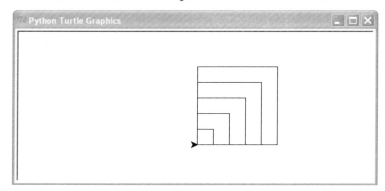

DRAWING FILLED SQUARES

To draw a filled square, first we need to reset the canvas, begin filling, and then call the square function again, with this code:

```
>>> t.reset()
>>> t.begin_fill()
>>> mysquare(50)
```

You should see an empty square until you end filling:

```
>>> t.end_fill()
```

And your square should look like this:

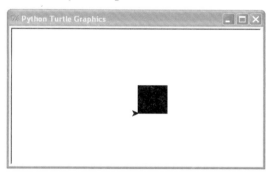

Let's change this function so that we can draw either a filled or an unfilled square. To do so, we need another parameter and slightly more complicated code.

```
>>> def mysquare(size, filled):
        if filled == True:
            t.begin_fill()
        for x in range(1, 5):
            t.forward(size)
            t.left(90)
        if filled == True:
            t.end_fill()
```

On the first line, we change the definition of our function to take two parameters: size and filled. Next, we check to see whether the value of filled is set to True with if filled == True. If it is, we call begin_fill, to tell the turtle to fill the shape we drew. We then loop four times (for x in range(0, 4)) to draw the four sides of the rectangle (moving forward and left), before checking again to see whether `filled` is `True` with `if filled == True`. If it is, we turn filling off again with `t.end_fill`, and the turtle fills the square with color.

Now we can draw a filled square with this line:

```
>>> mysquare(50, True)
```

Or we can create an unfilled square with this line:

```
>>> mysquare(150, False)
```

After these two calls to the `mysquare` function, we get the following image, which looks a bit like a square eye.

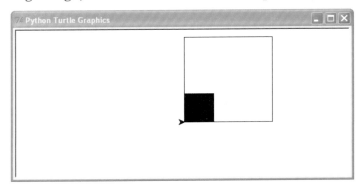

But there's no sense in stopping here. You can draw all sorts of shapes and fill them with color.

DRAWING FILLED STARS

For our final example, we'll add some color to the star we drew earlier. The original code looked like this:

```
for x in range(1, 19):
    t.forward(100)
    if x % 2 == 0:
        t.left(175)
    else:
        t.left(225)
```

Now we'll make a `mystar` function. We'll use the `if` statements from the `mysquare` function and add the `size` parameter.

```
>>> def mystar(size, filled):
        if filled == True:
            t.begin_fill()
        for x in range(1, 19):
            t.forward(size)
            if x % 2 == 0:
                t.left(175)
            else:
                t.left(225)
        if filled == True:
            t.end_fill()
```

In the first two lines of this function, we check to see if `filled` is `True`, and if it is we begin filling. We check again in the last two lines, and if `filled` is `True`, we stop filling. Also, as with the `mysquare` function, we pass the size of the star in the parameter `size`, and use that value when we call `t.forward`.

Now let's set the color to gold (90 percent red, 75 percent green, and 0 percent blue), and then call the function again.

```
>>> t.color(0.9, 0.75, 0)
>>> mystar(120, True)
```

The turtle will draw this filled star:

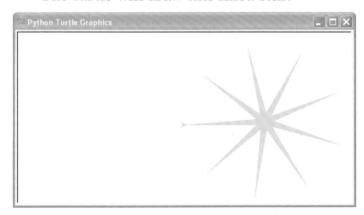

To add an outline to the star, change the color to black and redraw the star without filling:

```
>>> t.color(0,0,0)
>>> mystar(120, False)
```

And the star is now gold with a black outline, like this:

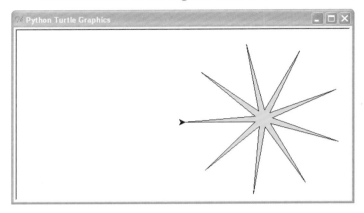

WHAT YOU LEARNED

In this chapter, you learned how to use the turtle module to draw a few basic geometric shapes, using for loops and if statements to control what the turtle does on the screen. We changed the color of the turtle's pen and filled the shapes that it drew. We also reused the drawing code in some functions to make it easier to draw shapes with different colors with a single call to a function.

PROGRAMMING PUZZLES

In the following experiments, you will draw your own shapes with the turtle. As always, the solutions can be found at *http://python-for-kids.com/*.

#1: DRAWING AN OCTAGON

We've drawn stars, squares, and rectangles in this chapter. How about creating a function to draw an eight-sided shape like an octagon? (Hint: Try turning the turtle 45 degrees.)

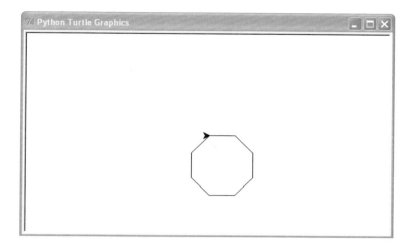

#2: DRAWING A FILLED OCTAGON

Now that you have a function to draw an octagon, modify it so that it draws a filled octagon. Try drawing an octagon with an outline, as we did with the star.

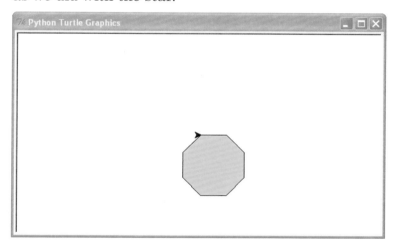

#3: ANOTHER STAR-DRAWING FUNCTION

Create a function to draw a star that will take two parameters: the size and number of points. The beginning of the function will look something like this:

```
def draw_star(size, points):
```

12
USING TKINTER FOR BETTER GRAPHICS

The problem with using a turtle to draw is . . . that . . . turtles . . . are . . . really . . . slow. Even when a turtle is going at top speed, it's still not going very fast. That's not really a problem for turtles, but it is a problem for computer graphics.

Computer graphics, especially in games, usually need to move fast. If you have a game console or you play games on your computer, think for a moment about the graphics you see on the screen. Two-dimensional (2D) graphics are flat—the characters generally move

only up and down or left and right—
as in many Nintendo DS, PlayStation
Portable (PSP), and mobile phone
games. In pseudo-three-dimensional
(3D) games—ones that are almost
3D—images look a little more real,
but the characters generally move
only in relation to a flat plane (this
is also known as *isometric graphics*).

And, finally, we have 3D games, where the pictures drawn on
the screen attempt to mimic reality. Whether the games use 2D,
pseudo-3D, or 3D graphics, all have one thing in common: the need
to draw on the computer screen very quickly.

If you've never tried to create your own animation, try this
simple project:

1. Get a blank pad of paper, and in the bottom corner of the first
   page, draw something (perhaps a stick figure).

2. On the corner of the next page, draw the same stick figure, but
   move its leg slightly.

3. On the next page, draw the stick figure again, with the leg
   moved a little more.

4. Gradually go through each page, drawing a modified stick figure on the bottom corner.

When you're finished, flip quickly through the pages, and you
should see your stick figure moving. This is the basic method used
with all animation, whether it's cartoons on TV or games on your
console or computer. An image is drawn, and then drawn again
with a slight change to create the illusion of movement. To make
an image look like it is moving, you need to display each *frame*, or
piece of the animation, very quickly.

Python offers different ways to create graphics. In addition to
the turtle module, you can use external modules (which need to
be installed separately), as well as the tkinter module, which you
should already have in your standard Python installation. tkinter
can be used to create full applications, like a simple word processor, as well as for simple drawing. In this chapter, we'll explore
how to use tkinter to create graphics.

CREATING A CLICKABLE BUTTON

For our first example, we'll use tkinter to create a basic application with a button. Enter this code:

```
>>> from tkinter import *
>>> tk = Tk()
>>> btn = Button(tk, text="click me")
>>> btn.pack()
```

On the first line, we import the contents of the tkinter module. Using from *module-name* import * allows us to use the contents of a module without using its name. In contrast, when using import turtle in previous examples, we needed to include the module name to access its contents:

```
import turtle
t = turtle.Pen()
```

When we use import *, we don't need to call turtle.Pen, as we did in Chapters 4 and 11. This isn't so useful with the turtle module, but it is when you are using modules with a lot of classes and functions, because it reduces the amount you need to type.

```
from turtle import *
t = Pen()
```

On the next line in our button example, we create a variable containing an object of the class Tk with tk = Tk(), just like we create a Pen object for the turtle. The tk object creates a basic window to which we can then add other things, such as buttons, input boxes, or a canvas to draw on. This is the main class provided by the tkinter module—without creating an object of the Tk class, you won't be able to do any graphics or animations.

On the third line, we create a button, with btn = Button and pass the tk variable as the first parameter, and "click me" as the text that the button will display, with (tk, text="click me"). Although we've added this button to the window, it won't be displayed until you enter the line btn.pack(), which tells the button to appear. It also lines everything up correctly on the screen, if there are other buttons or objects to display. The result should be something like this:

The *click me* button doesn't do much. You can click it all day, but nothing will happen until we change the code just a bit. (Be sure to close the window you created earlier!)

First, we create a function to print some text:

```
>>> def hello():
        print('hello there')
```

Then we modify our example to use this new function:

```
>>> from tkinter import *
>>> tk = Tk()
>>> btn = Button(tk, text="click me", command=hello)
>>> btn.pack()
```

Notice that we've made only a slight change to the previous version of this code: We've added the parameter command, which tells Python to use the hello function when the button is clicked.

Now when you click the button, you will see "hello there" written to the shell. This will appear each time the button is clicked. In the following example, I've clicked the button five times.

```
74 *Python Shell*
File Edit Debug Options Windows Help
Python 3.2.2 (default, Sep  4 2011, 09:51:08) [MSC v.1500 32 bit (Intel)] on win
32
Type "copyright", "credits" or "license()" for more information.
==== No Subprocess ====
>>> def hello():
        print('hello there')

>>> from tkinter import *
>>> tk = Tk()
>>> btn = Button(tk, text="click me", command=hello)
>>> btn.pack()
>>> hello there
hello there
hello there
hello there
hello there
                                                              Ln: 12 Col: 4
```

This is the first time we've used named parameters in any of our code examples, so let's talk about them a bit before continuing with our drawing.

USING NAMED PARAMETERS

Named parameters are just like normal parameters, except that, rather than using the specific order of the values provided to a function to determine which value belongs to which parameter (the first value is the first parameter, the second value is the second parameter, the third value is the third parameter, and so on), we explicitly name the values, so they can appear in any order.

Sometimes functions have a lot of parameters, and we may not always need to provide a value for every parameter. Named parameters are a way we can provide values for only the parameters that we need to give values.

For example, suppose we have a function called person that takes two parameters: width and height.

```
>>> def person(width, height):
        print('I am %s feet wide, %s feet high' % (width, height))
```

Normally, we might call this function like this:

```
>>> person(4, 3)
I am 4 feet wide, 3 feet high
```

Using named parameters, we could call this function and specify the parameter name with each value:

```
>>> person(height=3, width=4)
I am 4 feet wide, 3 feet high
```

Named parameters will become particularly useful as we do more with the tkinter module.

CREATING A CANVAS FOR DRAWING

Buttons are nice tools, but they're not particularly useful when we want to draw things on the screen. When it's time to really draw something, we need a different component: a canvas object, which is an object of the class Canvas (provided by the tkinter module).

When creating a canvas, we pass the width and height (in pixels) of the canvas to Python. Otherwise, the code is similar to the button code. Here's an example:

```
>>> from tkinter import *
>>> tk = Tk()
>>> canvas = Canvas(tk, width=500, height=500)
>>> canvas.pack()
```

As with the button example, a window will appear when you enter tk = Tk(). On the last line, we pack the canvas with canvas.pack(), which changes the size of the canvas to a width of 500 pixels and a height of 500 pixels, as specified in the third line of code.

Also as with the button example, the pack function tells the canvas to display itself in the correct position within the window. If that function isn't called, nothing will display properly.

DRAWING LINES

To draw a line on the canvas, we use pixel coordinates. *Coordinates* determine the positions of pixels on a surface. On a tkinter canvas, coordinates describe how far across the canvas (from left to right) and how far down the canvas (top to bottom) to place the pixel.

For example, since our canvas is 500 pixels wide by 500 pixels high, the coordinates of the bottom-right corner of the screen are (500, 500). To draw the line shown in the following image, we would use the starting coordinates (0, 0) and ending coordinates (500, 500).

We specify the coordinates using the create_line function, as shown here:

```
>>> from tkinter import *
>>> tk = Tk()
>>> canvas = Canvas(tk, width=500, height=500)
>>> canvas.pack()
>>> canvas.create_line(0, 0, 500, 500)
1
```

The create_line function returns 1, which is an identifier—we'll learn more about that later. If we had done the same thing with the turtle module, we would have needed the following code:

```
>>> import turtle
>>> turtle.setup(width=500, height=500)
>>> t = turtle.Pen()
>>> t.up()
>>> t.goto(-250, 250)
>>> t.down()
>>> t.goto(500, -500)
```

So the tkinter code is already an improvement. It's slightly shorter and a bit simpler.

Now let's look at some of the functions available on the canvas object that we can use for some more interesting drawings.

DRAWING BOXES

With the turtle module, we drew a box by moving forward, turning, moving forward, turning again, and so on. Eventually, we were able to draw a rectangular or square box by changing how far we moved forward.

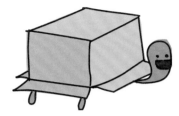

The tkinter module makes it a lot easier to draw a square or rectangle. All you need to know are the coordinates for the corners. Here's an example (you can close the other windows now):

```
>>> from tkinter import *
>>> tk = Tk()
>>> canvas = Canvas(tk, width=400, height=400)
>>> canvas.pack()
>>> canvas.create_rectangle(10, 10, 50, 50)
```

In this code, we use tkinter to create a canvas that is 400 pixels wide by 400 pixels high, and we then draw a square in the top-left corner of the window, like this:

The parameters we pass to canvas.create_rectangle in the last line of the code are the coordinates for the top-left and bottom-right corners of the square. We provide these coordinates as the distance from the left-hand side of the canvas and the distance from the top of the canvas. In this case, the first two coordinates (the top-left corner) are 10 pixels across from the left and 10 pixels down from the top (those are the first numbers: 10, 10). The bottom-right corner of the square is 50 pixels across from the left and 50 pixels down (the second numbers: 50, 50).

We'll refer to these two sets of coordinates as *x1, y1* and *x2, y2*. To draw a rectangle, we can increase the distance of the second corner from the side of the canvas (increasing the value of the *x2* parameter), like this:

```
>>> from tkinter import *
>>> tk = Tk()
>>> canvas = Canvas(tk, width=400, height=400)
>>> canvas.pack()
>>> canvas.create_rectangle(10, 10, 300, 50)
```

In this example, the top-left coordinates of the rectangle (its position on the screen) are (10, 10), and the bottom-right coordinates are (300, 50). The result is a rectangle that is the same height as our original square (50 pixels), but a lot wider.

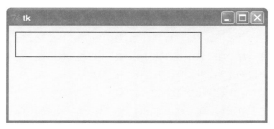

We can also draw a rectangle by increasing the distance of the second corner from the top of the canvas (increasing the value of the *y2* parameter), like this:

```
>>> from tkinter import *
>>> tk = Tk()
>>> canvas = Canvas(tk, width=400, height=400)
>>> canvas.pack()
>>> canvas.create_rectangle(10, 10, 50, 300)
```

In this call to the create_rectangle function, we are basically saying, in order:

- Go 10 pixels across the canvas (from the top left).
- Go 10 pixels down the canvas. This is the starting corner of the rectangle.

- Draw the rectangle across to 50 pixels.
- Draw down to 300 pixels.

The end result should look something like this:

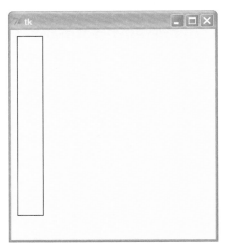

DRAWING A LOT OF RECTANGLES

How about filling the canvas with different-sized rectangles? We can do this by importing the module random and then creating a function that uses a random number for the coordinates at the top-left and bottom-right corners of the rectangle.

We'll use the function provided by the random module called randrange. When we give this function a number, it returns a random integer between 0 and the number we give it. For example, calling randrange(10) would return a number between 0 and 9, randrange(100) would return a number between 0 and 99, and so on.

Here's how we use randrange in a function. Create a new window by selecting **File ▸ New Window**, and enter the following code:

```
from tkinter import *
import random
tk = Tk()
canvas = Canvas(tk, width=400, height=400)
canvas.pack()
```

```
def random_rectangle(width, height):
    x1 = random.randrange(width)
    y1 = random.randrange(height)
    x2 = x1 + random.randrange(width)
    y2 = y1 + random.randrange(height)
    canvas.create_rectangle(x1, y1, x2, y2)
```

We first define our function (def random_rectangle) as taking two parameters: width and height. Next, we create variables for the top-left corner of the rectangle using the randrange function, passing the width and the height as parameters with x1 = random.randrange(width) and y1 = random.randrange(height), respectively. In effect, with the second line of this function, we're saying, "Create a variable called x1, and set its value to a random number between 0 and the value in the parameter width."

The next two lines create variables for the bottom-right corner of the rectangle, taking into account the top-left coordinates (either x1 or y1) and adding a random number to those values. The third line of the function is effectively saying, "Create the variable x2 by adding a random number to the value that we already calculated for x1."

Finally, with canvas.create_rectangle, we use the variables x1, y1, x2, and y2 to draw the rectangle on the canvas.

To try our random_rectangle function, we'll pass it the width and height of the canvas. Add the following code below the function you've just entered:

```
random_rectangle(400, 400)
```

Save the code you've entered (select **File ▸ Save** and enter a filename such as *randomrect.py*) and then select **Run ▸ Run Module**. Once you've seen the function working, fill the screen with rectangles by creating a loop to call random_rectangle a number of times. Let's try a for loop of 100 random rectangles. Add the following code, save your work, and try running it again:

```
for x in range(0, 100):
    random_rectangle(400, 400)
```

This code produces a bit of a mess, but it's kind of like modern art:

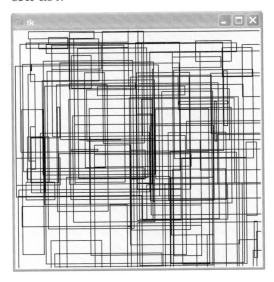

SETTING THE COLOR

Of course, we want to add color to our graphics. Let's change the random_rectangle function to pass in a color for the rectangle as an additional parameter (fill_color). Enter this code in a new window, and when you save, call the file *colorrect.py*:

```
from tkinter import *
import random
tk = Tk()
canvas = Canvas(tk, width=400, height=400)
canvas.pack()

def random_rectangle(width, height, fill_color):
    x1 = random.randrange(width)
    y1 = random.randrange(height)
    x2 = random.randrange(x1 + random.randrange(width))
    y2 = random.randrange(y1 + random.randrange(height))
    canvas.create_rectangle(x1, y1, x2, y2, fill=fill_color)
```

The create_rectangle function now takes a parameter fill_color, which specifies the color to use when drawing the rectangle.

We can pass named colors into the function like this (using a canvas 400 pixels wide by 400 pixels high) to create a bunch of different-colored rectangles. If you try this example, you might

like to copy and paste to save on typing.
To do so, select the text to copy, press
CTRL-C to copy it, click a blank line, and
press CTRL-V to paste. Add this code to
colorrect.py, just below the function):

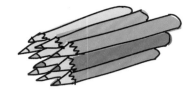

```
random_rectangle(400, 400, 'green')
random_rectangle(400, 400, 'red')
random_rectangle(400, 400, 'blue')
random_rectangle(400, 400, 'orange')
random_rectangle(400, 400, 'yellow')
random_rectangle(400, 400, 'pink')
random_rectangle(400, 400, 'purple')
random_rectangle(400, 400, 'violet')
random_rectangle(400, 400, 'magenta')
random_rectangle(400, 400, 'cyan')
```

Many of these named colors will display the color you expect
to see, but others may produce an error message (depending on
whether you're using Windows, Mac OS X, or Linux).

But what about a custom color that isn't exactly the same as
a named color? Recall in Chapter 11 that we set the color of the
turtle's pen using percentages of the colors red, green, and blue.
Setting the amount of each primary color (red, green, and blue)
to use in a color combination with tkinter is slightly more complicated, but we'll work through it.

When working with the turtle module, we created gold using
90 percent red, 75 percent green, and no blue. In tkinter, we can
create the same gold color using this line:

```
random_rectangle(400, 400, '#ffd800')
```

The hash mark (#) before the value ffd800 tells Python we're providing a *hexadecimal* number. Hexadecimal is a way of representing
numbers that is commonly used in computer programming. It uses
a base of 16 (0 through 9 then A through F) rather than decimal,
which has a base of 10 (0 through 9). If you haven't learned about
bases in mathematics, just know that you can convert a normal decimal number to hexadecimal using a *format placeholder* in a string:
%x (see "Embedding Values in Strings" on page 30). For example,
to convert the decimal number 15 to hexadecimal, you could do this:

```
>>> print('%x' % 15)
f
```

To make sure our number has at least two digits, we can change the format placeholder slightly, to this:

```
>>> print('%02x' % 15)
0f
```

The tkinter module provides an easy way to get a hexadecimal color value. Try adding the following code to *colorrect.py* (you can remove the other calls to the random_rectangle function).

```
from tkinter import *
colorchooser.askcolor()
```

This shows you a color chooser:

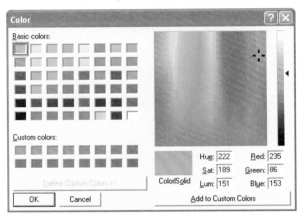

When you select a color and click **OK**, a tuple will be displayed. This tuple contains another tuple with three numbers and a string:

```
>>> colorchooser.askcolor()
((235.91796875, 86.3359375, 153.59765625), '#eb5699')
```

The three numbers represent the amounts of red, green, and blue. In tkinter, the amount of each primary color to use in a color combination is represented by a number between 0 and 255 (which is different from using a percentage for each primary color with the turtle module). The string in the tuple contains the hexadecimal version of those three numbers.

You can either copy and paste the string value to use or store the tuple as a variable, and then use the index position of the hexadecimal value.

Let's use the random_rectangle function to see how this works.

```
>>> c = colorchooser.askcolor()
>>> random_rectangle(400, 400, c[1])
```

Here's the result:

DRAWING ARCS

An arc is a segment of the circumference of a circle or another curve, but in order to draw one with tkinter, you need to draw it inside a rectangle using the create_arc function, with code like this:

```
canvas.create_arc(10, 10, 200, 100, extent=180, style=ARC)
```

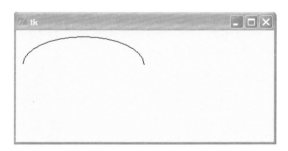

If you've closed all the tkinter windows, or restarted IDLE, make sure to reimport tkinter and then re-create the canvas with this code:

```
>>> from tkinter import *
>>> tk = Tk()
>>> canvas = Canvas(tk, width=400, height=400)
>>> canvas.pack()
>>> canvas.create_arc(10, 10, 200, 100, extent=180, style=ARC)
```

This code places the top-left corner of the rectangle that will contain the arc at the coordinates (10, 10), which is 10 pixels across and 10 pixels down, and its bottom-right corner at coordinates (200, 100), or 200 pixels across and 100 pixels down. The next parameter, extent, is used to specify the degrees of the angle of the arc. Recall from Chapter 4 that degrees are a way of measuring the distance to travel around a circle. Here are examples of two arcs, where we travel 45 degrees and 270 degrees around a circle:

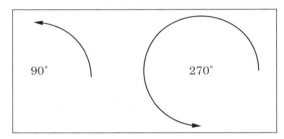

The following code draws several different arcs down the page so that you can see what happens when we use different degrees with the create_arc function.

```
>>> from tkinter import *
>>> tk = Tk()
>>> canvas = Canvas(tk, width=400, height=400)
>>> canvas.pack()
>>> canvas.create_arc(10, 10, 200, 80, extent=45, style=ARC)
>>> canvas.create_arc(10, 80, 200, 160, extent=90, style=ARC)
>>> canvas.create_arc(10, 160, 200, 240, extent=135, style=ARC)
>>> canvas.create_arc(10, 240, 200, 320, extent=180, style=ARC)
>>> canvas.create_arc(10, 320, 200, 400, extent=359, style=ARC)
```

NOTE *We use 359 degrees in the final circle, rather than 360, because tkinter considers 360 to be the same as 0 degrees, and would draw nothing if we used 360.*

DRAWING POLYGONS

A polygon is any shape with three or more sides. There are regularly shaped polygons like triangles, squares, rectangles, pentagons, hexagons, and so on, as well as irregular ones with uneven edges, many more sides, and odd shapes.

When drawing polygons with tkinter, you need to provide coordinates for each point of the polygon. Here's how we can draw a triangle:

```
from tkinter import *
tk = Tk()
canvas = Canvas(tk, width=400, height=400)
canvas.pack()
canvas.create_polygon(10, 10, 100, 10, 100, 110, fill="",
outline="black")
```

This example draws a triangle by starting with the x and y coordinates (10, 10), then moving across to (100, 10), and finishing at (100, 110). Here's the result:

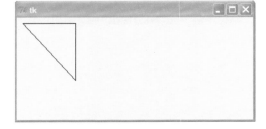

We can add another irregular polygon (a shape with uneven angles or sides) using this code:

```
canvas.create_polygon(200, 10, 240, 30, 120, 100, 140, 120, fill="",
outline="black")
```

This code begins with the coordinates (200, 10), moves to (240, 30), then to (120, 100), and finally to (140, 120). tkinter automatically joins the line back to the first coordinate. And here's the result of running the code:

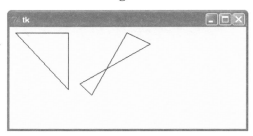

DISPLAYING TEXT

In addition to drawing shapes, you can also write on the canvas using create_text. This function takes only two coordinates (the x and y positions of the text), along with a named parameter for the text to display. In the following code, we create our canvas as before and then display a sentence positioned at the coordinates (150, 100). Save this code as *text.py*.

```
from tkinter import *
tk = Tk()
canvas = Canvas(tk, width=400, height=400)
canvas.pack()
canvas.create_text(150, 100, text='There once was a man from Toulouse,')
```

The create_text function takes some other useful parameters, such as a text fill color. In the following code, we call the create_text function with coordinates (130, 120), the text we want to display, and a red fill color.

```
canvas.create_text(130, 120, text='Who rode around on a moose.',
fill='red')
```

You can also specify the font (the type-face used for the displayed text) as a tuple with the font name and the size of the text. For example, the tuple for the Times font of size 20 is ('Times', 20). In the following code, we display text using the Times font set at size 15, the Helvetica font at size 20, and the Courier font at sizes 22 and then 30.

```
canvas.create_text(150, 150, text='He said, "It\'s my curse,',
font=('Times', 15))
canvas.create_text(200, 200, text='But it could be worse,',
font=('Helvetica', 20))
canvas.create_text(220, 250, text='My cousin rides round',
font=('Courier', 22))
canvas.create_text(220, 300, text='on a goose."', font=('Courier', 30))
```

And here's the result of these functions using the three speci-fied fonts at five different sizes:

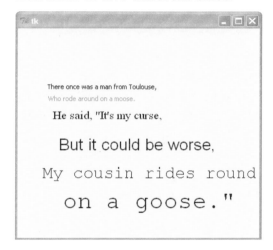

DISPLAYING IMAGES

To display an image on a canvas using tkinter, first load the image and then use the create_image function on the canvas object.

Any image that you load must be in a directory that's acces-sible to Python. For this example, we put our image *test.gif* in the *C:* directory, which is the root directory (the base directory) of the *C:* drive, but you could put it anywhere.

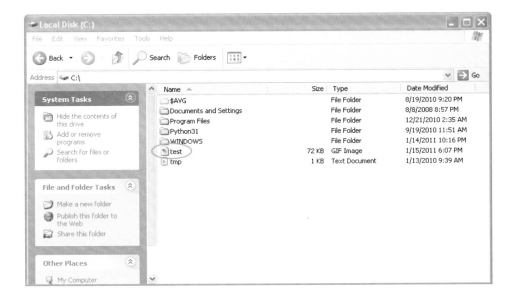

If you're using a Mac or Linux system, you can put the image in your Home directory. If you aren't able to put files on your *C:* drive, you can put the image on your desktop.

With tkinter, *you can load only GIF images, that is, image files with the extension .gif. You can display other types of images, such as PNG (.png) and JPG (.jpg), but you'll need to use a different module, such as the Python Imaging Library* (http://www.pythonware .com/products/pil/).

We can display the *test.gif* image like this:

```
from tkinter import *
tk = Tk()
canvas = Canvas(tk, width=400, height=400)
canvas.pack()
my_image = PhotoImage(file='c:\\test.gif')
canvas.create_image(0, 0, anchor=NW, image=my_image)
```

In the first four lines, we set up the canvas as with the previous examples. In the fifth line, the image is loaded into the variable my_image. We create PhotoImage with the directory 'c:\\test.gif'. If you saved your image to the desktop, you should create the PhotoImage with that directory, something like this:

```
my_image = PhotoImage(file='C:\\Users\\Joe Smith\\Desktop\\test.gif')
```

Once the image has been loaded into the variable, `canvas.create_image(0, 0, anchor=NW, image=my_image)` displays it using the `create_image` function. The coordinates (0, 0) are where the image will be displayed, and `anchor=NW` tells the function to use the top-left (`NW`, for northwest) edge of the image as the starting point when drawing (otherwise, it will use the center of the image as the starting point by default). The final named parameter, `image`, points at the variable for the loaded image. Here's the result:

CREATING BASIC ANIMATION

We've covered how to create static drawings—pictures that don't move. What about creating animation?

Animation is not necessarily a specialty of the `tkinter` module, but it can handle the basics. For example, we can create a filled triangle and then make it move across the screen using this code (don't forget, select **File ▸ New Window**, save your work, and then run the code with **Run ▸ Run Module**):

```
import time
from tkinter import *
tk = Tk()
canvas = Canvas(tk, width=400, height=200)
canvas.pack()
canvas.create_polygon(10, 10, 10, 60, 50, 35)
```

```
for x in range(0, 60):
    canvas.move(1, 5, 0)
    tk.update()
    time.sleep(0.05)
```

When you run this code, the triangle will start moving across the screen to the end of its path:

How does this work? As before, we've used the first three lines after importing tkinter to do the basic setup to display a canvas. In the fourth line, we create the triangle with this function:

```
canvas.create_polygon(10, 10, 10, 60, 50, 35)
```

NOTE   *When you enter this line, a number will be printed to the screen. This is an identifier for the polygon. We can use it to refer to the shape later, as described in the following example.*

Next, we create a simple for loop to count from 0 to 59, beginning with `for x in range(0, 60):`. The block of code inside the loop moves the triangle across the screen. The `canvas.move` function will move any drawn object by adding values to its x and y coordinates. For example, with `canvas.move(1, 5, 0)`, we move the object with ID 1 (the identifier for the  triangle) 5 pixels across and 0 pixels down. To move it back again, we could use the function call `canvas.move(1, -5, 0)`.

The function `tk.update()` forces tkinter to update the screen (redraw it). If we didn't use `update`, tkinter would wait until the loop finished before moving the triangle, which means you would see it jump to the last position, rather than move smoothly across the canvas. The final line of the loop, time.sleep(0.05), tells Python to sleep for one-twentieth of a second (0.05 seconds), before continuing.

To make the triangle move diagonally down the screen, we can modify this code by calling move(1, 5, 5). To try this, close the canvas, and create a new file (**File ▸ New Window**) for the following code:

```
import time
from tkinter import *
tk = Tk()
canvas = Canvas(tk, width=400, height=400)
canvas.pack()
canvas.create_polygon(10, 10, 10, 60, 50, 35)
for x in range(0, 60):
    canvas.move(1, 5, 5)
    tk.update()
    time.sleep(0.05)
```

This code differs from the original in two ways:

- We make the height of the canvas 400, rather than 200, with canvas = Canvas(tk, width=400, height=400).

- We add 5 to the triangle's x and y coordinates with canvas.move(1, 5, 5).

Once you save your code and run it, here's the triangle's position at the end of the loop:

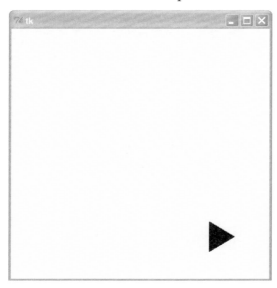

To move the triangle diagonally back up the screen to its starting position, use -5, -5 (add this code to the bottom of the file):

```
for x in range(0, 60):
    canvas.move(1, -5, -5)
    tk.update()
    time.sleep(0.05)
```

MAKING AN OBJECT REACT TO SOMETHING

We can make the triangle react when someone presses a key by using *event bindings*. *Events* are things that occur while a program is running, such as someone moving the mouse, pressing a key, or closing a window. You can tell tkinter to watch for these events and then do something in response.

To begin handling events (making Python do something when an event occurs), we first create a function. The binding part comes when we tell tkinter that a particular function is bound (or associated) to a specific event; in other words, it will be automatically called by tkinter to handle that event.

For example, to make the triangle move when the ENTER key is pressed, we can define this function:

```
def movetriangle(event):
    canvas.move(1, 5, 0)
```

The function takes a single parameter (event), which tkinter uses to send information to the function about the event. We now tell tkinter that this function should be used for a particular event, using the bind_all function on the canvas. The full code now looks like this:

```
from tkinter import *
tk = Tk()
canvas = Canvas(tk, width=400, height=400)
canvas.pack()
canvas.create_polygon(10, 10, 10, 60, 50, 35)
def movetriangle(event):
    canvas.move(1, 5, 0)
canvas.bind_all('<KeyPress-Return>', movetriangle)
```

The first parameter in this function describes the event that we want tkinter to watch for. In this case, it's called <KeyPress-Return>, which is a press of the ENTER or RETURN key. We tell tkinter that the movetriangle function should be called whenever this KeyPress event occurs. Run this code, click the canvas with your mouse, and then try pressing ENTER on your keyboard.

How about changing the direction of the triangle depending on different key presses, such as the arrow keys? That's no problem. We just need to change the movetriangle function to the following:

```python
def movetriangle(event):
    if event.keysym == 'Up':
        canvas.move(1, 0, -3)
    elif event.keysym == 'Down':
        canvas.move(1, 0, 3)
    elif event.keysym == 'Left':
        canvas.move(1, -3, 0)
    else:
        canvas.move(1, 3, 0)
```

The event object passed to movetriangle contains several variables. One of these variables is called keysym (for key symbol), which is a string that holds the value of the actual key pressed. The line if event.keysym == 'Up': says that if the keysym variable contains the string 'Up', we should call canvas.move with the parameters (1, 0, -3), as we do in the following line. If keysym contains 'Down', as in elif event.keysym == 'Down':, we call it with the parameters (1, 0, 3), and so on.

Remember that the first parameter is the identifying number for the shape drawn on the canvas, the second is the value to add to the x (horizontal) coordinate, and the third is the value to add to the y (vertical) coordinate.

We then tell tkinter that the movetriangle function should be used to handle events from four different keys (up, down, left, and right). The following shows how the code looks at this point. When you enter this code, it will again be a lot easier if you create a new shell window by selecting **File ▸ New Window**. Before running the code, save it with a meaningful filename, such as *movingtriangle.py*.

```
from tkinter import *
tk = Tk()
canvas = Canvas(tk, width=400, height=400)
canvas.pack()
canvas.create_polygon(10, 10, 10, 60, 50, 35)
def movetriangle(event):
❶    if event.keysym == 'Up':
❷        canvas.move(1, 0, -3)
❸    elif event.keysym == 'Down':
❹        canvas.move(1, 0, 3)
❺    elif event.keysym == 'Left':
❻        canvas.move(1, -3, 0)
❼    else:
❽        canvas.move(1, 3, 0)
canvas.bind_all('<KeyPress-Up>', movetriangle)
canvas.bind_all('<KeyPress-Down>', movetriangle)
canvas.bind_all('<KeyPress-Left>', movetriangle)
canvas.bind_all('<KeyPress-Right>', movetriangle)
```

On the first line of the movetriangle function, we check whether the keysym variable contains 'Up' at ❶. If it does, we move the triangle upward using the move function with the parameters 1, 0, -3 at ❷. The first parameter is the identifier of the triangle, the second is the amount to move to the right (we don't want to move horizontally, so the value is 0), and the third is the amount to move downward (−3 pixels).

We then check whether keysym contains 'Down' at ❸, and if so, we move the triangle down (3 pixels) at ❹. The final check is whether the value is 'Left' at ❺, and if so, we move the triangle left (−3 pixels) at ❻. If none of the values are matched, the final else at ❼ moves the triangle right at ❽.

Now the triangle should move in the direction of the pressed arrow key.

MORE WAYS TO USE THE IDENTIFIER

Whenever we use a create_ function from the canvas, such as create_polygon or create_rectangle, an identifier is returned. This identifying number can be used with other canvas functions, as we did earlier with the move function:

```
>>> from tkinter import *
>>> tk = Tk()
```

```
>>> canvas = Canvas(tk, width=400, height=400)
>>> canvas.pack()
>>> canvas.create_polygon(10, 10, 10, 60, 50, 35)
1
>>> canvas.move(1, 5, 0)
```

The problem with this example is that `create_polygon` won't always return 1. For example, if you've created other shapes, it might return 2, 3, or even 100 for that matter (depending on the number of shapes that have been created). If we change the code to store the value returned as a variable, and then use the variable (rather than just referring to the number 1), the code will work no matter what number is returned:

```
>>> mytriangle = canvas.create_polygon(10, 10, 10, 60, 50, 35)
>>> canvas.move(mytriangle, 5, 0)
```

The `move` function allows us to move objects around the screen using their identifier. But there are other canvas functions that can also change something we've drawn. For example, the `itemconfig` function of the canvas can be used to change some of the parameters of a shape, such as its fill and outline colors.

Say we create a red triangle:

```
>>> from tkinter import *
>>> tk = Tk()
>>> canvas = Canvas(tk, width=400, height=400)
>>> canvas.pack()
>>> mytriangle = canvas.create_polygon(10, 10, 10, 60, 50, 35,
fill='red')
```

We can change the triangle to another color using `itemconfig` and use the identifier as the first parameter. The following code says, "Change the fill color of the object identified by the number in variable `mytriangle` to blue."

```
>>> canvas.itemconfig(mytriangle, fill='blue')
```

We could also give the triangle a different-colored outline, again using the identifier as the first parameter:

```
>>> canvas.itemconfig(mytriangle, outline='red')
```

Later, we'll learn how to make other
changes to a drawing, such as hide it and
make it visible again. You'll find it useful
to be able to change a drawing once it's displayed on the screen when we start writing
games in the next chapter.

WHAT YOU LEARNED

In this chapter, you used the tkinter module to draw simple geometric shapes on a canvas, display images, and perform basic
animation. You learned how to use event bindings to make drawings react to someone pressing a key, which will be useful once we
start working on programming a game. You learned how the create
functions in tkinter return an identifying number, which can be
used to modify shapes after they've been drawn, such as to move
them around on the screen or change their color.

PROGRAMMING PUZZLES

Try the following to play with the tkinter module and basic animation. Visit *http://python-for-kids.com/* for solutions.

#1: FILL THE SCREEN WITH TRIANGLES

Create a program using tkinter to fill the screen with triangles.
Then change the code to fill the screen with different-colored
(filled) triangles instead.

#2: THE MOVING TRIANGLE

Modify the code for the moving triangle ("Creating Basic Animation" on page 183) to make it move across the screen to the right,
then down, then back to the left, and then back to its starting
position.

#3: THE MOVING PHOTO

Try displaying a photo of yourself on the canvas using tkinter.
Make sure it's a GIF image! Can you make it move across the
screen?

PART II

BOUNCE!

13

BEGINNING YOUR FIRST GAME: BOUNCE!

So far, we've covered the basics of computer programming. You've learned how to use variables to store
information, if statements for conditional code, and for
loops for repeating code. You know how to create functions to reuse your code, and how to use classes and
objects to divide your code into smaller chunks that
make it easier to understand. You've learned how to
draw graphics on the screen with both the turtle and
tkinter modules. Now it's time to use that knowledge
to create your first game.

WHACK THE BOUNCING BALL

We're going to develop a game with a bouncing ball and a paddle. The ball will fly around the screen, and the player will bounce it off the paddle. If the ball hits the bottom of the screen, the game comes to an end. Here's a preview of the finished game:

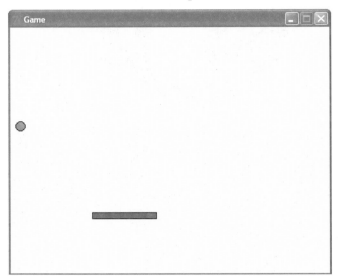

Our game may look quite simple, but the code will be a bit trickier than what we've written so far because there are a lot of things that it needs to handle. For example, it needs to animate the paddle and the ball, and detect when the ball hits the paddle or the walls.

In this chapter, we'll begin creating the game by adding a game canvas and a bouncing ball. In the next chapter, we'll complete the game by adding the paddle.

CREATING THE GAME CANVAS

To create your game, first open a new file in the Python shell (select **File ▸ New Window**). Then import tkinter and create a canvas to draw on:

```
from tkinter import *
import random
import time
```

```
tk = Tk()
tk.title("Game")
tk.resizable(0, 0)
tk.wm_attributes("-topmost", 1)
canvas = Canvas(tk, width=500, height=400, bd=0, highlightthickness=0)
canvas.pack()
tk.update()
```

This is a little different from previous examples. First, we import the time and random modules with import random and import time, for use a bit later in the code.

With tk.title("Game"), we use the title function of the tk object we created with tk = Tk() to give the window a title. Then we use resizable to make the window a fixed size. The parameters 0, 0 say "the size of the window cannot be changed either horizontally or vertically." Next, we call wm_attributes to tell tkinter to place the window containing our canvas in front of all other windows ("-topmost").

Notice that when we create a canvas object with canvas =, we pass in a few more named parameters than with previous examples. For example, both bd=0 and highlightthickness=0 make sure that there's no border around the outside of the canvas, which makes it look better on our game screen.

The line canvas.pack() tells the canvas to size itself according to the width and height parameters given in the preceding line. Finally, tk.update() tells tkinter to initialize itself for the animation in our game. Without this last line, nothing would work quite as expected.

Make sure you save your code as you go. Give it a meaningful filename the first time you save it, such as *paddleball.py*.

CREATING THE BALL CLASS

Now we'll create the class for the ball. We'll begin with the code we need for the ball to draw itself on the canvas. Here's what we need to do:

- Create a class called Ball that takes parameters for the canvas and the color of the ball we're going to draw.
- Save the canvas as an object variable because we'll draw our ball on it.
- Draw a filled circle on the canvas using the value of the color parameter as the fill color.
- Save the identifier that tkinter returns when it draws the circle (oval) because we're going use this to move the ball around the screen.
- Move the oval to the middle of the canvas.

This code should be added just after the first two lines in the file (after import time):

```
from tkinter import *
import random
import time

❶ class Ball:
❷     def __init__(self, canvas, color):
❸         self.canvas = canvas
❹         self.id = canvas.create_oval(10, 10, 25, 25, fill=color)
❺         self.canvas.move(self.id, 245, 100)

    def draw(self):
        pass
```

First, we name our class Ball at ❶. Then we create an initialization function (as described in Chapter 8) that takes the parameters canvas and color at ❷. At ❸, we set the object variable canvas to the value of the parameter canvas.

At ❹, we call the create_oval function with five parameters: x and y coordinates for the top-left corner (10 and 10), x and y coordinates for the bottom-right corner (25 and 25), and finally, the fill color for the oval.

The `create_oval` function returns an identifier for the shape that is drawn, which we store in the object variable id. At ❺, we move the oval to the middle of the canvas (position 245, 100), and the canvas knows what to move, because we use the stored shape identifier (the object variable id) to identify it.

On the last two lines of the Ball class, we create the draw function with `def draw(self)`, and the body of the function is simply the pass keyword. At the moment it does nothing. We'll add more to this function shortly.

Now that we've created our Ball class, we need to create an object of this class (remember that a class describes what it can do, but the object is the thing that actually does it). Add the following code to the bottom of the program to create a red ball object:

```
ball = Ball(canvas, 'red')
```

If you run this program now using **Run ▸ Run Module**, the canvas will appear for a split second and then vanish. To stop the window from closing immediately, we need to add an animation loop, which is called the *main loop* of our game.

A main loop is the central part of a program that generally controls most of what it does. Our main loop, for the moment, just tells tkinter to redraw the screen. The loop keeps running forever (or at least until we close the window), constantly telling tkinter to redraw the screen, and then sleeping for one hundredth of a second. We'll add this code to the end of our program:

```
ball = Ball(canvas, 'red')

while 1:
    tk.update_idletasks()
    tk.update()
    time.sleep(0.01)
```

Now if you run the code, the ball should appear almost in the center of the canvas:

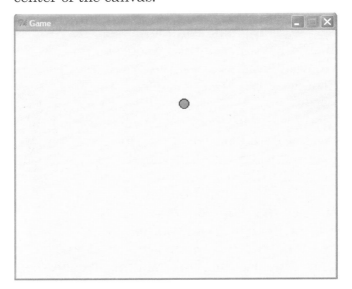

ADDING SOME ACTION

Now that we have the Ball class set up, it's time to animate the ball. We'll make it move, bounce, and change direction.

MAKING THE BALL MOVE

To move the ball, change the draw function as follows:

```
class Ball:
    def __init__(self, canvas, color):
        self.canvas = canvas
        self.id = canvas.create_oval(10, 10, 25, 25, fill=color)
        self.canvas.move(self.id, 245, 100)

    def draw(self):
        self.canvas.move(self.id, 0, -1)
```

Since __init__ saved the canvas parameter as the object variable canvas, we use that variable with self.canvas, and call the function move on the canvas.

We pass three parameters to move: the id of the oval, and the numbers 0 and -1. The 0 says don't move horizontally, and the -1 says move 1 pixel up the screen.

We're making this small change because it's a good idea to try things out as we go. Imagine if we wrote the entire code for our game at once, and then discovered that it didn't work. Where would we start looking to figure out why?

The other change is to the main loop at the bottom of our program. In the block of the while loop (that's our main loop!), we add a call to the ball object's draw function, like so:

```
while 1:
    ball.draw()
    tk.update_idletasks()
    tk.update()
    time.sleep(0.01)
```

If you run this code now, the ball should move up the canvas and vanish, because the code forces tkinter to redraw the screen quickly—the commands update_idletasks and update tell tkinter to hurry up and draw what is on the canvas.

The command time.sleep is a call to the sleep function of the time module, which tells Python to sleep for one hundredth of a second (0.01). This is to make sure that our program won't run so fast that the ball vanishes before you even see it.

So the loop is basically saying: move the ball a little, redraw the screen with the new position, sleep for a moment, and then start over again.

NOTE *You may see error messages written to the shell when you close the game window. This is because when you close the window, the code is breaking out of the while loop, and Python is complaining about it.*

Your game should now look like this:

```
from tkinter import *
import random
import time

class Ball:
    def __init__(self, canvas, color):
        self.canvas = canvas
        self.id = canvas.create_oval(10, 10, 25, 25, fill=color)
        self.canvas.move(self.id, 245, 100)
```

```
    def draw(self):
        self.canvas.move(self.id, 0, -1)

tk = Tk()
tk.title("Game")
tk.resizable(0, 0)
tk.wm_attributes("-topmost", 1)
canvas = Canvas(tk, width=500, height=400, bd=0, highlightthickness=0)
canvas.pack()
tk.update()

ball = Ball(canvas, 'red')

while 1:
    ball.draw()
    tk.update_idletasks()
    tk.update()
    time.sleep(0.01)
```

MAKING THE BALL BOUNCE

A ball that vanishes off the top of the screen isn't particularly useful for a game, so let's make it bounce. First, we save a few additional object variables in the initialization function of the Ball class, like this:

```
    def __init__(self, canvas, color):
        self.canvas = canvas
        self.id = canvas.create_oval(10, 10, 25, 25, fill=color)
        self.canvas.move(self.id, 245, 100)
        self.x = 0
        self.y = -1
        self.canvas_height = self.canvas.winfo_height()
```

We've added three more lines to our program. With self.x = 0, we set the object variable x to 0, and then with self.y = -1, we set the variable y to -1. Finally, we set the object variable canvas_height by calling the canvas function winfo_height. This function returns the current height of the canvas.

Next, we change the draw function again:

```
    def draw(self):
❶       self.canvas.move(self.id, self.x, self.y)
❷       pos = self.canvas.coords(self.id)
```

❸

❹

```
     if pos[1] <= 0:
         self.y = 1
     if pos[3] >= self.canvas_height:
         self.y = -1
```

At ❶, we change the call to the canvas's move function by passing the object variables x and y. Next, we create a variable called pos at ❷, by calling the canvas function coords. This function returns the current x and y coordinates of anything drawn on the canvas as long as you know its identifying number. In this case, we pass coords the object variable id, which contains the oval's identifier.

The coords function returns the coordinates as a list of four numbers. If we print the results of calling this function, we'll see something like this:

```
print(self.canvas.coords(self.id))
[255.0, 29.0, 270.0, 44.0]
```

The first two numbers in the list (255.0 and 29.0) contain the top-left coordinates of the oval (*x1* and *y1*); the second two (270.0 and 44.0) are the bottom-right *x2* and *y2* coordinates. We'll use these values in the next few lines of code.

At ❸, we see if the *y1* coordinate (that's the top of the ball!) is less than or equal to 0. If so, we set the y object variable to 1. In effect, we're saying if you hit the top of the screen, stop subtracting one from the vertical position, and therefore stop moving up.

At ❹, we see if the *y2* coordinate (that's the bottom of the ball!) is greater than or equal to the variable canvas_height. If it is, we set the y object variable back to -1.

Run this code now, and the ball should bounce up and down the canvas until you close the window.

CHANGING THE BALL'S STARTING DIRECTION

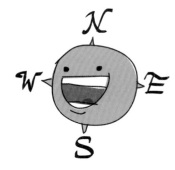

Making a ball bounce slowly up and down isn't much of a game, so let's enhance things a bit by changing the ball's starting direction—the angle that it flies off when the game starts. In the __init__ function, change these lines:

```
self.x = 0
self.y = -1
```

to the following (make sure you have the right number of spaces—there are eight—at the beginning of each line):

```
❶     starts = [-3, -2, -1, 1, 2, 3]
❷     random.shuffle(starts)
❸     self.x = starts[0]
❹     self.y = -3
```

At ❶, we create the variable starts with a list of six numbers, and then mix up the list at ❷ by calling random.shuffle. At ❸, we set the value of x to the first item in the list, so that x can be any number in the list, from −3 to 3.

If we then change y to −3 at ❹ (to speed up the ball), we need to make a few more additions to be sure that the ball won't just vanish off the side of the screen. Add the following line to the end of the __init__ function to save the width of the canvas to a new object variable, canvas_width:

```
self.canvas_width = self.canvas.winfo_width()
```

We'll use this new object variable in the draw function to see if the ball has hit the left or right side of the canvas:

```
if pos[0] <= 0:
    self.x = 3
if pos[2] >= self.canvas_width:
    self.x = -3
```

Since we're setting x to 3 and −3, we'll do the same with y, so that the ball moves at the same speed in all directions. Your draw function should now look like this:

```
def draw(self):
    self.canvas.move(self.id, self.x, self.y)
    pos = self.canvas.coords(self.id)
    if pos[1] <= 0:
        self.y = 3
    if pos[3] >= self.canvas_height:
        self.y = -3
    if pos[0] <= 0:
        self.x = 3
    if pos[2] >= self.canvas_width:
        self.x = -3
```

Save and run the code, and the ball should bounce around the screen without vanishing. And here is what the full program should look like now:

```
from tkinter import *
import random
import time

class Ball:
    def __init__(self, canvas, color):
        self.canvas = canvas
        self.id = canvas.create_oval(10, 10, 25, 25, fill=color)
        self.canvas.move(self.id, 245, 100)
        starts = [-3, -2, -1, 1, 2, 3]
        random.shuffle(starts)
        self.x = starts[0]
        self.y = -3
        self.canvas_height = self.canvas.winfo_height()
        self.canvas_width = self.canvas.winfo_width()

    def draw(self):
        self.canvas.move(self.id, self.x, self.y)
        pos = self.canvas.coords(self.id)
        if pos[1] <= 0:
            self.y = 3
        if pos[3] >= self.canvas_height:
            self.y = -3
        if pos[0] <= 0:
            self.x = 3
        if pos[2] >= self.canvas_width:
            self.x = -3
```

```
tk = Tk()
tk.title("Game")
tk.resizable(0, 0)
tk.wm_attributes("-topmost", 1)
canvas = Canvas(tk, width=500, height=400, bd=0, highlightthickness=0)
canvas.pack()
tk.update()

ball = Ball(canvas, 'red')

while 1:
    ball.draw()
    tk.update_idletasks()
    tk.update()
    time.sleep(0.01)
```

WHAT YOU LEARNED

In this chapter, we started creating our first game using the tkinter module. We created a class for a ball and animated it so that it moves around the screen. We used coordinates to check when the ball hits the sides of the canvas, so that we can make it bounce. We also used the shuffle function in the random module, so our ball doesn't always start moving in the exact same direction. In the next chapter, we'll complete the game by adding the paddle.

14

FINISHING YOUR FIRST GAME: BOUNCE!

In the previous chapter, we got started creating our first game: Bounce! We created a canvas and added a bouncing ball to our game code. But our ball will bounce around the screen forever (or at least until you turn your computer off), which doesn't make for much of a game. Now we'll add a paddle for the player to use. We'll also add an element of chance to the game, which will make it a bit more challenging and fun to play.

ADDING THE PADDLE

There's not much fun to be had with a bouncing ball when there's nothing to hit it with. Time to create a paddle!

Begin by adding the following code just after the Ball class, to create a paddle (you'll stick this in a new line below the Ball draw function):

```
    def draw(self):
        self.canvas.move(self.id, self.x, self.y)
        pos = self.canvas.coords(self.id)
        if pos[1] <= 0:
            self.y = 3
        if pos[3] >= self.canvas_height:
            self.y = -3
        if pos[0] <= 0:
            self.x = 3
        if pos[2] >= self.canvas_width:
            self.x = -3

class Paddle:
    def __init__(self, canvas, color):
        self.canvas = canvas
        self.id = canvas.create_rectangle(0, 0, 100, 10, fill=color)
        self.canvas.move(self.id, 200, 300)

    def draw(self):
        pass
```

This added code is almost exactly the same as that of the Ball class, except that we call create_rectangle (rather than create_oval), and we move the rectangle to position 200, 300 (200 pixels across and 300 pixels down).

Next, at the bottom of your code listing, create an object of the Paddle class, and then change the main loop to call the paddle's draw function, as shown here:

```
paddle = Paddle(canvas, 'blue')
ball = Ball(canvas, 'red')

while 1:
    ball.draw()
    paddle.draw()
```

```
tk.update_idletasks()
tk.update()
time.sleep(0.01)
```

If you run the game now, you should see the bouncing ball and a stationary rectangular paddle:

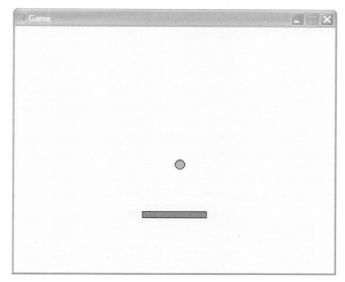

MAKING THE PADDLE MOVE

To make the paddle move left and right, we'll use event bindings to bind the left and right arrow keys to new functions in the Paddle class. When the player presses the left arrow key, the x variable will be set to -2 (to move left). Pressing the right arrow key sets the x variable to 2 (to move right).

The first step is to add the x object variable to the __init__ function of our Paddle class, and also a variable for the canvas width, as we did with the Ball class:

```
def __init__(self, canvas, color):
    self.canvas = canvas
    self.id = canvas.create_rectangle(0, 0, 100, 10, fill=color)
    self.canvas.move(self.id, 200, 300)
    self.x = 0
    self.canvas_width = self.canvas.winfo_width()
```

Now we need the functions for changing the direction between left (turn_left) and right (turn_right). We'll add these just after the draw function:

```
def turn_left(self, evt):
    self.x = -2

def turn_right(self, evt):
    self.x = 2
```

We can bind these functions to the correct key in the __init__ function of the class with these two lines. We used binding in "Making an Object React to Something" on page 187 to make Python call a function when a key is pressed. In this case, we bind the turn_left function of our Paddle class to the left arrow key using the event name '<KeyPress-Left>'. We then bind the turn_right function to the right arrow key using the event name '<KeyPress-Right>'. Our __init__ function now looks like this:

```
def __init__(self, canvas, color):
    self.canvas = canvas
    self.id = canvas.create_rectangle(0, 0, 100, 10, fill=color)
    self.canvas.move(self.id, 200, 300)
    self.x = 0
    self.canvas_width = self.canvas.winfo_width()
    self.canvas.bind_all('<KeyPress-Left>', self.turn_left)
    self.canvas.bind_all('<KeyPress-Right>', self.turn_right)
```

The draw function for the Paddle class is similar to that for the Ball class:

```
def draw(self):
    self.canvas.move(self.id, self.x, 0)
    pos = self.canvas.coords(self.id)
    if pos[0] <= 0:
        self.x = 0
    elif pos[2] >= self.canvas_width:
        self.x = 0
```

We use the canvas's move function to move the paddle in the direction of the x variable with self.canvas.move(self.id, self.x, 0). Then we get the paddle's coordinates to see if it has hit the left or right side of the screen using the value in pos.

Rather than bouncing like the ball, the paddle should stop moving. So, when the left x coordinate (pos[0]) is less than or equal to 0 (<= 0), we set the x variable to 0 with self.x = 0. In the same way, when the right x coordinate (pos[2]) is greater than or equal to the canvas width (>= self.canvas_width), we also set the x variable to 0 with self.x = 0.

NOTE *If you run the program now, you'll need to click the canvas before the game will recognize the left and right arrow key actions. Clicking the canvas gives the canvas focus, which means it knows to take charge when someone presses a key on the keyboard.*

FINDING OUT WHEN THE BALL HITS THE PADDLE

At this point in our code, the ball won't hit the paddle; in fact, the ball will fly straight through the paddle. The ball needs to know when it has hit the paddle, just as the ball needs to know when it has hit a wall.

We could solve this problem by adding code to the draw function (where we have code that checks for walls), but it's a better idea to move this sort of code into new functions to break things into smaller chunks. If we put too much code in one place (inside one function, for example), we can make the code much more difficult to understand. Let's make the necessary changes.

First, we change the ball's __init__ function so that we can pass in the paddle object as a parameter:

```
class Ball:
❶    def __init__(self, canvas, paddle, color):
        self.canvas = canvas
❷        self.paddle = paddle
        self.id = canvas.create_oval(10, 10, 25, 25, fill=color)
        self.canvas.move(self.id, 245, 100)
        starts = [-3, -2, -1, 1, 2, 3]
        random.shuffle(starts)
        self.x = starts[0]
        self.y = -3
        self.canvas_height = self.canvas.winfo_height()
        self.canvas_width = self.canvas.winfo_width()
```

Notice at ❶ that we change the parameters of __init__ to include the paddle. Then at ❷, we assign the paddle parameter to the object variable paddle.

Having saved the paddle object, we need to change the code where we create the ball object. This change is at the bottom of the program, just before the main loop:

```
paddle = Paddle(canvas, 'blue')
ball = Ball(canvas, paddle, 'red')

while 1:
    ball.draw()
    paddle.draw()
    tk.update_idletasks()
    tk.update()
    time.sleep(0.01)
```

The code we need to see if the ball has struck the paddle is a little more complicated than the code to check for walls. We'll call this function hit_paddle and add it to the draw function of the Ball class, where we see if the ball has hit the bottom of the screen:

```
def draw(self):
    self.canvas.move(self.id, self.x, self.y)
    pos = self.canvas.coords(self.id)
    if pos[1] <= 0:
        self.y = 3
    if pos[3] >= self.canvas_height:
        self.y = -3
    if self.hit_paddle(pos) == True:
        self.y = -3
    if pos[0] <= 0:
        self.x = 3
    if pos[2] >= self.canvas_width:
        self.x = -3
```

As you can see in the new code we added, if hit_paddle returns True, we change the direction of the ball by setting the y object variable to -3 with self.y = -3. But don't try to run the game now—we haven't created the hit_paddle function yet. Let's do that now.

Add the hit_paddle function just before the draw function.

```
❶     def hit_paddle(self, pos):
❷         paddle_pos = self.canvas.coords(self.paddle.id)
❸         if pos[2] >= paddle_pos[0] and pos[0] <= paddle_pos[2]:
❹             if pos[3] >= paddle_pos[1] and pos[3] <= paddle_pos[3]:
                  return True
          return False
```

First, we define the function with the parameter pos at ❶. This line contains the ball's current coordinates. Then, at ❷, we get the paddle's coordinates and store them in the variable paddle_pos.

At ❸, we have the first part of our if-then statement, and we say, "If the right side of the ball is greater than the left side of the paddle, and the left side of the ball is less than the right side of the paddle . . ." Here, pos[2] contains the x coordinate for the ball's right side, and pos[0] contains the x coordinate for its left side. The variable paddle_pos[0] contains the x coordinate for the paddle's left side, and paddle_pos[2] contains its x coordinate for the right side. The following diagram shows how these coordinates look when the ball is about to hit the paddle.

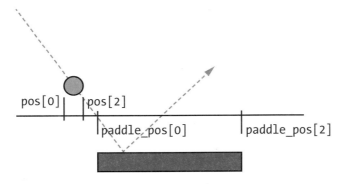

The ball is falling toward the paddle, but in this case, you see that the right side of the ball (pos[2]) hasn't yet crossed over the left side of the paddle (that's paddle_pos[0]).

At ❹, we see if the bottom of the ball (pos[3]) is between the paddle's top (paddle_pos[1]) and bottom (paddle_pos[3]). In the next diagram, you can see that the bottom of the ball (pos[3]) has yet to hit the top of the paddle (paddle_pos[1]).

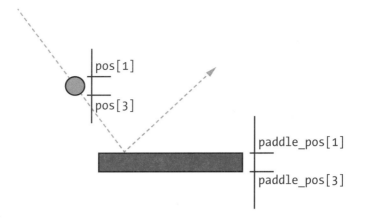

So, based on the current position of the ball, the hit_paddle function would return false.

Why do we need to see if the bottom of the ball is between the top and bottom of the paddle? Why not just see if the bottom of the ball has hit the top of the paddle? Because each time we move the ball across the canvas, we move in 3-pixel jumps. If we just checked to see if the ball had reached the top of the paddle (pos[1]), we might have jumped past that position. In that case, the ball would continue traveling, and it would pass through the paddle without stopping.

ADDING AN ELEMENT OF CHANCE

Now it's time to turn our program into a game rather than just a bouncing ball and a paddle. Games need an element of chance—some way for the player to lose. In our current game, the ball will bounce forever, so there's nothing to lose.

We'll finish our game by adding code that says that the game ends if the ball hits the bottom of the canvas (in other words, once it hits the ground).

First, we add the `hit_bottom` object variable to the bottom of the Ball class's __init__ function:

```
self.canvas_height = self.canvas.winfo_height()
self.canvas_width = self.canvas.winfo_width()
self.hit_bottom = False
```

Then we change the main loop at the bottom of the program, like this:

```
while 1:
    if ball.hit_bottom == False:
        ball.draw()
        paddle.draw()
    tk.update_idletasks()
    tk.update()
    time.sleep(0.01)
```

Now the loop keeps checking `hit_bottom` to see if the ball has indeed hit the bottom of the screen. The code should continue moving the ball and paddle only if the ball hasn't touched the bottom, as you can see in our `if` statement. The game ends when the ball and paddle stop moving. (We no longer animate them.)

The final change is to the `draw` function of the Ball class:

```
def draw(self):
    self.canvas.move(self.id, self.x, self.y)
    pos = self.canvas.coords(self.id)
    if pos[1] <= 0:
        self.y = 3
    if pos[3] >= self.canvas_height:
        self.hit_bottom = True
    if self.hit_paddle(pos) == True:
        self.y = -3
    if pos[0] <= 0:
        self.x = 3
    if pos[2] >= self.canvas_width:
        self.x = -3
```

We altered the `if` statement to see if the ball has hit the bottom of the screen (that is, if it is greater than or equal to `canvas_height`). If so, in the following line, we set `hit_bottom` to `True`, rather than changing the value of the y variable, because there's no need to bounce the ball once it hits the bottom of the screen.

When you run the game now and miss hitting the ball with the paddle, all movement on your screen should stop, and the game will end once the ball touches the bottom of the canvas:

Your program should now look like the following code. If you have trouble getting your game to work, check what you've entered against this code.

```
from tkinter import *
import random
import time

class Ball:
    def __init__(self, canvas, paddle, color):
        self.canvas = canvas
        self.paddle = paddle
        self.id = canvas.create_oval(10, 10, 25, 25, fill=color)
        self.canvas.move(self.id, 245, 100)
        starts = [-3, -2, -1, 1, 2, 3]
        random.shuffle(starts)
        self.x = starts[0]
        self.y = -3
        self.canvas_height = self.canvas.winfo_height()
        self.canvas_width = self.canvas.winfo_width()
        self.hit_bottom = False
```

```python
def hit_paddle(self, pos):
    paddle_pos = self.canvas.coords(self.paddle.id)
    if pos[2] >= paddle_pos[0] and pos[0] <= paddle_pos[2]:
        if pos[3] >= paddle_pos[1] and pos[3] <= paddle_pos[3]:
            return True
    return False

def draw(self):
    self.canvas.move(self.id, self.x, self.y)
    pos = self.canvas.coords(self.id)
    if pos[1] <= 0:
        self.y = 3
    if pos[3] >= self.canvas_height:
        self.hit_bottom = True
    if self.hit_paddle(pos) == True:
        self.y = -3
    if pos[0] <= 0:
        self.x = 3
    if pos[2] >= self.canvas_width:
        self.x = -3

class Paddle:
    def __init__(self, canvas, color):
        self.canvas = canvas
        self.id = canvas.create_rectangle(0, 0, 100, 10, fill=color)
        self.canvas.move(self.id, 200, 300)
        self.x = 0
        self.canvas_width = self.canvas.winfo_width()
        self.canvas.bind_all('<KeyPress-Left>', self.turn_left)
        self.canvas.bind_all('<KeyPress-Right>', self.turn_right)

    def draw(self):
        self.canvas.move(self.id, self.x, 0)
        pos = self.canvas.coords(self.id)
        if pos[0] <= 0:
            self.x = 0
        elif pos[2] >= self.canvas_width:
            self.x = 0

    def turn_left(self, evt):
        self.x = -2

    def turn_right(self, evt):
        self.x = 2
```

```
tk = Tk()
tk.title("Game")
tk.resizable(0, 0)
tk.wm_attributes("-topmost", 1)
canvas = Canvas(tk, width=500, height=400, bd=0, highlightthickness=0)
canvas.pack()
tk.update()

paddle = Paddle(canvas, 'blue')
ball = Ball(canvas, paddle, 'red')

while 1:
    if ball.hit_bottom == False:
        ball.draw()
        paddle.draw()
    tk.update_idletasks()
    tk.update()
    time.sleep(0.01)
```

WHAT YOU LEARNED

In this chapter, we finished creating our first game using the tkinter module. We created classes for the paddle used in our game, and used coordinates to check when the ball hits the paddle or the walls of our game canvas. We used event bindings to bind the left and right arrow keys to the movement of the paddle, and used the main loop to call the draw function, to animate it. Finally, we changed our code to give our game an element of chance, so that when the player misses the ball, the game is over when the ball hits the bottom of the canvas.

PROGRAMMING PUZZLES

At the moment, our game is a bit simple. There's a lot you could change to create a more professional game. Try enhancing your code in the following ways to make it more interesting, and then check your answers at *http://python-for-kids.com/*.

#1: DELAY THE GAME START

Our game starts a bit quickly, and you need to click the canvas before it will recognize pressing the left and right arrow keys on your keyboard. Can you add a delay to the start of the game in order to give the player enough time to click the canvas? Or even better, can you add an event binding for a mouse click, which starts the game only then?

Hint 1: You've already added event bindings to the Paddle class, so that might be a good place to start.

Hint 2: The event binding for the left mouse button is the string '<Button-1>'.

#2: A PROPER "GAME OVER"

Everything just freezes when the game ends, and that's not very player-friendly. Try adding the text "Game Over" when the ball hits the bottom of the screen. You can use the create_text function, but you might also find the named parameter state useful (it takes values such as normal and hidden). Have a look at itemconfig in "More Ways to Use the Identifier" on page 188. As an additional challenge, add a delay so that the text doesn't appear right away.

#3: ACCELERATE THE BALL

If you play tennis, you know that when a ball hits your racket, it sometimes flies away faster than the speed at which it arrived, depending on how hard you swing. The ball in our game goes at the same speed, whether or not the paddle is moving. Try changing the program so that the paddle's speed is passed on to the speed of the ball.

#4: RECORD THE PLAYER'S SCORE

How about recording the score? Every time the ball hits the paddle, the score should increase. Try displaying the score at the top-right corner of the canvas. You might want to look back at itemconfig in "More Ways to Use the Identifier" on page 188 for a hint.

PART III

MR. STICK MAN RACES FOR THE EXIT

15
CREATING GRAPHICS FOR THE MR. STICK MAN GAME

It's a good idea to develop a plan when creating a game (or any program). Your plan should include a description of what the game is about, as well as a description of the game's major elements and characters. When it's time to start programming, your description will help keep you focused on what you are trying to develop. Your game might not turn out exactly like the original description—and that's okay as well.

In this chapter, we'll begin developing a fun game called Mr. Stick Man Races for the Exit.

MR. STICK MAN GAME PLAN

Here's the description of our new game:

- Secret agent Mr. Stick Man is trapped in the lair of Dr. Innocuous, and you want to help him escape through the exit on the top floor.

- The game has a stick figure that can run from left to right and jump up. There are platforms on each floor that he must jump to.

- The goal of the game is to reach the door to the exit, before it's too late and the game ends.

Based on this description, we know we'll need several images, including ones for Mr. Stick Man, the platforms, and the door. We'll obviously need code to pull all this together, but before we get there, we'll create the graphics for our game in this chapter. That way, we'll have something to work with in the next chapter.

How will we draw the elements in our game? We could use graphics like the ones that we created for the bouncing ball and paddle in the previous chapters, but those are far too simple for this game. Instead, we're going to create sprites.

Sprites are the things in a game—typically a character of some kind. Sprites are usually *prerendered*, meaning they are drawn in advance (before the program runs) rather than being created by the program itself using polygons, as in our Bounce! game. Mr. Stick Man will be a sprite, and the platforms will be sprites, too. In order to create these images, you'll need to install a graphics program.

GETTING GIMP

Several graphics programs are available, but for this game, we need one that supports *transparency* (sometimes called the *alpha channel*), which lets images have sections where no colors are drawn on the screen. We need images with transparent parts because when one image passes over or near another as it moves across the screen, we don't want the background of one image to wipe out part of another. For example, in this image, the checkerboard pattern in the background represents the transparent area:

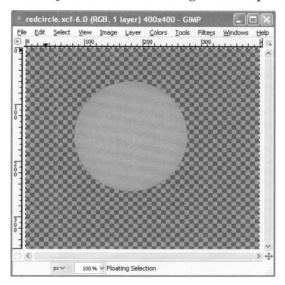

So if we copy the entire image and paste it over the top of another image, the background won't wipe anything out:

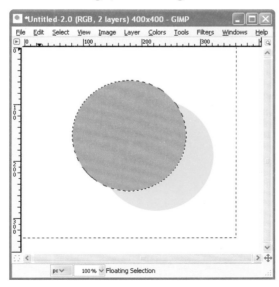

GIMP (*http://www.gimp.org/*), short for GNU Image Manipulation Program, is a free graphics program for Linux, Mac OS X, and Windows that supports transparent images. Download and install it as follows:

- If you're using Windows, you'll be able to find Windows installers on the GIMP-WIN project page at *http://gimp-win .sourceforge.net/stable.html*.

- If you're using Ubuntu, install GIMP by opening the Ubuntu Software Center and entering *gimp* in the search box. Click the Install button for the GIMP Image Editor when it appears in the results.

- If you're using Mac OS X, download an application bundle from *http://gimp.lisanet.de/Website/Download.html*.

You should also create a directory for your game. To do so, right-click your desktop anywhere there is empty space and select **New ▸ Folder** (on Ubuntu, the option is **Create New Folder**; on Mac OS X, it's **New Folder**). In the dialog, enter *stickman* for the folder name.

CREATING THE GAME ELEMENTS

Once you have your graphics program installed, you're ready to draw. We'll create these images for our game elements:

- Images for a stick figure that can run left and right and jump
- Images for the platform, in three different sizes
- Images for the door: one open and one closed
- An image for the game's background (because a plain white or gray background makes for a boring game)

Before we start drawing, we need to prepare our images with transparent backgrounds.

PREPARING A TRANSPARENT IMAGE

To set up an image with transparency—an alpha channel—start up GIMP, and then follow these steps:

1. Select **File ▸ New**.

2. In the dialog, enter *27* pixels for the image width and *30* pixels for its height.

3. Select **Layer ▸ Transparency ▸ Add Alpha Channel**.

4. Select **Select ▸ All**.

5. Select **Edit ▸ Cut**.

The end result should be an image filled with a checkerboard of dark gray and light gray, as shown here (zoomed in):

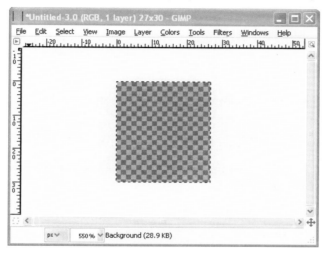

Now we can begin creating our secret agent: Mr. Stick Man.

DRAWING MR. STICK MAN

To draw our first stick figure image, click the Paintbrush tool in the GIMP Toolbox, and then select the brush that looks like a small dot in the Brushes toolbar (usually at the bottom right of the screen), as shown on the right.

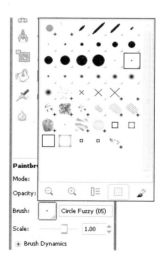

We'll draw three different images (or *frames*) for our stick figure to show him running and jumping to the right. We'll use these frames to animate Mr. Stick Man, as we did for the animation in Chapter 12.

If you zoom in to look at these images, they might look like this:

Your images don't need to look exactly the same, but they should have the stick figure with three different positions of movement. Remember that each one is 27 pixels wide by 30 pixels tall.

MR. STICK MAN RUNNING TO THE RIGHT

First, we'll draw a sequence of frames for Mr. Stick Man running to the right. Create the first image as follows:

1. Draw the first image (the leftmost image in the preceding illustration).
2. Select **File ▸ Save As**.
3. In the dialog, enter *figure-R1.gif* for the name. Then click the small plus (+) button labeled **Select File Type**.
4. Select **GIF image** in the list that appears.
5. Save the file to the *stickman* directory you created earlier (click **Browse for Other Folders** to find the correct directory).

Follow the same steps to create a new 27 pixel by 30 pixel image, and then draw the next Mr. Stick Man image. Save this image as *figure-R2.gif*. Repeat the process for the final image, and save it as *figure-R3.gif*.

MR. STICK MAN RUNNING TO THE LEFT

Rather than re-creating our drawings for the stick figure moving to the left, we can use GIMP to flip our frames of Mr. Stick Man moving to the right.

In GIMP, open each image in sequence, and then select **Tools ▸ Transform Tools ▸ Flip**. When you click the image, you should see it flip from side to side. Save the images as *figure-L1.gif*, *figure-L2 .gif*, and *figure-L3.gif*.

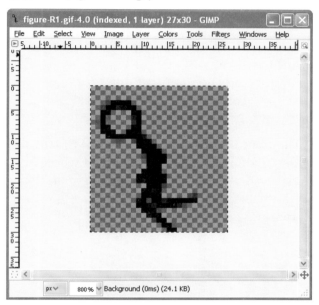

Now we've created six images for Mr. Stick Man, but we still need images for the platforms and the door for the exit.

DRAWING THE PLATFORMS

We'll create three platforms in different sizes: 100 pixels wide by 10 pixels tall, 66 pixels wide by 10 pixels tall, and 32 pixels wide by 10 pixels tall. You can draw the platforms any way that you like, but make sure that their backgrounds are transparent, as with the stick figure images.

Here's what the three platform images might look like zoomed in:

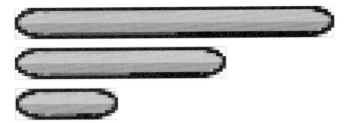

As with the stick figure images, save these in the *stickman* directory. Call the largest platform *platform1.gif*, the middle-sized one *platform2.gif*, and the smallest one *platform3.gif*.

DRAWING THE DOOR

The size of the door should be proportional to the size of Mr. Stick Man (27 pixels wide by 30 pixels tall), and we need two images: one for the closed door and another for the open door. The doors might look like this (again zoomed in):

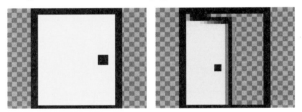

To create these images, follow these steps:

1. Click the foreground color box (at the bottom of the GIMP Toolbox) to display the color chooser. Select the color you want for your door. On the right is an example with yellow selected.

2. Choose the Bucket tool (shown selected in the Toolbox), and fill the screen with the color you chose.

3. Change the foreground color to black.

4. Choose either the Pencil or Paintbrush tool (to the right of the Bucket tool), and draw the black outline of the door and the doorknob.

5. Save these in the *stickman* directory, and call them *door1.gif* and *door2.gif.*

DRAWING THE BACKGROUND

The final image we need to create is the background. We'll make this image 100 pixels wide by 100 pixels tall. It does not need a transparent background because we'll fill it with a single color that will be the background "wallpaper" behind all the other elements of the game.

To create the background, select **File ▸ New** and give the image's size as 100 pixels wide and 100 pixels tall. Choose a suitably evil color for the wallpaper of a villain's lair. I chose a darker shade of pink.

You can dress up your wallpaper with flowers, stripes, stars, and such—whatever you think looks suitable for the game. For example, if you want to add stars to the wallpaper, choose another color, select the Pencil tool, and draw your first star. Then use the Selection tool to select a box around the star, and copy and paste it around the image (select **Edit ▸ Copy**, and then **Edit ▸ Paste**). You should be able to drag the pasted image around the screen by clicking it. Here's an example with some stars, and the Selection tool selected in the Toolbox:

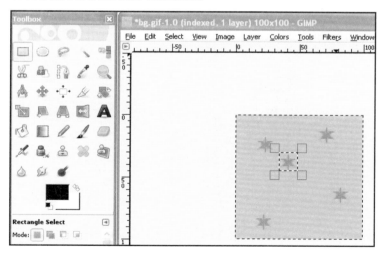

Once you're happy with your drawing, save the image as *background.gif* in the *stickman* directory.

TRANSPARENCY

With our graphics created, you can get a better of idea of why our images (other than the background) need transparency. What would happen if we placed Mr. Stick Man in front of our background wallpaper and he didn't have a transparent background? Here's the answer:

The white background of Mr. Stick Man wipes out part of the wallpaper. But if we use our transparent image, we get this:

Nothing in the background is obscured by the stick figure image, except for whatever he covers himself. That's much more professional!

WHAT YOU LEARNED

In this chapter, you learned how to write a basic plan for a game (Mr. Stick Man Races for the Exit in this case) and figured out where to begin. Because we need graphical elements before we can make a game, we used a graphics program to create the basic graphics for our game. In the process, you learned how to make the backgrounds of these images transparent so they don't cover up other images on the screen.

In the next chapter, we'll create some of the classes for our game.

16

DEVELOPING THE
MR. STICK MAN GAME

Now that we've created the images for our Mr. Stick
Man Races for the Exit game, we can begin to develop
the code. The description of the game in the previous
chapter gives us a basic idea of what we need: a stick
figure that can run and jump, and platforms that he
must jump to.

　　We'll need code to display the stick figure and
move it across the screen, as well as to draw platforms.
But before we write that code, we need to create the
canvas to display our background image.

CREATING THE GAME CLASS

First, we'll create a class called Game, which will be our program's main controller. The Game class will have an __init__ function for initializing the game and a mainloop function for doing the animation.

SETTING THE WINDOW TITLE AND CREATING THE CANVAS

In the first part of the __init__ function, we'll set the window title and create the canvas. As you'll see, this part of the code is similar to the code that we wrote for the Bounce! game in Chapter 13. Open your editor and enter the following code, and then save your file as *stickmangame.py*. Make sure you save it in the directory we created in Chapter 15 (called *stickman*).

```python
from tkinter import *
import random
import time

class Game:
    def __init__(self):
        self.tk = Tk()
        self.tk.title("Mr. Stick Man Races for the Exit")
        self.tk.resizable(0, 0)
        self.tk.wm_attributes("-topmost", 1)
        self.canvas = Canvas(self.tk, width=500, height=500, \
                highlightthickness=0)
        self.canvas.pack()
        self.tk.update()
        self.canvas_height = 500
        self.canvas_width = 500
```

In the first half of this program (from from tkinter import * to self.tk.wm_attributes), we create the tk object and then set the window title with self.tk.title to ("Mr. Stick Man Races for the Exit"). We make the window fixed (so it can't be resized) by calling the resizable function, and then we move the window in front of all other windows with the wm_attributes function.

Next, we create the canvas with the self.canvas = Canvas line, and call the pack and update functions of the tk object. Finally, we create two variables for our Game class, height and width, to store the height and width of the canvas.

NOTE *The backslash (\) in the* self.canvas = Canvas *line is used only to separate the long line of code. It's not required, but I've included it here for readability since the entire line won't fit on the page.*

FINISHING THE __INIT__ FUNCTION

Now enter the rest of the __init__ function into the *stickfiguregame .py* file that you just created. This code will load the background image and then display it on the canvas:

```
        self.tk.update()
        self.canvas_height = 500
        self.canvas_width = 500
❶       self.bg = PhotoImage(file="background.gif")
❷       w = self.bg.width()
        h = self.bg.height()
❸       for x in range(0, 5):
❹           for y in range(0, 5):
❺               self.canvas.create_image(x * w, y * h, \
                        image=self.bg, anchor='nw')
❻       self.sprites = []
        self.running = True
```

At ❶, we create the variable bg, which contains a PhotoImage object—the background image file called *background.gif* that we created in Chapter 15. Next, beginning at ❷, we store the width and height of the image in the variables w and h. The PhotoImage class functions width and height return the size of the image once it has been loaded.

Next come two loops inside this function. To understand what they do, imagine that you have a small square rubber stamp, an ink pad, and a large piece of paper. How are you going to fill the paper with colored squares using the stamp? Well, you could just randomly cover the page with stamps until it's filled. The result would be a mess, and it would take a while to complete, but it would fill the page. Or you could start stamping down the page in a column and then move back to the top and start stamping down the page in the next column, as shown on the right.

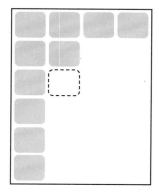

The background image we created in the previous chapter is our stamp. We know that the canvas is 500 pixels across and 500 pixels down, and that we created a background image of 100 pixels square. This tells us that we need five columns across and five rows down to fill the screen with images. We use the loop at ❸ to calculate the columns across, and the loop at ❹ to calculate rows going down.

At ❺, we multiply the first loop variable x by the width of the image (x * w) to determine how far across we're drawing, and then multiply the second loop variable y by the height of the image (y * h) to calculate how far down to draw. We use the create_image function of the canvas object (self.canvas.create_image) to draw the image on the screen using those coordinates.

Finally, beginning with ❻, we create the variables sprites, which holds an empty list, and running, which contains the Boolean value True. We'll use these variables later in our game code.

CREATING THE MAINLOOP FUNCTION

We'll use the mainloop function in the Game class to animate our game. This function looks a lot like the main loop (or animation loop) we created for the Bounce! game in Chapter 13. Here it is:

```
        for x in range(0, 5):
            for y in range(0, 5):
                self.canvas.create_image(x * w, y * h, \
                    image=self.bg, anchor='nw')
        self.sprites = []
        self.running = True

    def mainloop(self):
❶      while 1:
❷          if self.running == True:
❸              for sprite in self.sprites:
❹                  sprite.move()
❺          self.tk.update_idletasks()
            self.tk.update()
            time.sleep(0.01)
```

At ❶, we create a while loop that will run until the game window is closed. Next, at ❷, we check to see if the variable running is equal to True. If it is, we loop through any sprites in the list of sprites (self.sprites) at ❸, calling the function move for each one at ❹. (Of course, we have yet to create any sprites, so this code wouldn't do anything if you ran the program now, but it will be useful later.)

The last three lines of the function, beginning at ❺, force the tk object to redraw the screen and sleep for a fraction of a second, as we did with the Bounce! game in Chapter 13.

So that you can run this code, add the following two lines (note that there's no indentation required for these two lines) and save the file.

```
g = Game()
g.mainloop()
```

NOTE   *Be sure to add this code to the bottom of your game file. Also, make sure that your images are in the same directory as the Python file. If you created the* stickman *directory in Chapter 15 and saved all your images there, the Python file for this game should be there as well.*

This code creates an object of the Game class and saves it as the variable g. We then call the mainloop function on the new object to draw the screen.

Once you've saved the program, run it in IDLE by choosing **Run ▸ Run Module**. You will see a window appear with the background image filling the canvas.

We've added a nice background for our game, and created an animation loop that will draw sprites for us (once we've created them).

CREATING THE COORDS CLASS

Now we'll create the class that we'll use to specify the position of something on our game screen. This class will store the top-left (x1 and y1) and bottom-right (x2 and y2) coordinates of any component of our game.

Here's how you might record the position of the stick figure image using these coordinates:

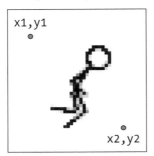

We'll call our new class Coords, and it will contain only an __init__ function, where we pass the four parameters (x1, y1, x2, and y2). Here's the code to add (put it at the beginning of the *stickmangame.py* file):

```
class Coords:
    def __init__(self, x1=0, y1=0, x2=0, y2=0):
        self.x1 = x1
        self.y1 = y1
        self.x2 = x2
        self.y2 = y2
```

Notice that each parameter is saved as an object variable of the same name (x1, y1, x2, and y2). We'll be using objects of this class shortly.

CHECKING FOR COLLISIONS

Once we know how to store the position of our game sprites, we need a way to tell if one sprite has collided with another, like when Mr. Stick Man jumps around the screen and bangs into one of the platforms. To make this problem easier to solve, we can break it down into two smaller problems: checking if sprites are colliding vertically and checking if sprites are colliding horizontally. Then we can combine our two smaller solutions to easily see if two sprites are colliding in any direction!

SPRITES COLLIDING HORIZONTALLY

First, we'll create the within_x function to determine if one set of x coordinates (x1 and x2) has crossed over another set of x coordinates (again, x1 and x2). There's more than one way to do this, but here's a simple approach which you can add just below the Coords class:

```
class Coords:
    def __init__(self, x1=0, y1=0, x2=0, y2=0):
        self.x1 = x1
        self.y1 = y1
        self.x2 = x2
        self.y2 = y2

def within_x(co1, co2):
    if co1.x1 > co2.x1 and co1.x1 < co2.x2:          ❶
        return True                                   ❷
    elif co1.x2 > co2.x1 and co1.x2 < co2.x2:         ❸
        return True                                   ❹
    elif co2.x1 > co1.x1 and co2.x1 < co1.x2:         ❺
        return True
    elif co2.x2 > co1.x1 and co2.x2 < co1.x2:         ❻
        return True
    else:                                             ❼
        return False                                  ❽
```

The within_x function takes the parameters co1 and co2, both Coords objects. At ❶, we check to see if the leftmost position of the first coordinate object (co1.x1) is between the leftmost position (co2.x1) and the rightmost position (co2.x2) of the second coordinate object. We return True at ❷ if it is.

Let's take a look at two lines with overlapping x coordinates to understand how this works. Each line starts at x1 and finishes at x2.

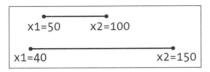

The first line in this diagram (co1) starts at pixel position 50 (x1) and finishes at 100 (x2). The second line (co2) starts at position 40 and finishes at 150. In this case, because the x1 position of the first line is between the x1 and x2 positions of the second line, the first if statement in the function would be true for these two sets of coordinates.

With the elif at ❸, we see whether the rightmost position of the first line (co1.x2) is between the leftmost position (co2.x1) and rightmost position (co2.x2) of the second. If it is, we return True at ❹. The two elif statements at ❺ and ❻ do almost the same thing: They check the leftmost and rightmost positions of the second line (co2) against the first (co1).

If none of the if statements match, we reach else at ❼, and return False at ❽. This is effectively saying, "No, the two coordinate objects do not cross over each other horizontally."

To see an example of the function working, look back at the diagram showing the first and second lines. The x1 and x2 positions of the first coordinate object are 40 and 100, and the x1 and x2 positions of the second coordinate object are 50 and 150. Here's what happens when we call the within_x function that we wrote:

```
>>> c1 = Coords(40, 40, 100, 100)
>>> c2 = Coords(50, 50, 150, 150)
>>> print(within_x(c1, c2))
True
```

The function returns True. This is the first step to being able to determine whether one sprite has bumped into another. For example, when we create a class for Mr. Stick Man and for the platforms, we will be able to tell if their x coordinates have crossed one another.

It's not really good programming practice to have lots of `if` or `elif` statements that return the same value. To solve this problem, we can shorten the `within_x` function by surrounding each of its conditions with parentheses, separated by the or keyword. If you want a slightly neater function, with a few less lines of code, you can change the function so it looks like this:

```python
def within_x(co1, co2):
    if (co1.x1 > co2.x1 and co1.x1 < co2.x2) \
            or (co1.x2 > co2.x1 and co1.x2 < co2.x2) \
            or (co2.x1 > co1.x1 and co2.x1 < co1.x2) \
            or (co2.x2 > co1.x1 and co2.x2 < co1.x2):
        return True
    else:
        return False
```

To extend the `if` statement across multiple lines so that we don't end up with one really long line containing all the conditions, we use a backslash (\), as shown above.

SPRITES COLLIDING VERTICALLY

We also need to know if sprites collide vertically. The `within_y` function is very similar to the `within_x` function. To create it, we check whether the y1 position of the first coordinate has crossed over the y1 and y2 positions of the second, and then vice versa. Here's the function to add (put it below the `within_x` function)—this time we'll write it using the shorter version of the code (rather than lots of `if` statements):

```python
def within_y(co1, co2):
    if (co1.y1 > co2.y1 and co1.y1 < co2.y2) \
            or (co1.y2 > co2.y1 and co1.y2 < co2.y2) \
            or (co2.y1 > co1.y1 and co2.y1 < co1.y2) \
            or (co2.y2 > co1.y1 and co2.y2 < co1.y2):
        return True
    else:
        return False
```

PUTTING IT ALL TOGETHER: OUR FINAL COLLISION-DETECTION CODE

Once we've determined whether one set of x coordinates has crossed over another, and done the same for y coordinates, we can write functions to see whether a sprite has hit another sprite and on which side. We'll do this with the functions `collided_left`, `collided_right`, `collided_top`, and `collided_bottom`.

THE COLLIDED_LEFT FUNCTION

Here's the code for the `collided_left` function, which you can add below the two `within` functions we just created:

```
❶ def collided_left(co1, co2):
❷     if within_y(co1, co2):
❸         if co1.x1 <= co2.x2 and co1.x1 >= co2.x1:
❹             return True
❺     return False
```

This function tells us whether the left-hand side (the x1 value) of a first coordinate object has hit another coordinate object.

The function takes two parameters: co1 (the first coordinate object) and co2 (the second coordinate object). As you can see at ❶, we check whether the two coordinate objects have crossed over vertically, using the within_y function at ❷. After all, there's no point in checking whether Mr. Stick Man has hit a platform if he is floating way above it, like this:

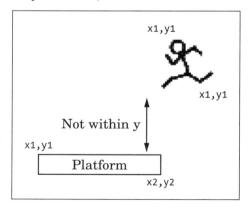

At ❸, we see if the value of the left-most position of the first coordinate object (co1.x1) has hit the x2 position of the second coordinate object (co2.x2)—that it is less than or equal to the x2 position. We also check to make sure that it hasn't gone past the x1 position. If it has hit the side, we return True at ❹. If none of the if statements are true, we return False at ❺.

THE COLLIDED_RIGHT FUNCTION

The collided_right function looks a lot like collided_left:

```
   def collided_right(co1, co2):
❶      if within_y(co1, co2):
❷          if co1.x2 >= co2.x1 and co1.x2 <= co2.x2:
❸              return True
❹      return False
```

As with collided_left, we check to see if the y coordinates have crossed over each other using the within_y function at ❶. We then check to see if the x2 value is between the x1 and x2 positions of the second coordinate object at ❷, and return True at ❸ if it is. Otherwise, we return False at ❹.

THE COLLIDED_TOP FUNCTION

The collided_top function is very similar to the two functions we just added.

```
   def collided_top(co1, co2):
❶      if within_x(co1, co2):
❷          if co1.y1 <= co2.y2 and co1.y1 >= co2.y1:
               return True
       return False
```

The difference is that this time, we check to see if the coordinates have crossed over horizontally, using the within_x function at ❶. Next, at ❷, we see if the topmost position of the first coordinate (co1.y1) has crossed over the y2 position of the second coordinate, but not its y1 position. If so, we return True (meaning that yes, the top of the first coordinate has hit the second coordinate).

THE COLLIDED_BOTTOM FUNCTION

Of course, you knew that one of these four functions had to be just a bit different, and it is. Here's the collided_bottom function:

```
def collided_bottom(y, co1, co2):
❶    if within_x(co1, co2):
❷        y_calc = co1.y2 + y
❸        if y_calc >= co2.y1 and y_calc <= co2.y2:
❹            return True
❺    return False
```

This function takes an additional parameter, y, a value that we add to the y position of the first coordinate. At ❶, we see if the coordinates have crossed over horizontally (as we did with collided_top). Next, we add the value of the y parameter to the first coordinate's y2 position, and store the result in the variable y_calc at ❷. If at ❸ the newly calculated value is between the y1 and y2 values of the second coordinate, we return True at ❹ because the bottom of coordinate co1 has hit the top of coordinate co2. However, if none of the if statements are true, we return False at ❺.

We need the additional y parameter because Mr. Stick Man could fall off a platform. Unlike with the other collided functions, we need to be able to test to see if he *would* collide at the bottom, rather than whether he already has. If he walks off a platform and keeps floating in midair, our game won't be very realistic; so as he walks, we check to see if he has collided with something on the left or right. However, when we check below him, we see if he would collide with the platform; if not, he needs to go crashing down!

CREATING THE SPRITE CLASS

We'll call the parent class for our game items Sprite. This class will provide two functions: move to move the sprite and coords to return the sprite's current position on the screen. Here's the code for the Sprite class.

```
class Sprite:
❶    def __init__(self, game):
❷        self.game = game
❸        self.endgame = False
❹        self.coordinates = None
```

```
❺      def move(self):
❻          pass
❼      def coords(self):
❽          return self.coordinates
```

The Sprite class's __init__ function defined at ❶ takes a single parameter: game. This parameter will be the game object. We need it so that any sprite we create will be able to access the list of other sprites in the game. We store the game parameter as an object variable at ❷.

At ❸, we store the object variable endgame, which we'll use to indicate the end of the game. (At the moment, it's set to False.) The final object variable, coordinates at ❹, is set to nothing (None).

The move function defined at ❺ does nothing in this parent class, so we use the pass keyword in the body of this function at ❻. The coords function at ❼ simply returns the object variable coordinates at ❽.

So our Sprite class has a move function that does nothing and a coords function that returns no coordinates. It doesn't sound very useful, does it? However, we know that any classes that have Sprite as their parent will always have move and coords functions. So, in the main loop of the game, when we loop through a list of sprites, we can call the function move, and it won't cause any errors. Why not? Because each sprite has that function.

NOTE   *Classes with functions that don't do very much are actually quite common in programming. In a way, they're a kind of agreement or contract that makes sure all the children of a class provide the same sort of functionality, even if in some cases the functions in the child classes do nothing.*

ADDING THE PLATFORMS

Now we'll add the platforms. We'll call our class for platform objects PlatformSprite, and it will be a child class of Sprite. The __init__ function for this class will take a game parameter (as the Sprite parent class does), as well as an image, x and y positions, and the image width and height. Here's the code for the `PlatformSprite` class:

```
❶ class PlatformSprite(Sprite):
❷    def __init__(self, game, photo_image, x, y, width, height):
❸        Sprite.__init__(self, game)
❹        self.photo_image = photo_image
❺        self.image = game.canvas.create_image(x, y, \
                  image=self.photo_image, anchor='nw')
❻        self.coordinates = Coords(x, y, x + width, y + height)
```

When we define the `PlatformSprite` class at ❶, we give it a single parameter: the name of the parent class (`Sprite`). The `__init__` function, at ❷, has seven parameters: `self`, `game`, `photo_image`, `x`, `y`, `width`, and `height`.

At ❸, we call the `__init__` function of the parent class, `Sprite`, using `self` and `game` as the parameter values, because other than the `self` keyword, the `Sprite` class's `__init__` function takes only one parameter: `game`.

At this point, if we were to create a `PlatformSprite` object, it would have all the object variables from its parent class (`game`, `endgame`, and `coordinates`), simply because we've called the `__init__` function in `Sprite`.

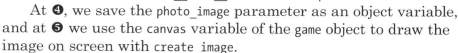

At ❹, we save the `photo_image` parameter as an object variable, and at ❺ we use the `canvas` variable of the game object to draw the image on screen with `create_image`.

Finally, we create a `Coords` object with the x and y parameters as the first two arguments. We then add the `width` and `height` parameters to these parameters for the second two arguments at ❻.

Even though the `coordinates` variable is set to `None` in the `Sprite` parent class, we have changed it in our `PlatformSprite` child class to a real `Coords` object, containing the real location of the platform image on the screen.

ADDING A PLATFORM OBJECT

Let's add a platform to the game to see how it looks. Change the last two lines of the game file (*stickmangame.py*) as follows:

```
❶ g = Game()
❷ platform1 = PlatformSprite(g, PhotoImage(file="platform1.gif"), \
     0, 480, 100, 10)
❸ g.sprites.append(platform1)
❹ g.mainloop()
```

As you can see, lines ❶ and ❹ have not changed, but at ❷, we create an object of the PlatformSprite class, passing it the variable for our game (g), along with a PhotoImage object (which uses the first of our platform images, *platform1.gif*). We also pass it the position where we want to draw the platform (0 pixels across and 480 pixels down, near the bottom of the canvas), along with the height and width of our image (100 pixels across and 10 pixels high). We add this sprite to the list of sprites in our game object at ❸.

If you run the game now, you should see a platform drawn at the bottom-left side of the screen, like this:

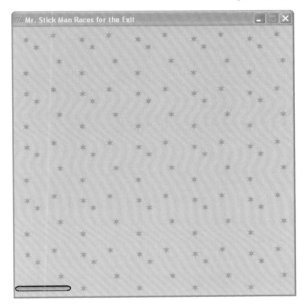

ADDING A BUNCH OF PLATFORMS

Let's add a whole bunch of platforms. Each platform will have different x and y positions, so that they will be drawn scattered around the screen. Here's the code to use:

```
g = Game()
platform1 = PlatformSprite(g, PhotoImage(file="platform1.gif"), \
    0, 480, 100, 10)
platform2 = PlatformSprite(g, PhotoImage(file="platform1.gif"), \
    150, 440, 100, 10)
platform3 = PlatformSprite(g, PhotoImage(file="platform1.gif"), \
    300, 400, 100, 10)
platform4 = PlatformSprite(g, PhotoImage(file="platform1.gif"), \
    300, 160, 100, 10)
```

```
platform5 = PlatformSprite(g, PhotoImage(file="platform2.gif"), \
    175, 350, 66, 10)
platform6 = PlatformSprite(g, PhotoImage(file="platform2.gif"), \
    50, 300, 66, 10)
platform7 = PlatformSprite(g, PhotoImage(file="platform2.gif"), \
    170, 120, 66, 10)
platform8 = PlatformSprite(g, PhotoImage(file="platform2.gif"), \
    45, 60, 66, 10)
platform9 = PlatformSprite(g, PhotoImage(file="platform3.gif"), \
    170, 250, 32, 10)
platform10 = PlatformSprite(g, PhotoImage(file="platform3.gif"), \
    230, 200, 32, 10)
g.sprites.append(platform1)
g.sprites.append(platform2)
g.sprites.append(platform3)
g.sprites.append(platform4)
g.sprites.append(platform5)
g.sprites.append(platform6)
g.sprites.append(platform7)
g.sprites.append(platform8)
g.sprites.append(platform9)
g.sprites.append(platform10)
g.mainloop()
```

We create a lot of PlatformSprite objects, saving them as variables platform1, platform2, platform3, and so on, up to platform10. We then add each platform to the variable sprites, which we created in our Game class. If you run the game now, it should look like this:

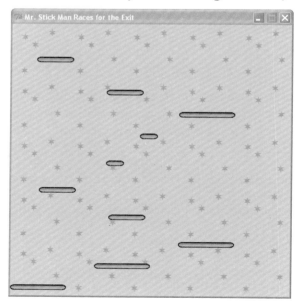

We've created the basics of our game! Now we're ready to add our main character, Mr. Stick Man.

WHAT YOU LEARNED

In this chapter, you created the Game class and drew the background image onto the screen like a kind of wallpaper. You learned how to determine whether a horizontal or vertical position is within the bounds of two other horizontal or vertical positions by creating the functions within_x and within_y. You then used these functions to create new functions to determine whether one coordinate object had collided with another. We'll use these functions in the next chapters when we animate Mr. Stick Man and need to detect whether he has collided with a platform as he moves around the canvas.

We also created a parent class Sprite and its first child class, PlatformSprite, which we used to draw the platforms onto the canvas.

PROGRAMMING PUZZLES

The following coding puzzles are some ways that you can experiment with the game's background image. Check your answers at *http://python-for-kids.com/*.

#1: CHECKERBOARD

Try changing the Game class so that the background image is drawn like a checkerboard:

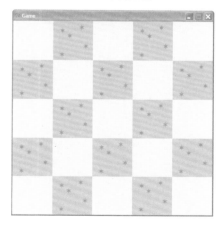

#2: TWO-IMAGE CHECKERBOARD

Once you've figured out how to create a checkerboard effect, try using two alternating images. Come up with another wallpaper image (using your graphics program), and then change the Game class so it displays a checkerboard with two alternating images instead of one image and the blank background.

#3: BOOKSHELF AND LAMP

You can create different wallpaper images to make the background of the game look more interesting. Create a copy of the background image, and then draw a simple bookshelf on it. Or you could draw a table with a lamp or a window. Then dot these images around the screen by changing the Game class so that it loads (and displays) three or four different wallpaper images.

17
CREATING MR. STICK MAN

In this chapter, we'll create the main character of our Mr. Stick Man Races for the Exit game. This will require the most complicated coding we've done so far, because Mr. Stick Man needs to run left and right, jump, stop when he runs into a platform, and fall when he runs off the edge of a platform. We'll use event bindings for the left and right arrow keys to make the stick figure run left and right, and we'll have him jump when the player presses the spacebar.

INITIALIZING THE STICK FIGURE

The __init__ function for our new stick figure class will look a lot like it does in the other classes in our game so far. We start by giving our new class a name: StickFigureSprite. As with previous classes, this class has a parent class: Sprite.

```
class StickFigureSprite(Sprite):
    def __init__(self, game):
        Sprite.__init__(self, game)
```

This code looks like what we wrote for the PlatformSprite class in Chapter 16, except that we're not using any additional parameters (other than self and game). The reason is that, unlike with the PlatformSprite class, there will be only one StickFigureSprite object used in the game.

LOADING THE STICK FIGURE IMAGES

Because we have a lot of platform objects on the screen, which each can use a different-sized image, we pass the platform image as a parameter of the PlatformSprite's __init__ function (kind of like saying, "Here, Platform Sprite, use this image when you draw yourself on the screen."). But since there's only one stick figure on the screen, it doesn't make sense to load the image outside the sprite and then pass it in as a parameter. The StickFigureSprite class will know how to load its own images.

The next few lines of the __init__ function do this very job: They load each of the three left images (which we'll use to animate the stick figure running left) and the three right images (used to animate the stick figure running right). We need to load these images now, because we don't want to have to load them every time we display the stick figure on the screen (doing so would take too long and make our game run slowly).

```
class StickFigureSprite(Sprite):
    def __init__(self, game):
        Sprite.__init__(self, game)
❶      self.images_left = [
            PhotoImage(file="figure-L1.gif"),
            PhotoImage(file="figure-L2.gif"),
            PhotoImage(file="figure-L3.gif")
        ]
❷      self.images_right = [
            PhotoImage(file="figure-R1.gif"),
            PhotoImage(file="figure-R2.gif"),
            PhotoImage(file="figure-R3.gif")
        ]
❸      self.image = game.canvas.create_image(200, 470, \
                image=self.images_left[0], anchor='nw')
```

This code loads each of the three left images, which we'll
use to animate the stick figure running left, and the three right
images, which we'll use to animate the stick figure running right.

At ❶ and ❷, we create the object variables images_left and
images_right. Each contains a list of PhotoImage objects that we created in Chapter 15, showing the stick figure facing left and right.

We draw the first image at ❸ with images_left[0] using the
canvas's create_image function at position (200, 470), which puts the
stick figure in the middle of the game screen, at the bottom of the
canvas. The create_image function returns a number that identifies
the image on the canvas. We store this identifier in the object variable image for later use.

SETTING UP VARIABLES

The next part of the __init__ function sets up some more variables
that we'll be using later in this code.

```
        self.images_right = [
            PhotoImage(file="figure-R1.gif"),
            PhotoImage(file="figure-R2.gif"),
            PhotoImage(file="figure-R3.gif")
        ]
        self.image = game.canvas.create_image(200, 470, \
            image=self.images_left[0], anchor='nw')
❶      self.x = -2
❷      self.y = 0
❸      self.current_image = 0
```

```
❹          self.current_image_add = 1
❺          self.jump_count = 0
❻          self.last_time = time.time()
❼          self.coordinates = Coords()
```

At ❶ and ❷, the object variables x and y will store the amount we'll be adding to the stick figure's horizontal (x1 and x2) or vertical (y1 and y2) coordinates when he is moving around the screen.

As you learned in Chapter 13, in order to animate something with the tkinter module, we add values to the object's x or y position to move it around the canvas. By setting x to −2, and y to 0, we subtract 2 from the x position later in the code and add nothing to the vertical position, to make the stick figure run to the left.

NOTE   *Remember that a negative x number means move left on the canvas, and a positive x number means move right. A negative y number means move up, and a positive y number means move down.*

At ❸, we create the object variable current_image to store the image's index position as currently displayed on the screen. Our list of left-facing images, images_left, contains *figure-L1.gif*, *figure-L2.gif*, and *figure-L3.gif*. Those are index positions 0, 1, and 2.

At ❹, the variable current_image_add will contain the number we'll add to that index position stored in current_image to get the next index position. For example, if the image at index position 0 is displayed, we add 1 to get the next image at index position 1, and then add 1 again to get the final image in the list at index position 2. (You'll see how we use this variable for animation in the next chapter.)

The variable jump_count at ❺ is a counter we'll use while the stick figure is jumping. The variable last_time will record the last time we changed the image when animating our stick figure. We store the current time using the time function of the time module at ❻.

At ❼, we set the coordinates object variable to an object of the Coords class, with no initialization parameters set (x1, y1, x2, and y2 are all 0). Unlike with the platforms, the stick figure's coordinates will change, so we'll set these values later.

BINDING TO KEYS

In the final part of the __init__ function, the bind functions bind a key to something in our code that needs to be run when the key is pressed.

```
self.jump_count = 0
self.last_time = time.time()
self.coordinates = Coords()
game.canvas.bind_all('<KeyPress-Left>', self.turn_left)
game.canvas.bind_all('<KeyPress-Right>', self.turn_right)
game.canvas.bind_all('<space>', self.jump)
```

We bind <KeyPress-Left> to the function turn_left, <KeyPress-Right> to the function turn_right, and <space> to the function jump. Now we need to create those functions to make the stick figure move.

TURNING THE STICK FIGURE LEFT AND RIGHT

The turn_left and turn_right functions make sure that the stick figure is not jumping, and then set the value of the object variable x to move him left and right. (If our character is jumping, our game doesn't allow us to change his direction in midair.)

```
game.canvas.bind_all('<KeyPress-Left>', self.turn_left)
game.canvas.bind_all('<KeyPress-Right>', self.turn_right)
game.canvas.bind_all('<space>', self.jump)
```

```
❶    def turn_left(self, evt):
❷        if self.y == 0:
❸            self.x = -2

❹    def turn_right(self, evt):
❺        if self.y == 0:
❻            self.x = 2
```

Python calls the turn_left function when the player presses the left arrow key, and it passes an object with information about what the player did as a parameter. This object is called an *event object*, and we give it the parameter name evt.

The event object isn't important for our purposes, but we need to include it as a parameter of our functions (at ❶ and ❹) or we'll get an error because Python is expecting it to be there. The event object contains things like the x and y positions of the mouse (mouse event), a code identifying a particular key (keyboard event), and other information. For this game, none of that information is useful, so we can safely ignore it.

To see if the stick figure is jumping, we check the value of the y object variable at ❷ and ❺. If the value is not 0, the stick figure is jumping. In this example, if the value of y is 0, we set x to −2 to run left (❸) or we set it to 2 to run right (❻), because setting the value to −1 or 1 wouldn't make the stick figure move across the screen fast enough. (Once you have the animation working for your stick figure, try changing this value to see what difference it makes.)

MAKING THE STICK FIGURE JUMP

The jump function is very similar to the turn_left and turn_right functions.

```
def turn_right(self, evt):
    if self.y == 0:
        self.x = 2

def jump(self, evt):
    if self.y == 0:
        self.y = -4
        self.jump_count = 0
```

This function takes a parameter evt (the event object), which we can ignore because we don't need any more information about the event. If this function is called, we know it's because the spacebar was pressed.

Because we want our stick figure to jump only if he is not already jumping, at ❶ we check to see if y is equal to 0. If the stick figure is not jumping, at ❷ we set y to −4 (to move him

vertically up the screen), and we set jump_count to 0 at ❸. We'll use jump_count to make sure the stick figure doesn't just keep jumping forever. Instead, we'll let him jump for a specific count and then have him come down again, as if gravity were pulling him. We'll add this code in the next chapter.

WHAT WE HAVE SO FAR

Let's review the definitions of the classes and functions we now have in our game, and where they should be in your file.

At the top of your program, you should have your import statements, followed by the Game and Coords classes. The Game class will be used to create an object which will be the main controller for our game, and objects of the Coords class are used to hold the positions of things in our game (like the platforms and Mr. Stick Man):

```
from tkinter import *
import random
import time

class Game:
    ...
class Coords:
    ...
```

Next, you should have the within functions (which tell whether the coordinates of one sprite are "within" the same area of another sprite), the Sprite parent class (which is the parent class of all the sprites in our game), the PlatformSprite class, and the beginning of the StickFigureSprite class. PlatformSprite was used to create platform objects, which our stick figure will jump across, and we created one object of the StickFigureSprite class, to represent the main character in our game:

```
def within_x(co1, co2):
    ...
def within_y(co1, co2):
    ...
def collided_left(co1, co2):
    ...
def collided_right(co1, co2):
    ...
def collided_top(co1, co2):
    ...
```

```
def collided_bottom(y, co1, co2):
    ...
class Sprite:
    ...
class PlatformSprite(Sprite):
    ...
class StickFigureSprite(Sprite):
    ...
```

Finally, at the end of your program, you should have code that creates all the objects in our game so far: the game object itself and the platforms. The final line is where we call the mainloop function.

```
g = Game()
platform1 = PlatformSprite(g, PhotoImage(file="platform1.gif"), \
    0, 480, 100, 10)
...
g.sprites.append(platform1)
...
g.mainloop()
```

If your code looks a bit different, or you're having trouble getting it working, you can always skip ahead to the end of Chapter 18, where you'll find the full listing for the entire game.

WHAT YOU LEARNED

In this chapter, we began working on the class for our stick figure. At the moment, if we created an object of this class, it wouldn't really do much besides loading the images it needs for animating the stick figure, and setting up a few object variables to be used later in the code. This class contains a couple of functions for changing the values in those object variables based on keyboard events (when the player presses the left or right arrow, or the spacebar).

In the next chapter, we'll finish our game. We'll write the functions for the StickFigureSprite class to display and animate the stick figure, and move him around the screen. We'll also add the exit (the door) that Mr. Stick Man is trying to reach.

18

COMPLETING THE
MR. STICK MAN GAME

In the previous three chapters, we've been developing our game: Mr. Stick Man Races for the Exit. We created the graphics, and then wrote code to add the background image, platforms, and stick figure. In this chapter, we'll fill in the missing pieces to animate the stick figure and add the door.

You'll find the full listing for the complete game at the end of this chapter. If you get lost or become confused when writing some of this code, compare your code with that listing to see where you might have gone wrong.

ANIMATING THE STICK FIGURE

So far, we've created a basic class for our stick figure, loading the images we'll be using and binding keys to some functions. But none of our coding will do anything particularly interesting if you run our game at this point.

Now we'll add the remaining functions to the StickFigureSprite class we created in Chapter 17: animate, move, and coords. The animate function will draw the different stick figure images, move will determine where the character needs to move to, and coords will return the stick figure's current position. (Unlike with the platform sprites, we need to recalculate the position of the stick figure as he moves around the screen.)

CREATING THE ANIMATE FUNCTION

First, we'll add the animate function, which will need to check for movement and change the image accordingly.

CHECKING FOR MOVEMENT

We don't want to change the stick figure image too quickly in our animation or its movement won't look realistic. Think about a flip animation, drawn in the corner of a notepad—if you flip the pages too quickly, you may not get the full effect of what you've drawn.

The first half of the animate function checks to see if the stick figure is running left or right, and then uses the last_time variable to decide whether to change the current image. This variable will help us control the speed of our animation. The function will go after the jump function, which we added to our StickFigureSprite class in Chapter 17.

```
    def jump(self, evt):
        if self.y == 0:
            self.y = -4
            self.jump_count = 0

    def animate(self):
❶       if self.x != 0 and self.y == 0:
❷           if time.time() - self.last_time > 0.1:
```

```
❸        self.last_time = time.time()
❹        self.current_image += self.current_image_add
❺        if self.current_image >= 2:
❻            self.current_image_add = -1
❼        if self.current_image <= 0:
❽            self.current_image_add = 1
```

In the if statement at ❶, we check to see if x is not 0 in order
to determine whether the stick figure is moving (either left or right),
and we check to see if y is 0 in order to determine that the stick
figure is not jumping. If this if statement is true, we need to animate our stick figure; if not, he's standing still, so there's no need
to keep drawing. If the stick figure isn't moving, we drop out of the
function, and the rest of the code in this listing is ignored.

At ❷, we calculate the amount of time since the animate
function was last called, by subtracting the value of the last_time
variable from the current time, using time.time(). This calculation
is used to decide whether to draw the next image in the sequence,
and if the result is greater than a tenth of a second (0.1), we continue with the block of code at ❸. We set the last_time variable to
the current time, basically resetting the stopwatch to start timing
again for the next change of image.

At ❹, we add the value of the object variable current_image_add
to the variable current_image, which stores the index position of
the currently displayed image. Remember that we created the
current_image_add variable in the stick figure's __init__ function in
Chapter 17, so when the animate function is first called, the value
of the variable has already been set to 1.

At ❺, we check to see if the value of the index position in
current_image is greater than or equal to 2, and if so, we change the
value of current_image_add to −1 at ❻. The process is similar at ❼—
once we reach 0, we need to start counting up again, which we do
at ❽.

NOTE   *If you're having trouble figuring out how to indent this code, here's
a hint: There are 8 spaces at the beginning of ❶ and 20 spaces at
the beginning of ❽.*

To help you understand what's going on in the function so far,
imagine that you have a sequence of colored blocks in a line on the
floor. You move your finger from one block to the next, and each
block that your finger points to (1, 2, 3, 4, and so on) has a number

(the current_image variable). The number of the block your finger moves to (it points at one block at a time) is the number stored in the variable current_image_add. When your finger moves one way up the line of blocks, you're adding 1 each time, and when it hits the end of the line and moves back down, you're subtracting 1 (that is, adding −1).

The code we've added to our animate function performs this process, but instead of colored blocks, we have the three stick figure images for each direction stored in a list. The index positions of these images are 0, 1, and 2. As we animate the stick figure, once we reach the last image, we start counting down, and once we reach the first image, we need to start counting up again. As a result, we create the effect of a running figure.

The following shows how we move through the list of images, using the index positions we calculate in the animate function.

Position 0	Position 1	Position 2	Position 1	Position 0	Position 1
Counting up	Counting up	Counting up	Counting down	Counting down	Counting up

CHANGING THE IMAGE

In the next half of the animate function, we change the currently displayed image, using the calculated index position.

```
    def animate(self):
        if self.x != 0 and self.y == 0:
            if time.time() - self.last_time > 0.1:
                self.last_time= time.time()
                self.current_image += self.current_image_add
                if self.current_image >= 2:
                    self.current_image_add = -1
                if self.current_image <= 0:
                    self.current_image_add = 1
❶        if self.x < 0:
❷            if self.y != 0:
❸                self.game.canvas.itemconfig(self.image, \
                        image=self.images_left[2])
❹            else:
❺                self.game.canvas.itemconfig(self.image, \
                        image=self.images_left[self.current_image])
```

```
❻          elif self.x > 0:
❼              if self.y != 0:
❽                  self.game.canvas.itemconfig(self.image, \
                        image=self.images_right[2])
❾              else:
❿                  self.game.canvas.itemconfig(self.image, \
                        image=self.images_right[self.current_image])
```

At ❶, if x is less than 0, the stick figure is moving left, so Python moves into the block of code shown at ❷ through ❺, which checks whether y is not equal to 0 (meaning the stick figure is jumping). If y is not equal to 0 (the stick figure is moving up or down—in other words, jumping), we use the canvas's `itemconfig` function to change the displayed image to the last image in our list of left-facing images at ❸ (`images_left[2]`). Because the stick figure is jumping, we'll use the image showing him in full stride to make the animation look a bit more realistic:

If the stick figure is not jumping (that is, y is equal to 0), the `else` statement starting at ❹ uses `itemconfig` to change the displayed image to whatever index position is in the variable `current_image`, as shown in the code at ❺.

At ❻, we see if the stick figure is running right (x is greater than 0), and Python moves into the block shown at ❼ through ❿. This code is very similar to the first block, again checking whether the stick figure is jumping, and drawing the correct image if so, except that it uses the `images_right` list.

GETTING THE STICK FIGURE'S POSITION

Because we'll need to determine where the stick figure is on the screen (since he is moving around), the `coords` function will differ from the other `Sprite` class functions. We'll use the `coords` function of the canvas to determine where the stick figure is, and then use those values to set the x1, y1 and x2, y2 values of the coordinates variable we created in the __init__ function at the beginning of Chapter 17. Here's the code, which can be added after the animate function:

```
        if self.x < 0:
            if self.y != 0:
                self.game.canvas.itemconfig(self.image, \
                        image=self.images_left[2])
            else:
                self.game.canvas.itemconfig(self.image, \
                        image=self.images_left[self.current_image])
        elif self.x > 0:
            if self.y != 0:
                self.game.canvas.itemconfig(self.image, \
                        image=self.images_right[2])
            else:
                self.game.canvas.itemconfig(self.image, \
                        image=self.images_right[self.current_image])

    def coords(self):
❶      xy = self.game.canvas.coords(self.image)
❷      self.coordinates.x1 = xy[0]
❸      self.coordinates.y1 = xy[1]
❹      self.coordinates.x2 = xy[0] + 27
❺      self.coordinates.y2 = xy[1] + 30
        return self.coordinates
```

When we created the Game class in Chapter 16, one of the object variables was the canvas. At ❶, we use the coords function of this canvas variable, with self.game.canvas.coords, to return the x and y positions of the current image. This function uses the number stored in the object variable image, the identifier for the image drawn on the canvas.

We store the resulting list in the variable xy, which now contains two values: the top-left x position stored as the x1 variable of coordinates at ❷, and the top-left y position stored as the y1 variable of coordinates at ❸.

Because all of the stick figure images we created are 27 pixels wide by 30 pixels high, we can determine what the x2 and y2 variables should be by adding the width at ❹ and the height at ❺ to the x and y numbers, respectively.

Finally, on the last line of the function, we return the object variable coordinates.

MAKING THE STICK FIGURE MOVE

The final function of the StickFigureSprite class, move, is in charge of actually moving our game character around the screen. It also needs to be able to tell us when the character has bumped into something.

STARTING THE MOVE FUNCTION

Here's the code for the first part of the move function—this will go after coords:

```
def coords(self):
    xy = self.game.canvas.coords(self.image)
    self.coordinates.x1 = xy[0]
    self.coordinates.y1 = xy[1]
    self.coordinates.x2 = xy[0] + 27
    self.coordinates.y2 = xy[1] + 30
    return self.coordinates

def move(self):
❶    self.animate()
❷    if self.y < 0:
❸        self.jump_count += 1
❹        if self.jump_count > 20:
❺            self.y = 4
❻    if self.y > 0:
❼        self.jump_count -= 1
```

At ❶, this part of the function calls the animate function we created earlier in this chapter, which changes the currently displayed image if necessary. At ❷, we see whether the value of y is less than 0. If it is, we know that the stick figure is jumping because a negative value will move him up the screen. (Remember that 0 is at the top of the canvas, and the bottom of the canvas is pixel position 500.)

At ❸, we add 1 to jump_count, and at ❹, we say that if the value of jump_count reaches 20, we should change y to 4 to start the stick figure falling again (❺).

At ❻, we see if the value of y is greater than 0 (meaning the character must be falling), and if it is, we subtract 1 from jump_count because once we've counted up to 20, we need to count back down again. (Move your hand slowly up in the air while counting to 20,

then move it back down again while counting down from 20, and you'll get a sense of how calculating the stick figure jumping up and down is supposed to work.)

In the next few lines of the move function, we call the coords function, which tells us where our character is on the screen and stores its result in the variable co. We then create the variables left, right, top, bottom, and falling. We'll use each in the remainder of this function.

```
if self.y > 0:
    self.jump_count -= 1
co = self.coords()
left = True
right = True
top = True
bottom = True
falling = True
```

Notice that each variable has been set to the Boolean value True. We'll use these as indicators to check whether the character has hit something on the screen or is falling.

HAS THE STICK FIGURE HIT THE BOTTOM OR TOP OF THE CANVAS?

The next section of the move function checks whether our character has hit the bottom or top of the canvas. Here's the code:

```
  bottom = True
  falling = True
❶ if self.y > 0 and co.y2 >= self.game.canvas_height:
❷     self.y = 0
❸     bottom = False
```

```
❹    elif self.y < 0 and co.y1 <= 0:
❺        self.y = 0
❻        top = False
```

If the character is falling down the screen, y will be greater than 0, so we need to make sure it hasn't yet hit the bottom of the canvas (or it will vanish off the bottom of the screen). To do so, at ❶, we see if its y2 position (the bottom of the stick figure) is greater than or equal to the canvas_height variable of the game object. If it is, we set the value of y to 0 at ❷ to stop the stick figure from falling, and then set the bottom variable to False at ❸, which tells the remaining code that we no longer need to see if the stick figure has hit the bottom.

The process of determining whether the stick figure has hit the top of the screen is very similar to the way we determine whether he has hit the bottom. To do so, at ❹, we first see if the stick figure is jumping (y is less than 0), then we see if his y1 position is less than or equal to 0, meaning he has hit the top of the canvas. If both conditions are true, we set y equal to 0 at ❺ to stop the movement. We also set the top variable to False at ❻ to tell the remaining code that we no longer need to see if the stick figure has hit the top.

HAS THE STICK FIGURE HIT THE SIDE OF THE CANVAS?

We follow almost exactly the same process as in the preceding code to determine whether the stick figure has hit the left and right sides of the canvas, as follows:

```
      elif self.y < 0 and co.y1 <= 0:
          self.y = 0
          top = False
❶     if self.x > 0 and co.x2 >= self.game.canvas_width:
❷         self.x = 0
❸         right = False
❹     elif self.x < 0 and co.x1 <= 0:
❺         self.x = 0
❻         left = False
```

The code at ❶ is based on the fact that we know the stick figure is running to the right if x is greater than 0. We also know whether he has hit the right-hand side of the screen by seeing if the x2 position (co.x2) is greater than or equal to the width of the canvas stored in game_width. If both statements are true, we set x equal to 0 (to stop the stick figure from running), and we set the right variable to False at ❸.

COLLIDING WITH OTHER SPRITES

Once we've determined whether the figure has hit the sides of the screen, we need to see if he has hit anything else on the screen. We use the following code to loop through the list of sprite objects stored in the game object to see if the stick figure has hit any of them.

```
        elif self.x < 0 and co.x1 <= 0:
            self.x = 0
            left = False
❶       for sprite in self.game.sprites:
❷           if sprite == self:
❸               continue
❹           sprite_co = sprite.coords()
❺           if top and self.y < 0 and collided_top(co, sprite_co):
❻               self.y = -self.y
❼               top = False
```

At ❶, we loop through the list of sprites, assigning each one in turn to the variable sprite. At ❷, we say that if the sprite is equal to self (that's another way of saying, "if this sprite is the same as me"), we don't need to determine whether the stick figure has collided because he would have only hit himself. If the sprite variable is equal to self, we use continue to jump to the next sprite in the list.

Next, we get the coordinates of the new sprite by calling its coords function at ❹ and storing the results in the variable sprite_co. Then the code at ❺ checks for the following:

- The stick figure has not hit the top of the canvas (the top variable is still true).
- The stick figure is jumping (the value of y is less than 0).
- The top of the stick figure has collided with the sprite from the list (using the collided_top function we created in Chapter 16).

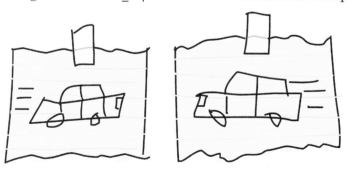

If all of these conditions are true, we want the sprite to start falling back down again, so at ❻, we reverse the value of the y using minus (-). The top variable is set to False at ❼, because once the stick figure has hit the top, we don't need to keep checking for a collision.

COLLIDING AT THE BOTTOM

The next part of the loop checks to see if the bottom of our character has hit something:

```
        if top and self.y < 0 and collided_top(co, sprite_co):
            self.y = -self.y
            top = False
❶      if bottom and self.y > 0 and collided_bottom(self.y, \
            co, sprite_co):
❷          self.y = sprite_co.y1 - co.y2
❸          if self.y < 0:
❹              self.y = 0
❺          bottom = False
❻          top = False
```

There are three similar checks at ❶: whether the bottom variable is still set, whether the character is falling (y is greater than 0), and whether the bottom of our character has hit the sprite. If all three checks are true, we subtract the bottom y value (y2) of the stick figure from the top y value of the sprite (y1) at ❷. This might seem strange, so let's see why we do this.

Imagine that our game character has fallen off a platform. He moves down the screen 4 pixels each time the mainloop function runs, and the foot of the stick figure is 3 pixels above another platform. Let's say the stick figure's bottom (y2) is at position 57 and the top of the platform (y1) is at position 60. In this case, the collided_bottom function would return true, because its code will add the value of y (which is 4) to the stick figure's y2 variable, resulting in 61.

However, we don't want Mr. Stick Man to stop falling as soon as it looks like he will hit a platform or the bottom of the screen, because that would be like taking a huge jump off a step and stopping in midair, an inch above the ground. That may be a neat trick, but it won't look right in our game. Instead, if we subtract the character's y2 value (of 57) from the platform's y1 value (of 60) we get 3, the amount the stick figure should drop in order to land properly on the top of the platform.

At ❸, we make sure that the calculation doesn't result in a negative number; if it does, we set y equal to 0 at ❹. (If we let the number be negative, the stick figure would fly back up again, and we don't want that to happen in this game.)

Finally, we set the top ❻ and bottom ❺ flags to False, so we no longer need to check whether the stick figure has collided at the top or bottom with another sprite.

We'll do one more bottom check to see whether the stick figure has run off the edge of a platform. Here's the code for this if statement:

```
if self.y < 0:
    self.y = 0
bottom = False
top = False
if bottom and falling and self.y == 0 \
        and co.y2 < self.game.canvas_height \
        and collided_bottom(1, co, sprite_co):
    falling = False
```

Five checks here must all be true in order for the falling variable to be set to False:

- We still need to check that the bottom flag is set to True.
- We need to check whether the stick figure should be falling (the falling flag is still set to True).
- The stick figure isn't already falling (y is 0).
- The bottom of the sprite hasn't hit the bottom of the screen (it's less than the canvas height).
- The stick figure has hit the top of a platform (collided_bottom returns True).

Then we set the falling variable to False.

CHECKING LEFT AND RIGHT

We've checked whether the stick figure has hit a sprite at the bottom or the top. Now we need to check whether he has hit the left or right side, with this code:

```
if bottom and falling and self.y == 0 \
        and co.y2 < self.game.canvas_height \
        and collided_bottom(1, co, sprite_co):
    falling = False
```

```
❶            if left and self.x < 0 and collided_left(co, sprite_co):
❷                self.x = 0
❸                left = False
❹            if right and self.x > 0 and collided_right(co, sprite_co):
❺                self.x = 0
❻                right = False
```

At ❶, we see if we should
still be looking for collisions to
the left (left is still set to True)
and whether the stick figure
is moving to the left (x is less
than 0). We also check to see
if the stick figure has collided with a sprite using the

collided_left function. If these three conditions are true, we set x
equal to 0 at ❷ (to make the stick figure stop running), and set left
to False at ❸, so that we no longer check for collisions on the left.

The code is similar for collisions to the right, as shown at ❹.
We set x equal to 0 again at ❺, and right to False at ❻, to stop
checking for right-hand collisions.

Now, with checks for collisions in all four directions, our for
loop should look like this:

```
        elif self.x < 0 and co.x1 <= 0:
            self.x = 0
            left = False
    for sprite in self.game.sprites:
        if sprite == self:
            continue
        sprite_co = sprite.coords()
        if top and self.y < 0 and collided_top(co, sprite_co):
            self.y = -self.y
            top = False
        if bottom and self.y > 0 and collided_bottom(self.y, \
                co, sprite_co):
            self.y = sprite_co.y1 - co.y2
            if self.y < 0:
                self.y = 0
            bottom = False
            top = False
        if bottom and falling and self.y == 0 \
                and co.y2 < self.game.canvas_height \
                and collided_bottom(1, co, sprite_co):
            falling = False
```

```
        if left and self.x < 0 and collided_left(co, sprite_co):
            self.x = 0
            left = False
        if right and self.x > 0 and collided_right(co, sprite_co):
            self.x = 0
            right = False
```

We need to add only a few more lines to the move function, as follows:

```
        if right and self.x > 0 and collided_right(co, sprite_co):
            self.x = 0
            right = False
❶      if falling and bottom and self.y == 0 \
            and co.y2 < self.game.canvas_height:
❷          self.y = 4
❸      self.game.canvas.move(self.image, self.x, self.y)
```

At ❶, we check whether both the falling and bottom variables are set to True. If so, we've looped through every platform sprite in the list without colliding at the bottom.

The final check in this line determines whether the bottom of our character is less than the canvas height—that is, above the ground (the bottom of the canvas). If the stick figure hasn't collided with anything and he is above the ground, he is standing in mid-air, so he should start falling (in other words, he has run off the end of a platform). To make him run off the end of any platform, we set y equal to 4 at ❷.

At ❸, we move the image across the screen, according to the values we set in the variables x and y. The fact that we've looped through the sprites checking for collisions may mean that we've set both variables to 0, because the stick figure has collided on the left and with the bottom. In that case, the call to the move function of the canvas will do nothing.

It may also be the case that Mr. Stick Man has walked off the edge of a platform. If that happens, y will be set to 4, and Mr. Stick Man will fall downward.

Phew, that was a long function!

TESTING OUR STICK FIGURE SPRITE

Having created the StickFigureSprite class, let's try it out by adding the following two lines just before the call to the mainloop function.

```
❶ sf = StickFigureSprite(g)
❷ g.sprites.append(sf)
  g.mainloop()
```

At ❶, we create a StickFigureSprite object and set it equal to the variable sf. As we did with the platforms, we add this new variable to the list of sprites stored in the game object at ❷.

Now run the program. You will find that Mr. Stick Man can run, jump from platform to platform, and fall!

THE DOOR!

The only thing missing from our game is the door to the exit. We'll finish up by creating a sprite for the door, adding code to detect the door, and giving our program a door object.

CREATING THE DOORSPRITE CLASS

You guessed it—we need to create one more class: DoorSprite. Here's the start of the code:

```
class DoorSprite(Sprite):
❶    def __init__(self, game, photo_image, x, y, width, height):
❷        Sprite.__init__(self, game)
❸        self.photo_image = photo_image
❹        self.image = game.canvas.create_image(x, y, \
                image=self.photo_image, anchor='nw')
❺        self.coordinates = Coords(x, y, x + (width / 2), y + height)
❻        self.endgame = True
```

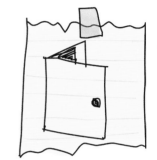

As shown at ❶, the __init__ function of the DoorSprite class has parameters for self, a game object, a photo_image object, the x and y coordinates, and the width and height of the image. At ❷, we call __init__ as with our other sprite classes.

At ❸, we save the parameter photo_image using an object variable with the same name, as we did with PlatformSprite. We create a display image using the canvas create_image function and save the identifying number returned by that function using the object variable image at ❹.

At ❺, we set the coordinates of DoorSprite to the x and y parameters (which become the x1 and y1 positions of the door), and then calculate the x2 and y2 positions. We calculate the x2 position by adding half of the width (the width variable, divided by 2) to the x parameter. For example, if x is 10 (the x1 coordinate is also 10), and the width is 40, the x2 coordinate would be 30 (10 plus half of 40).

Why use this confusing little calculation? Because, unlike with the platforms, where we want Mr. Stick Man to stop running as soon as he collides with the side of the platform, we want him to stop in front of the door. (It won't look good if Mr. Stick Man stops running next to the door!) You'll see this in action when you play the game and make it to the door.

Unlike the x1 position, the y1 position is simple to calculate. We just add the value of the height variable to the y parameter, and that's it.

Finally, at ❻, we set the endgame object variable to True. This says that when the stick figure reaches the door, the game should end.

DETECTING THE DOOR

Now we need to change the code in the StickFigureSprite class of the move function that determines when the stick figure has collided with a sprite on the left or the right. Here's the first change:

```
if left and self.x < 0 and collided_left(co, sprite_co):
    self.x = 0
    left = False
    if sprite.endgame:
        self.game.running = False
```

We check to see if the sprite that the stick figure has collided with has an endgame variable that is set to True. If it does, we set the running variable to False, and everything stops—we've reached the end of the game.

We'll add these same lines to the code that checks for a collision on the right. Here's the code:

```
if right and self.x > 0 and collided_right(co, sprite_co):
    self.x = 0
    right = False
    if sprite.endgame:
        self.game.running = False
```

ADDING THE DOOR OBJECT

Our final addition to the game code is an object for the door. We'll add this before the main loop. Just before creating the stick figure object, we'll create a door object, and then add it to the list of sprites. Here's the code:

```
g.sprites.append(platform7)
g.sprites.append(platform8)
g.sprites.append(platform9)
g.sprites.append(platform10)
door = DoorSprite(g, PhotoImage(file="door1.gif"), 45, 30, 40, 35)
g.sprites.append(door)
sf = StickFigureSprite(g)
g.sprites.append(sf)
g.mainloop()
```

We create a door object using the variable for our game object, g, followed by a PhotoImage (the door image we created in Chapter 15). We set the x and y parameters to 45 and 30 to put the door on a platform near the top of the screen, and set the width and height to 40 and 35. We add the door object to the list of sprites, as with all the other sprites in the game.

You can see the result when Mr. Stick Man reaches the door. He stops running in front of the door, rather than next to it, as shown here:

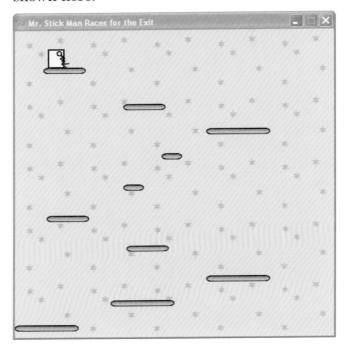

THE FINAL GAME

The full listing of our game is now a bit more than 200 lines of code. The following is the complete code for the game. If you have trouble getting your game to work, compare each function (and each class) to this listing and see where you've gone wrong.

```python
from tkinter import *
import random
import time

class Game:
    def __init__(self):
        self.tk = Tk()
        self.tk.title("Mr. Stick Man Races for the Exit")
        self.tk.resizable(0, 0)
```

```
        self.tk.wm_attributes("-topmost", 1)
        self.canvas = Canvas(self.tk, width=500, height=500, \
                highlightthickness=0)
        self.canvas.pack()
        self.tk.update()
        self.canvas_height = 500
        self.canvas_width = 500
        self.bg = PhotoImage(file="background.gif")
        w = self.bg.width()
        h = self.bg.height()
        for x in range(0, 5):
            for y in range(0, 5):
                self.canvas.create_image(x * w, y * h, \
                        image=self.bg, anchor='nw')
        self.sprites = []
        self.running = True

    def mainloop(self):
        while 1:
            if self.running == True:
                for sprite in self.sprites:
                    sprite.move()
            self.tk.update_idletasks()
            self.tk.update()
            time.sleep(0.01)

class Coords:
    def __init__(self, x1=0, y1=0, x2=0, y2=0):
        self.x1 = x1
        self.y1 = y1
        self.x2 = x2
        self.y2 = y2

def within_x(co1, co2):
    if (co1.x1 > co2.x1 and co1.x1 < co2.x2) \
            or (co1.x2 > co2.x1 and co1.x2 < co2.x2) \
            or (co2.x1 > co1.x1 and co2.x1 < co1.x2) \
            or (co2.x2 > co1.x1 and co2.x2 < co1.x2):
        return True
    else:
        return False

def within_y(co1, co2):
    if (co1.y1 > co2.y1 and co1.y1 < co2.y2) \
            or (co1.y2 > co2.y1 and co1.y2 < co2.y2) \
            or (co2.y1 > co1.y1 and co2.y1 < co1.y2) \
            or (co2.y2 > co1.y1 and co2.y2 < co1.y2):
        return True
```

```
        else:
            return False

    def collided_left(co1, co2):
        if within_y(co1, co2):
            if co1.x1 <= co2.x2 and co1.x1 >= co2.x1:
                return True
        return False

    def collided_right(co1, co2):
        if within_y(co1, co2):
            if co1.x2 >= co2.x1 and co1.x2 <= co2.x2:
                return True
        return False

    def collided_top(co1, co2):
        if within_x(co1, co2):
            if co1.y1 <= co2.y2 and co1.y1 >= co2.y1:
                return True
        return False

    def collided_bottom(y, co1, co2):
        if within_x(co1, co2):
            y_calc = co1.y2 + y
            if y_calc >= co2.y1 and y_calc <= co2.y2:
                return True
        return False

    class Sprite:
        def __init__(self, game):
            self.game = game
            self.endgame = False
            self.coordinates = None
        def move(self):
            pass
        def coords(self):
            return self.coordinates

    class PlatformSprite(Sprite):
        def __init__(self, game, photo_image, x, y, width, height):
            Sprite.__init__(self, game)
            self.photo_image = photo_image
            self.image = game.canvas.create_image(x, y, \
                    image=self.photo_image, anchor='nw')
            self.coordinates = Coords(x, y, x + width, y + height)
```

```
class StickFigureSprite(Sprite):
    def __init__(self, game):
        Sprite.__init__(self, game)
        self.images_left = [
            PhotoImage(file="figure-L1.gif"),
            PhotoImage(file="figure-L2.gif"),
            PhotoImage(file="figure-L3.gif")
        ]
        self.images_right = [
            PhotoImage(file="figure-R1.gif"),
            PhotoImage(file="figure-R2.gif"),
            PhotoImage(file="figure-R3.gif")
        ]
        self.image = game.canvas.create_image(200, 470, \
                image=self.images_left[0], anchor='nw')
        self.x = -2
        self.y = 0
        self.current_image = 0
        self.current_image_add = 1
        self.jump_count = 0
        self.last_time = time.time()
        self.coordinates = Coords()
        game.canvas.bind_all('<KeyPress-Left>', self.turn_left)
        game.canvas.bind_all('<KeyPress-Right>', self.turn_right)
        game.canvas.bind_all('<space>', self.jump)

    def turn_left(self, evt):
        if self.y == 0:
            self.x = -2

    def turn_right(self, evt):
        if self.y == 0:
            self.x = 2

    def jump(self, evt):
        if self.y == 0:
            self.y = -4
            self.jump_count = 0

    def animate(self):
        if self.x != 0 and self.y == 0:
            if time.time() - self.last_time > 0.1:
                self.last_time= time.time()
                self.current_image += self.current_image_add
```

```
            if self.current_image >= 2:
                self.current_image_add = -1
            if self.current_image <= 0:
                self.current_image_add = 1
        if self.x < 0:
            if self.y != 0:
                self.game.canvas.itemconfig(self.image, \
                        image=self.images_left[2])
            else:
                self.game.canvas.itemconfig(self.image, \
                        image=self.images_left[self.current_image])
        elif self.x > 0:
            if self.y != 0:
                self.game.canvas.itemconfig(self.image, \
                        image=self.images_right[2])
            else:
                self.game.canvas.itemconfig(self.image, \
                        image=self.images_right[self.current_image])

    def coords(self):
        xy = self.game.canvas.coords(self.image)
        self.coordinates.x1 = xy[0]
        self.coordinates.y1 = xy[1]
        self.coordinates.x2 = xy[0] + 27
        self.coordinates.y2 = xy[1] + 30
        return self.coordinates

    def move(self):
        self.animate()
        if self.y < 0:
            self.jump_count += 1
            if self.jump_count > 20:
                self.y = 4
        if self.y > 0:
            self.jump_count -= 1
        co = self.coords()
        left = True
        right = True
        top = True
        bottom = True
        falling = True
        if self.y > 0 and co.y2 >= self.game.canvas_height:
            self.y = 0
            bottom = False
        elif self.y < 0 and co.y1 <= 0:
            self.y = 0
            top = False
```

```python
            if self.x > 0 and co.x2 >= self.game.canvas_width:
                self.x = 0
                right = False
            elif self.x < 0 and co.x1 <= 0:
                self.x = 0
                left = False
            for sprite in self.game.sprites:
                if sprite == self:
                    continue
                sprite_co = sprite.coords()
                if top and self.y < 0 and collided_top(co, sprite_co):
                    self.y = -self.y
                    top = False
                if bottom and self.y > 0 and collided_bottom(self.y, \
                        co, sprite_co):
                    self.y = sprite_co.y1 - co.y2
                    if self.y < 0:
                        self.y = 0
                    bottom = False
                    top = False
                if bottom and falling and self.y == 0 \
                        and co.y2 < self.game.canvas_height \
                        and collided_bottom(1, co, sprite_co):
                    falling = False
                if left and self.x < 0 and collided_left(co, sprite_co):
                    self.x = 0
                    left = False
                    if sprite.endgame:
                        self.game.running = False
                if right and self.x > 0 and collided_right(co, sprite_co):
                    self.x = 0
                    right = False
                    if sprite.endgame:
                        self.game.running = False
        if falling and bottom and self.y == 0 \
                and co.y2 < self.game.canvas_height:
            self.y = 4
        self.game.canvas.move(self.image, self.x, self.y)

class DoorSprite(Sprite):
    def __init__(self, game, photo_image, x, y, width, height):
        Sprite.__init__(self, game)
        self.photo_image = photo_image
        self.image = game.canvas.create_image(x, y, \
                image=self.photo_image, anchor='nw')
        self.coordinates = Coords(x, y, x + (width / 2), y + height)
        self.endgame = True
```

```
g = Game()
platform1 = PlatformSprite(g, PhotoImage(file="platform1.gif"), \
    0, 480, 100, 10)
platform2 = PlatformSprite(g, PhotoImage(file="platform1.gif"), \
    150, 440, 100, 10)
platform3 = PlatformSprite(g, PhotoImage(file="platform1.gif"), \
    300, 400, 100, 10)
platform4 = PlatformSprite(g, PhotoImage(file="platform1.gif"), \
    300, 160, 100, 10)
platform5 = PlatformSprite(g, PhotoImage(file="platform2.gif"), \
    175, 350, 66, 10)
platform6 = PlatformSprite(g, PhotoImage(file="platform2.gif"), \
    50, 300, 66, 10)
platform7 = PlatformSprite(g, PhotoImage(file="platform2.gif"), \
    170, 120, 66, 10)
platform8 = PlatformSprite(g, PhotoImage(file="platform2.gif"), \
    45, 60, 66, 10)
platform9 = PlatformSprite(g, PhotoImage(file="platform3.gif"), \
    170, 250, 32, 10)
platform10 = PlatformSprite(g, PhotoImage(file="platform3.gif"), \
    230, 200, 32, 10)
g.sprites.append(platform1)
g.sprites.append(platform2)
g.sprites.append(platform3)
g.sprites.append(platform4)
g.sprites.append(platform5)
g.sprites.append(platform6)
g.sprites.append(platform7)
g.sprites.append(platform8)
g.sprites.append(platform9)
g.sprites.append(platform10)
door = DoorSprite(g, PhotoImage(file="door1.gif"), 45, 30, 40, 35)
g.sprites.append(door)
sf = StickFigureSprite(g)
g.sprites.append(sf)
g.mainloop()
```

WHAT YOU LEARNED

In this chapter, we completed our game, Mr. Stick Man Races for the Exit. We created a class for our animated stick figure and wrote functions to move him around the screen and animate him as he moves (changing from one image to the next to give the illusion of running). We've used basic collision detection to tell when he has hit the left or right sides of the canvas, and when he has hit another sprite, such as a platform or a door. We've also added collision code to tell when he hits the top of the screen or the bottom, and to make sure that when he runs off the edge of a platform, he tumbles down accordingly. We added code to tell when Mr. Stick Man has reached the door, so the game comes to an end.

PROGRAMMING PUZZLES

There's a lot more we can do to improve the game. At the moment, it's very simple, so we can add code to make it more professional looking and more interesting to play. Try adding the following features and then check your code at *http://python-for-kids.com/*.

#1: "YOU WIN!"

Like the "Game Over" text in the Bounce! game we completed in Chapter 14, add the "You Win!" text when the stick figure reaches the door, so players can see that they have won.

#2: ANIMATING THE DOOR

In Chapter 15, we created two images for the door: one open and one closed. When Mr. Stick Man reaches the door, the door image should change to the open door, Mr. Stick Man should vanish, and the door image should revert to the closed door. This will give the illusion that Mr. Stick Man is exiting and closing the door as he leaves. You can do this by changing the DoorSprite class and the StickFigureSprite class.

#3: MOVING PLATFORMS

Try adding a new class called MovingPlatformSprite. This platform should move from side to side, making it more difficult for Mr. Stick Man to reach the door at the top.

AFTERWORD
WHERE TO GO FROM HERE

You've learned some basic programming concepts in your tour of Python, and now you'll find it much easier to work with other programming languages. While Python is incredibly useful, one language is not always the best tool for every task, so don't be afraid to try other ways to program your computer. Here, we'll look at some alternatives for games and graphics programming, and then take a peek at some of the most commonly used programming languages.

GAMES AND GRAPHICS PROGRAMMING

If you want to do more with games or graphics programming, you'll find many options available. Here are just a few:

- BlitzBasic (*http://www.blitzbasic.com/*), which uses a special version of the BASIC programming language designed specifically for games
- Adobe Flash, a type of animation software designed to run in the browser, which has its own programming language called ActionScript (*http://www.adobe.com/devnet/actionscript.html*)
- Alice (*http://www.alice.org/*), a 3D programming environment (for Microsoft Windows and Mac OS X only)
- Scratch (*http://scratch.mit.edu/*), a tool for developing games
- Unity3D (*http://unity3d.com/*), another tool for creating games

An online search will uncover a wealth of resources to help you get started with any of these options.

On the other hand, if you would like to continue playing with Python, you could use PyGame, the Python module designed for game development. Let's explore that option.

PYGAME

PyGame Reloaded (pgreloaded or `pygame2`) is the version of PyGame that works with Python 3 (earlier versions work only with Python 2). A good place to start reading is the pgreloaded tutorial at *http://code.google.com/p/pgreloaded/*.

NOTE   *As of this writing, there is no installer for pgreloaded on Mac OS X or Linux, so there is no straightforward way to use it on either of these operating systems.*

Writing a game with PyGame is a little more complicated than using `tkinter`. For example, in Chapter 12, we displayed an image using `tkinter` with this code:

```
from tkinter import *
tk = Tk()
canvas = Canvas(tk, width=400, height=400)
canvas.pack()
myimage = PhotoImage(file='c:\\test.gif')
canvas.create_image(0, 0, anchor=NW, image=myimage)
```

The same code using PyGame (loading a *.bmp* file rather than a *.gif* file) would look like this:

```
import sys
import time
import pygame2
import pygame2.sdl.constants as constants
import pygame2.sdl.image as image
import pygame2.sdl.video as video
❶ video.init()
❷ img = image.load_bmp("c:\\test.bmp")
❸ screen = video.set_mode(img.width, img.height)
❹ screen.fill(pygame2.Color(255, 255, 255))
❺ screen.blit(img, (0, 0))
❻ screen.flip()
❼ time.sleep(10)
❽ video.quit()
```

After importing the pygame2 modules, we call the init function on the PyGame video module at ❶, which is a bit like the call to create the canvas and then pack it in the tkinter example. We load a BMP image using the load_bmp function at ❷, and then create a screen object using the set_mode function, passing in the width and height of the loaded image as parameters at ❸. With the next (optional) line, we wipe the screen by filling it with white at ❹, and then use the blit function of the screen object to display the image at ❺. The parameters for this function are the img object and a tuple containing the position where we want to display the image (0 pixels across, 0 pixels down).

PyGame uses an *off-screen buffer* (also known as a *double-buffer*). An off-screen buffer is a technique used to draw graphics in an area of the computer's memory where it isn't visible, and then to copy that entire area into the visible display (onto your screen) all at once. Off-screen buffering reduces the flickering effect if you happen to be drawing a lot of different objects on a display. Copying from the off-screen buffer to the visible display is performed using the flip function at ❻.

Finally, we sleep for 10 seconds at ❼ because, unlike tkinter's canvas, the screen will immediately close if we don't stop it from doing so. At ❽, we clean up using video.quit so that PyGame will shut down properly. There's a lot more to PyGame, but this short example gives you an idea of what it's like.

PROGRAMMING LANGUAGES

If you're interested in other programming languages, some that are currently popular are Java, C/C++, C#, PHP, Objective-C, Perl, Ruby, and JavaScript. We'll take a brief tour of these languages and see how a Hello World program (like the Python version we started with in Chapter 1) would look in each one. Note that none of these languages are specifically intended for beginning programmers, and most are significantly different from Python.

JAVA

Java (*http://www.oracle.com/technetwork/java/index.html*) is a moderately complicated programming language with a large built-in library of modules (called *packages*). A lot of free documentation is available online. You can use Java on most operating systems. Java is also the language used on Android mobile phones.

Here's an example of Hello World in Java:

```
public class HelloWorld {
    public static final void main(String[] args) {
        System.out.println("Hello World");
    }
}
```

C/C++

C (*http://www.cprogramming.com/*) and C++ (*http://www.stroustrup/C++.html*) are complicated programming languages that are used on all operating systems. You'll find both free and commercial versions available. Both languages (though perhaps C++ more than C) have a steep learning curve. For example, you'll find that you need to manually code some features that Python provides (like telling the computer that you need to use a chunk of memory to store an object). Many commercial games and game consoles are programmed in some form of C or C++.

Here's an example of Hello World in C:

```
#include <stdio.h>
int main ()
{
  printf ("Hello World\n");
}
```

An example in C++ might look like this:

```
#include <iostream>
int main()
{
  std::cout << "Hello World\n";
  return 0;
}
```

C#

C# (*http://msdn.microsoft.com/en-us/vstudio/hh388566/*), pronounced "C sharp," is a moderately complicated programming language for Windows that is very similar to Java. It's a bit easier than C and C++.

Here's an example of Hello World in C#:

```
public class Hello
{
    public static void Main()
    {
        System.Console.WriteLine("Hello World");
    }
}
```

PHP

PHP (*http://www.php.net/*) is a programming language for building websites. You will need a web server (software used to deliver web pages to a web browser) with PHP installed, but all the software required is freely available for all the major operating systems. In order to work with PHP, you will need to learn HTML (a simple language for building web pages). You can find a free PHP tutorial at *http://php.net/manual/en/tutorial.php*, and an HTML tutorial at *http://www.w3schools.com/html*.

An HTML page that displays "Hello World" in a browser might look like this:

```
<html>
    <body>
        <p>Hello World</p>
    </body>
</html>
```

A PHP page to do the same thing might look like this:

```php
<?php
echo "Hello World\n";
?>
```

OBJECTIVE-C

Objective-C (*http://classroomm.com/objective-c/*) is very similar to C (in fact, it's an extension of the C programming language) and most commonly used on Apple computers. It's the programming language for the iPhone and iPad.

Here's an example of Hello World in Objective-C:

```objectivec
#import <Foundation/Foundation.h>
int main (int argc, const char * argv[]) {
    NSAutoreleasePool * pool = [[NSAutoreleasePool alloc] init];
    NSLog (@"Hello World");

    [pool drain];
    return 0;
}
```

PERL

The Perl programming language (*http://www.perl.org/*) is available for free for all major operating systems. It's usually used for developing websites (similar to PHP).

Here's an example of Hello World in Perl:

```perl
print("Hello World\n");
```

RUBY

Ruby (*http://www.ruby-lang.org/*) is a free programming language available on all major operating systems. It's mostly used for creating websites, specifically using the framework Ruby on Rails. (A *framework* is a set of libraries supporting the development of specific types of applications.)

Here's an example of Hello World in Ruby:

```ruby
puts "Hello World"
```

JAVASCRIPT

JavaScript (*https://developer.mozilla.org/en/javascript/*) is a programming language that is usually used inside web pages but is increasingly being used for game programming. The syntax is basically similar to Java, but perhaps it's a little easier to get started with JavaScript. (You can create a simple HTML page that contains a JavaScript program and run it inside a browser without needing a shell, command line, or anything else.) A good place to start learning JavaScript might be Codecademy at *http://www.codecademy.com/*.

A "Hello World" example in JavaScript will be different depending on whether you run it in a browser or in a shell. In a shell, the example looks like this:

```
print('Hello World');
```

In a browser, it might look like this:

```
<html>
    <body>
        <script type="text/javascript">
            alert("Hello World");
        </script>
    </body>
</html>
```

FINAL WORDS

Whether you stick with Python or decide to try out another programming language (and there are many more than those listed here), you should still find the concepts that you've discovered in this book useful. Even if you don't continue with computer programming, understanding some of the fundamental ideas can help with all sorts of activities, whether in school or later on, at work.

Good luck and have fun with your programming!

APPENDIX
PYTHON KEYWORDS

Keywords in Python (and in most programming languages) are words that have special meaning. They are used as part of the programming language itself, and therefore must not be used for anything else. For example, if you try to use keywords as variables, or use them in the wrong way, you will get strange (sometimes funny, sometimes confusing) error messages from the Python console.

This appendix describes each of the Python keywords. You should find this to be a handy reference as you continue to program.

AND

The keyword and is used to join two expressions together in a statement (like an if statement) to say that both expressions must be true. Here's an example:

```
if age > 10 and age < 20:
    print('Beware the teenager!!!!')
```

This code means that the value of the variable age must be greater than 10 *and* less than 20 before the message will be printed.

AS

The keyword as can be used to give another name to an imported module. For example, suppose you had a module with a very long name:

```
i_am_a_python_module_that_is_not_very_useful
```

It would be enormously annoying to need to type this module name every time you wanted to use it:

```
import i_am_a_python_module_that_is_not_very_useful
i_am_a_python_module_that_is_not_very_useful.do_something()
I have done something that is not useful.
i_am_a_python_module_that_is_not_very_useful.do_something_else()
I have done something else that is not useful!!
```

Instead, you can give the module a new, shorter name when you import it, and then simply use that new name (a bit like a nickname), as follows:

```
import i_am_a_python_module_that_is_not_very_useful as notuseful
notuseful.do_something()
I have done something that is not useful.
notuseful.do_something_else()
I have done something else that is not useful!!
```

ASSERT

assert is a keyword used to say that some code must be true. It's another way of catching errors and problems in code, usually in more advanced programs (which is why we don't use assert in this book). Here's a simple assert statement:

```
>>> mynumber = 10
>>> assert mynumber < 5
Traceback (most recent call last):
  File "<pyshell#1>", line 1, in <module>
    assert a < 5
AssertionError
```

In this example, we assert that the value of the variable mynumber is less than 5. It isn't, and so Python displays an error (called an AssertionError).

BREAK

The break keyword is used to stop some code from running. You might use a break inside a for loop, like this:

```
age = 10
for x in range(1, 100):
    print('counting %s' % x)
    if x == age:
        print('end counting')
        break
```

Since the variable age is set to 10 here, this code will print out the following:

```
counting 1
counting 2
counting 3
counting 4
counting 5
counting 6
counting 7
counting 8
counting 9
counting 10
end counting
```

Once the value of the variable x reaches 10, the code prints the text "end counting" and then breaks out of the loop.

CLASS

The keyword class is used to define a type of object, like a vehicle, animal, or person. Classes can have a function called __init__, which is used to perform all the tasks an object of the class needs when it is created. For example, an object of the class Car might need a variable color when it's created:

```
class Car:
    def __init__(self, color):
        self.color = color

car1 = Car('red')
car2 = Car('blue')
print(car1.color)
red
print(car2.color)
blue
```

CONTINUE

The continue keyword is a way to "jump" to the next item in a loop—so that the remaining code in the loop block is not executed. Unlike break we don't jump out of the loop, we just carry on with the next item. For example, if we had a list of items and wanted to skip items starting with *b*, we could use the following code:

```
❶ >>> my_items = ['apple', 'aardvark', 'banana', 'badger', 'clementine',
             'camel']
❷ >>> for item in my_items:
❸         if item.startswith('b'):
❹             continue
❺         print(item)

apple
aardvark
clementine
camel
```

We create our list of items at ❶, and then use a for loop to loop over the items and run a block of code for each at ❷. If the item starts with the letter *b* at ❸, we continue to the next item at ❹. Otherwise, at ❺ we print out the item.

DEF

The def keyword is used to define a function. For example, to create a function to convert a number of years into the equivalent number of minutes:

```
>>> def minutes(years):
        return years * 365 * 24 * 60
>>> minutes(10)
5256000
```

DEL

The del function is used to remove something. For example, if you had a list of things you wanted for your birthday in your diary, but then changed your mind about one of them, you might cross it off the list and add something new:

remote controlled car
new bike
~~computer game~~
roboreptile

In Python, the original list would look like this:

```
what_i_want = ['remote controlled car', 'new bike', 'computer game']
```

You could remove the computer game by using del and the index of the item you want to delete. You could then add the new item with the function append:

```
del what_i_want[2]
what_i_want.append('roboreptile')
```

And then print the new list:

```
print(what_i_want)
['remote controlled car', 'new bike', 'roboreptile']
```

ELIF

The keyword elif is used as part of an if statement. See the description of the if keyword for an example.

ELSE

The keyword else is used as part of an if statement. See the description of the if keyword for an example.

EXCEPT

The keyword except is used for catching problems in code. It's typically used in fairly complicated programs, so we don't use it in this book.

FINALLY

The keyword finally is used to make sure that if an error occurs, certain code runs (usually to tidy up any mess that a piece of code has left behind). This keyword isn't used in this book because it's for more advanced programming.

FOR

The for keyword is used to create a loop of code that runs a certain number of times. Here's an example:

```
for x in range(0, 5):
    print('x is %s' % x)
```

This for loop executes the block of code (the print statement) five times, resulting in the following output:

```
x is 0
x is 1
x is 2
x is 3
x is 4
```

FROM

When importing a module, you can import just the part you need using the from keyword. For example, the turtle module introduced in Chapter 4 has a class called Pen, which we use to create a Pen object (the canvas on which the turtle moves). Here's how we import the entire turtle module and then use the Pen class:

```
import turtle
t = turtle.Pen()
```

You could also just import the Pen class on its own, and then use it directly (without referring to the turtle module at all):

```
from turtle import Pen
t = Pen()
```

You might do this so that the next time you look at the top of that program, you can see all the functions and classes that you're using (which is particularly useful in larger programs that import a lot of modules). However, if you choose to do this, you won't be able to use the parts of the module you haven't imported. For example, the time module has functions called localtime and gmtime, but if you import only localtime and then try to use gmtime, you'll get an error:

```
>>> from time import localtime
>>> print(localtime())
(2007, 1, 30, 20, 53, 42, 1, 30, 0)
>>> print(gmtime())
Traceback (most recent call last):
  File "<stdin>", line 1, in <module>
NameError: name 'gmtime' is not defined
```

The error message name 'gmtime' is not defined means that Python doesn't know anything about the function gmtime, which is because you haven't imported it.

If there are a number of functions in a particular module that you want to use, and you don't want to refer to them by using the module name (for example, time.localtime, or time.gmtime), you can import everything in the module using an asterisk (*), like this:

```
>>> from time import *
>>> print(localtime())
(2007, 1, 30, 20, 57, 7, 1, 30, 0)
>>> print(gmtime())
(2007, 1, 30, 13, 57, 9, 1, 30, 0)
```

This form imports everything from the time module, and you can now refer to the individual functions by name.

GLOBAL

The idea of scope in programs is introduced in Chapter 7. Scope refers to the *visibility* of a variable. If a variable is defined outside a function, usually it can be seen (in other words, it's visible) inside the function. On the other hand, if the variable is defined inside a function, usually it can't be seen outside that function. The `global` keyword is one exception to this rule. A variable that is defined as global can be seen everywhere. Here's an example:

```
>>> def test():
        global a
        a = 1
        b = 2
```

What do you think happens when you call `print(a)` and then `print(b)`, after running the function test? The first will work, but the second will display an error message:

```
>>> test()
>>> print(a)
1
>>> print(b)
Traceback (most recent call last):
  File "<stdin>", line 1, in <module>
NameError: name 'b' is not defined
```

The variable a has been changed to global inside the function, so it's visible, even once the function has completed, but b is still visible only inside the function. (You must use the `global` keyword before setting the value of your variable.)

IF

The `if` keyword is used to make a decision about something. It can also be used with the keywords `else` and `elif` (else if). An `if` statement is a way of saying, "If something is true, then perform an action of some kind." Here's an example:

```
❶ if toy_price > 1000:
❷     print('That toy is overpriced')
❸ elif toy_price > 100:
❹     print('That toy is expensive')
❺ else:
❻     print('I can afford that toy')
```

This `if` statement says that if a toy price is over $1,000 at ❶, display a message that it is overpriced at ❷; otherwise, if the toy price is over $100 as at ❸, then display a message that it's expensive at ❹. If neither of those conditions is true as at ❺, it should display the message "I can afford that toy" at ❻.

IMPORT

The import keyword is used to tell Python to load a module so it can be used. For example, the following code tells Python to use the module sys:

```
import sys
```

IN

The in keyword is used in expressions to see if an item is within a collection of items. For example, can the number 1 be found in a list (a collection) of numbers?

```
>>> if 1 in [1,2,3,4]:
>>>     print('number is in list')
number is in list
```

Here's how to find out if the string 'pants' is in a list of clothing items:

```
>>> clothing_list = ['shorts', 'undies', 'boxers', 'long johns',
                'knickers']
>>> if 'pants' in clothing_list:
        print('pants is in the list')
else:
        print('pants is not in the list')
pants is not in the list
```

IS

The is keyword is a bit like the equal to operator (==), which is used to tell if two things are equal (for example 10 == 10 is true, and 10 == 11 is false). However, there is a fundamental difference between is and ==. If you are comparing two things, == may return true, while is may not (even if you think the things are the same). This is an advanced programming concept, and we stick with using == in this book.

LAMBDA

The lambda keyword is used to create anonymous, or inline, functions. This keyword is used in more advanced programs, and we don't discuss it in this book.

NOT

If something is true, the not keyword makes it false. For example, if we create a variable x and set it to the value True, and then print the value of this variable using not, we get the following result:

```
>>> x = True
>>> print(not x)
False
```

This doesn't seem very useful, until you start using the keyword in if statements. For example, to find out whether an item is not in a list, we could write something like this:

```
>>> clothing_list = ['shorts', 'undies', 'boxers', 'long johns',
                'knickers']
>>> if 'pants' not in clothing_list:
        print('You really need to buy some pants')
You really need to buy some pants
```

OR

The or keyword is used to join two conditions together in a statement (such as an if statement) to say that at least one of the conditions should be true. Here's an example:

```
if dino == 'Tyrannosaurus' or dino == 'Allosaurus':
    print('Carnivores')
elif dino == 'Ankylosaurus' or dino == 'Apatosaurus':
    print('Herbivores')
```

In this case, if the variable dino contains Tyrannosaurus or Allosaurus, the program prints "Carnivores." If it contains Ankylosaurus or Apatosaurus, the program prints "Herbivores."

PASS

Sometimes when you're developing a program, you want to write only small pieces of it, to try things out. The problem with doing this is that you can't have an `if` statement without the block of code that should be run if the expression in the `if` statement is true. You also cannot have a `for` loop without the block of code that should be run in the loop. For example, the following code works just fine:

```
>>> age = 15
>>> if age > 10:
        print('older than 10')

older than 10
```

But if you don't fill in the block of code (the body) for the `if` statement, you'll get an error message:

```
>>> age = 15
>>> if age > 10:

File "<stdin>", line 2
   ^
IndentationError: expected an indented block
```

This is the error message Python displays when you should have a block of code after a statement of some kind (it won't even let you type this kind of code if you're using IDLE). In cases like these, you can use the `pass` keyword to write a statement but not provide the block of code that goes with it.

For example, say you want to create a `for` loop with an `if` statement inside it. Perhaps you haven't decided what to put in the `if` statement yet—maybe you'll use the `print` function, put in a `break`, or something else. You can use `pass`, and the code will still work (even if it doesn't do exactly what you want yet).

Here's our `if` statement again, this time using the `pass` keyword:

```
>>> age = 15
>>> if age > 10:
        pass
```

The following code shows another use of the pass keyword:

```
>>> for x in range(0, 7):
>>>     print('x is %s' % x)
>>>     if x == 4:
            pass

x is 0
x is 1
x is 2
x is 3
x is 4
x is 5
x is 6
```

Python still checks whether the variable x contains the value 4 every time it executes the block of code in the loop, but it will do nothing as a consequence, so it will print every number in the range 0 to 7.

Later, you could add the code in the block for the if statement, replacing the pass keyword with something else, such as break:

```
>>> for x in range(1, 7):
        print('x is %s' % x)
        if x == 5:
            break

x is 1
x is 2
x is 3
x is 4
x is 5
```

The pass keyword is most commonly used when you're creating a function but don't want to write the code for the function yet.

RAISE

The raise keyword can be used to cause an error to happen. That might sound like a strange thing to do, but in advanced programming, it can actually be quite useful. (We don't use this keyword in this book.)

RETURN

The return keyword is used to return a value from a function. For example, you might create a function to calculate the number of seconds you've been alive up till your last birthday:

```
def age_in_seconds(age_in_years):
    return age_in_years * 365 * 24 * 60 * 60
```

When you call this function, the returned value can be assigned to another variable or printed:

```
>>> seconds = age_in_seconds(9)
>>> print(seconds)
283824000
>>> print(age_in_seconds())
378432000
```

TRY

The try keyword begins a block of code that ends with the except and finally keywords. Together, these try/except/finally blocks of code are used to handle errors in a program, such as to make sure that the program displays a useful message to the user, rather than an unfriendly Python error. These keywords aren't used in this book.

WHILE

The while keyword is a bit like for, except that a for loop counts through a range (of numbers), but a while loop keeps on running while an expression is true. Be careful with while loops because if the expression is always true, the loop will never end (this is called an *infinite loop*). Here's an example:

```
>>> x = 1
>>> while x == 1:
        print('hello')
```

If you run this code, it will loop forever, or at least until you close the Python shell or press CTRL-C to interrupt it. However, the following code will print "hello" nine times (each time adding 1 to the variable x, until x is no longer less than 10).

```
>>> x = 1
>>> while x < 10:
        print('hello')
        x = x + 1
```

WITH

The with keyword is used with an object to create a block of code in a similar way to the try and finally keywords. This keyword is not used in this book.

YIELD

The yield keyword is a little bit like return, except that it is used with a specific class of object called a generator. Generators create values on the fly (which is another way of saying that they create values on request), so in that respect, the range function behaves like a generator. This keyword is not used in this book.

GLOSSARY

Sometimes, when you're programming for the first time, you'll encounter a new term that just doesn't make much sense. That lack of understanding can get in the way of making any real progress. But there's a simple solution to that problem!

I've created this glossary to help you through those times when a new word or term holds you up. You'll find definitions of many of the programming terms used in this book, so look here if you encounter a word that you don't understand.

animation The process of displaying a sequence of images fast enough that it looks like something is moving.

block A group of computer statements in a program.

Boolean A type of value that can be either true or false. (In Python, it's True or False, with capital T and F.)

call Run the code in a function. When we use a function, we say we are "calling" it.

canvas An area of the screen for drawing on. canvas is a class provided by the tkinter module.

child When we're talking about classes, we describe the relationships between classes as that of parents and children. A child class inherits the characteristics of its parent class.

class A description or definition of a type of thing. In programming terms, a class is a collection of functions and variables.

click Press one of the mouse buttons to push an on-screen button, select a menu option, and so on.

collision In computer games, when one character in the game crashes into another character or object on the screen.

condition An expression in a program that is a bit like a question. Conditions evaluate to true or false.

coordinates The position of a pixel on the screen. This is usually described as a number of pixels across the screen (x) and a number of pixels down (y).

degrees A unit of measurement for angles.

data Usually refers to information stored and manipulated by a computer.

dialog A dialog is typically a small window in an application that presents some contextual information, such as an alert or an error message, or asks you to respond to a question. For example, when you choose to open a file, the window that appears is usually the File dialog.

dimensions In the context of graphics programming, *two-dimensional* or *three-dimensional* refers to how images are displayed on a computer monitor. Two-dimensional (2D) graphics are flat images on a screen that have width and height—like the old cartoons you might see on TV. Three-dimensional (3D) graphics are images on the screen that have width, height, and the appearance of depth—the sort of graphics you might see in a more realistic computer game.

directory   The location of a group of files on the hard disk of your computer.

embed   Replace values inside a string. The replaced values are sometimes called *placeholders*.

error   When something goes wrong with a program on your computer, this is an error. When programming with Python, you might see all sorts of messages displayed in response to an error. If you enter your code incorrectly you might see an `IndentationError`, for example.

event   Something that occurs when a program is running. For example, an event might be someone moving the mouse, clicking the mouse button, or typing on a keyboard.

exception   A type of error that can occur when running a program.

execute   Run some code, like a program, a small snippet of code, or a function.

frame   One of a series of images that makes up an animation.

function   A command in a programming language that is usually a collection of statements that perform some action.

hexadecimal   A way of representing numbers, particularly in computer programming. Hexadecimal numbers are base 16, which means the numbers go from 0 through 9 and then A, B, C, D, E, and F.

horizontal   The left and right directions on the screen (represented by x).

identifier   A number that uniquely names something in a program. For example, in Python's `tkinter` module, the identifier is used to refer to shapes drawn on the canvas.

image   A picture on the computer screen.

import   In Python terms, importing makes a module available for your program to use.

initialize   Refers to setting up the initial state of an object (that is, setting variables in the object when it is first created).

installation   The process of copying a software application's files onto your computer so that the application is available for use.

instance   The instance of a class—in other words, an object.

keyword   A special word used by a programming language. Keywords are also referred to as *reserved words*, which basically means you can't use them for anything else (for example, you can't use a keyword as the name of a variable).

loop   A repeated command or set of commands.

memory   A device or component in your computer that is used to temporarily store information.

module   A group of functions and variables.

null   The absence of value (in Python, also referred to as None).

object   The specific instance of a class. When you create an object of a class, Python sets aside some of your computer's memory to store information about a member of that class.

operator   An element in a computer program used for mathematics or for comparing values.

parameter   A value used with a function when calling it or when creating an object (when calling the Python _init_ function, for example). Parameters are sometimes referred to as *arguments*.

parent   When referring to classes and objects, the parent of a class is another class that functions and variables are inherited from. In other words, a child class inherits the characteristics of its parent class. When we're not talking Python, a parent is the person who tells you to brush your teeth before going to bed at night.

pixel   A single point on your computer screen—the smallest dot that the computer is capable of drawing.

program   A set of commands that tells a computer what to do.

scope   The part, or section, of a program where a variable can be "seen" (or used). (A variable inside a function may not be visible to code outside the function.)

shell In computing, a shell is a command-line interface of some kind. In this book, "the Python shell" refers to the IDLE application.

software A collection of computer programs.

sprite A character or an object in a computer game.

string A collection of alphanumeric characters (letters, numbers, punctuation, and whitespace).

syntax The arrangement and order of words in a program.

transparency In graphics programming, part of an image that isn't displayed, meaning it doesn't overwrite whatever is displayed behind it.

variable Something used to store values. A variable is like a label for information held in the computer's memory. Variables aren't permanently tied to a specific value, hence the name "variable," meaning it can change.

vertical The up and down directions on the screen (represented by y).

INDEX

UPDATES

Visit *http://python-for-kids.com/* for updates, errata, and other information.

More no-nonsense books from **NO STARCH PRESS**

SUPER SCRATCH PROGRAMMING ADVENTURE! (COVERS VERSION 2)

Learn to Program by Making Cool Games
by THE LEAD PROJECT
OCTOBER 2013, 160 PP., $24.95
ISBN 978-1-59327-531-0
full color

SURVIVE! INSIDE THE HUMAN BODY, VOL. 1

The Digestive System
by GOMDORI CO. *and* HYUN-DONG HAN
OCTOBER 2013, 184 PP., $17.95
ISBN 978-1-59327-471-9
full color

THE LEGO® MINDSTORMS® EV3 LABORATORY

Build, Program, and Experiment with Five Wicked Cool Robots!
by DANIELE BENEDETTELLI
OCTOBER 2013, 432 PP., $34.95
ISBN 978-1-59327-533-4

LEARN TO PROGRAM WITH SCRATCH

A Visual Introduction to Programming with Games, Art, Science, and Math
by MAJED MARJI
FEBRUARY 2014, 288 PP., $34.95
ISBN 978-1-59327-543-3
full color

ARDUINO WORKSHOP

A Hands-On Introduction with 65 Projects
by JOHN BOXALL
MAY 2013, 392 PP., $29.95
ISBN 978-1-59327-448-1

THE MANGA GUIDE™ TO PHYSICS

by HIDEO NITTA, KEITA TAKATSU, *and* TREND-PRO CO., LTD.
MAY 2009, 248 PP., $19.95
ISBN 978-1-59327-196-1

PHONE:
800.420.7240 OR
415.863.9900

EMAIL:
SALES@NOSTARCH.COM
WEB:
WWW.NOSTARCH.COM